D1714797

.

War in the Age of
Enlightenment, 1700–1789

War in the Age of Enlightenment, 1700–1789

ARMSTRONG STARKEY

Studies in Military History and International Affairs
Jeremy Black, Series Editor

Westport, Connecticut
London

Library of Congress Cataloging-in-Publication Data

Starkey, Armstrong.
  War in the age of the Enlightenment, 1700–1789 / Armstrong Starkey.
    p. cm.—(Studies in military history and international affairs, ISSN 1537–4432)
  Includes bibliographical references and index.
  ISBN 0–275–97240–2 (alk. paper)
    1. Military art and science—Europe—History—18th century.
  2. Enlightenment—Europe.   3. Europe—History, Military—18th century.
  I. Title. II Series.
  U43.E95S73 2003
  355'.0094'09033—dc21   2003042935

British Library Cataloguing-in-Publication Data is available.

Library of Congress Catalog Card Number: 2003042935
ISBN: 0–275–97240–2
ISSN: 1537–4432

First published in 2003

Praeger Publishers, 88 Post Road West, Westport, CT 06881
An imprint of Greenwood Publishing Group, Inc.
www.praeger.com

Printed in the United States of America

The paper used in this book complies with the
Permanent Paper Standard issued by the National
Information Standards Organization (Z39.48–1984).

10 9 8 7 6 5 4 3 2 1

Contents

Preface

In recent years, when colleagues have asked me about my research interests, I have replied that I have been considering the relationship between the Enlightenment and warfare. The response has frequently been: "I shouldn't have thought there was one." That says a lot about the perception of the Enlightenment shared by many academics who are nonspecialists in the period. Most of us at some time learn that the Enlightenment was a good thing. It was about peace, humanity, toleration, and freedom. Surely, war was antithetical to all of these positive goals. But was it? War is not a goal for most of us, but it is a means by which freedom or humanity may be protected. Eighteenth-century intellectuals understood this. They deplored, as do we, the horrors of war, but they recognized that there were times when it was necessary. Their attitudes toward war reflect a central tension in the Enlightenment, one that cannot be ignored if we are to fully understand the Enlightenment's contribution to the development of the modern world.

Political and military historians have frequently discussed the relationship between the Enlightenment and war. They have focused on two aspects: (1) the Enlightenment's contribution to the development of strategic thought (most recently discussed in the excellent work of Azar Gat) and (2) its contribution to the cause of humanity in war (perhaps best represented in the work of Geoffrey Best). It was the issue of humanity in war that inspired my interest in this study. A number of surveys of early modern warfare concluded that the conduct of war in the period 1700–1789 was more humane than during the preceding wars of religion or the succeeding revolutionary period. Often the Enlightenment was cited as a contributing factor, although there seemed to be little evidence that this was so. I believed that more needed to be done to explore a concrete connection between the ideas and values of the Enlightenment and the actual conduct of war. This is what I have attempted to do in this book.

Enlightenment specialists now approach the Enlightenment as a complex phenomenon, and I hope that my work will be viewed as consistent with this approach. There were many ambiguities in Enlightenment attitudes toward war. The articles in Denis Diderot's *Encyclopédie* testify to this complexity, for they range from denouncing war to providing a guide to the latest military thought. Complexity creates problems with definition. If the Enlightenment had room for all of these interests, what exactly was it? I do not propose to provide a definite answer. Indeed, I hope to add to the complexity. I have chosen to explore what I term the *culture of force,* that is, the ideas and values that guided the practice of war in the period. This culture was not simply a product of the Enlightenment. Religion continued to play an important role in European cultural life. The average soldier was better versed in scripture than in the *Encyclopédie.* The average officer might have read Rousseau—or at least have heard of him. He might have read a military manual containing new tactical ideas that might be found in the *Encyclopédie,* but he also was required to adhere to a code of values that seem to have nothing to do with the Enlightenment. Soldiers were, after all, defenders of the Old Regime.

Eighteenth-century Europe was relatively free from religious fanaticism and revolutionary zeal, but it was still a violent place. There were many wars, and these wars provoked revolutions. In many countries the civilian population bore the brunt of these conflicts. As a result, there were many instances of popular uprisings before the French Revolution, although most did not succeed. The stereotype of eighteenth-century "cabinet war," fought by mercenary armies for limited objectives and at low cost, requires correction. I hope that this book will contribute to a new interpretation of the nature of eighteenth-century warfare. This was also the first period of truly global warfare. Europeans came into contact with powerful non-European peoples who were capable of defending themselves against foreign aggression. These peoples often possessed different cultural attitudes toward war than those of their European opponents. Inevitably, warfare produced a measure of cultural exchange, which I have examined in the last chapter.

I am conscious of producing a small book on a big subject and do not claim to have the last word on the topics that I write about. The virtue of a book such as this is that it may contain food for thought. If it succeeds in this regard, it will have achieved my hopes for it.

A preface is also a place to acknowledge the assistance of others. First and foremost, I wish to thank Jeremy Black for his advice and encouragement. One day, while we were walking on the beach together, he even suggested the title. I also wish to thank Jean Chagniot for his help in an early correspondence. John Thornton gave me helpful advice about Africa. Two new colleagues in my own department, Cristina Zaccarini and Dennis Hidalgo, have provided me with helpful global perspectives. Eliz Alahrerdian of the Adelphi University Art Department drafted the map of the battle of Fontenoy. Adelphi University awarded me a sabbatical while I was writing this book. I also owe thanks to the staffs of many libraries: Adelphi University and its excellent interlibrary loan department; the New York Public Library; the British Library; the William L. Clements Library of the University of Michigan; the Huntington Library in San Marino, California; the Scottish Record Office; and the British Public Record Office at Kew. I especially wish to thank the staff of the library of the Society of the Cincinnati in Washington, D.C. I profited from their valuable collection of eighteenth-century military treatises and appreciated the warmth of their reception and the hospitality of Mr. William H. Greer, Jr. who has done so much to support the study of eighteenth-century military history.

CHAPTER 1

The Culture of Force

For a century born in war, Charles XII of Sweden was the symbol of the rashness of military heroism. Three years after his succession to the crown at age 15, his country was set upon by rapacious enemies. He subsequently spent his entire career in warfare, until his death in 1718. Charles's military genius frequently prevailed against overwhelming odds. He invaded and defeated Denmark, routed the Russian army at Narva in 1700, and deposed Augustus the Strong of Saxony as king of Poland. Charles's aggressive battlefield tactics provided a model for military reformers throughout the century, but Swedish resources ultimately proved to be inadequate for the defense of an extensive Baltic empire, particularly against the rising power of Russia under Peter the Great. The Great Northern War of 1700–1721 was a catastrophe for Sweden and established Russia as the most formidable military power of northern Europe. Charles's ill-fated invasion of Russia in 1709, ending in his defeat at the battle of Poltava and a period of exile in Turkey, initiated the looting of his inheritance by the czar and his allies. His contemporaries regarded him as a flawed hero, but modern historiography has on the whole been kind to Charles. His most distinguished modern biographer has portrayed him as an enlightened patriot whose career of arms was forced upon him by circumstances.[1]

Charles made a powerful impression on the people of his own century, for whom he assumed symbolic importance as a military hero and as a self-destructive, tragic figure. In England, Sweden's flirtation with Jacobitism made him a target of early-eighteenth-century political pamphlets, and he fared no better at the hands of more thoughtful writers. Alexander

Pope, who expressed the early Enlightenment's sense of a divine, rational, and beneficent universal order, linked Charles with Alexander the Great as madmen and enemies of humanity:

> Look next on Greatness; say where Greatness lies?
> "Where, but among heroes and the wise?"
> Heroes are much the same, the point's agreed,
> From Macedonia's madman to the Swede;
> The whole strange purpose of their lives, to find
> Or make an enemy of all mankind!
> Not one looks backward, onward still he goes,
> Yet n'er looks forward than his nose.[2]

Military heroism and conquest could not in themselves render a man great. Few eighteenth-century intellectuals would have disagreed with Pope on this fundamental point. Pope presented this standard of greatness:

> 'Tis phrase absurd to call a Villain Great:
> Who wickedly is wise, or madly brave,
> Is but the more a fool, the more a knave.
> Who noble ends by noble means obtains,
> Or failing, smiles in exile or in chains,
> Like good Aurelius let him reign, or bleed
> Like Socrates, that Man is great indeed.[3]

"The paths of glory lead but to the grave."[4] That sentiment is echoed throughout the literature of the eighteenth century. In *The Vanity of Human Wishes*, Samuel Johnson provided Charles XII's most memorable epitaph:

> His fall was destined to a barren strand,
> A petty fortress and a dubious hand;
> He left a name at which the world grew pale,
> To point a moral, or adorn a tale.[5]

But Johnson was not immune to the call of military glory. James Boswell contrasted Johnson's cool reflection that "A soldier's time is passed in distress and danger, or in idleness and corruption" with the expression of Johnson's warmer nature: "[W]henever he was warmed and animated by the presence of company, he, like other philosophers, whose minds are impregnated with poetical fancy, caught the common enthusiasm for splendid renown."[6]

"We talked of war. Johnson. 'Every man thinks meanly of himself for not having been a soldier, or not having been at sea.' Boswell. 'Lord Mansfield does not.' Johnson. 'Sir, if Lord Mansfield were in the company of general Officers or Admirals who have been in service, he would shrink; he'd wish to creep under the table.... No, Sir, were Socrates and Charles the Twelfth both present in any company, and Socrates to say, "Follow me, and hear a lecture on philosophy;" and Charles laying his hand on his sword, to say, "Follow me, and dethrone the Czar," a man would be ashamed to follow Socrates. Sir, the impression is universal; yet it is strange.' "

War fulfilled some need in the human soul. This was Johnson's acute observation on human nature. Most intellectuals were aware of the war-like passions that provoked conflict, and they despaired at the barrenness of the results. This awareness lay at the heart of their discussions of the problem of war. Furthermore, the conventional linkage of Charles XII with Alexander the Great during the first half of the eighteenth century pro-voked discussion of the nature of greatness. "Greatness" was a conven-tional ironic device used by writers who opposed Robert Walpole. "The Great Man" reflected not on his statesmanship but on his avarice. Henry Fielding took this to the extreme in his thinly veiled portrayal of Walpole as the highwayman Jonathan Wild. Claude-Adrien Helvétius extended this point to military conquerors: "The robber is a terror to the individual. The conqueror, like a tyrant, is the scourge of a nation. What makes us respect Alexander and Cortez, and despise Cartouch and Rassiat? The power of the one, and the impotence of the other."[7]

Voltaire wrote the definitive eighteenth-century biography of Charles XII. His portrait of Charles was one of heroic virtue carried to excess, of ruling passions unrestrained by reason. Charles suffered in comparison to Peter I of Russia, whose talents were those of a political figure rather than of a soldier. Throughout his career, Voltaire was fascinated by the rise of Russia as a great power, a phenomenon he attributed to the achievements of remarkable personalities who transformed a backward land through enlightened policies. In contrast, he believed that Charles, for all of his admirable traits, lacked substance and vision. In comparing Charles and Peter on the occasion of Poltava, Voltaire observed that "Charles bore the title 'Invincible' which he might lose at any moment, the nations had already given Peter the title 'Great' which he could not lose by any defeat, as he did not own it to any of his victories."[8] He concluded that Charles "was an extraordinary rather than a great man, and rather to be imitated than admired. But his life may be a lesson to kings and teach them that a peaceful life and a happy reign is more desirable than so much glory."[9] Voltaire never tired of making this point to his friend Frederick II of Prus-sia, who complained that the philosopher's strictures against war gave him the gout.[10]

In his historical and philosophical writings, Voltaire consistently main-tained that great rulers were those who looked first to the welfare of their people. His ideal ruler was Prince Leopold of Lorraine, "whose only care was to procure peace, wealth, learning and pleasures for his country."[11] This was a widely shared ideal. Frederick II's own chamberlain, Count Francesco Algarotti, observed that Charles XII, while brave on the battlefield, relied on others for direction. He might be compared to "a shell, which does sometimes prodigious execution, but it must be when under the direction of an able bombardier." Algarotti concluded that the "greatest man among the Swedish monarchs was Gustavus Vasa. He found the means of well regulating and directing the natural strength of his country; and did not attempt to push it beyond its proper bounds; but made so judicious a use of it within the kingdom, that without him it could neither have been extended so far beyond the limits of the realm by Gustavus Adolphus, nor so gloriously misguided as it was afterwards by Charles the Twelfth."[12]

Leopold of Lorraine and Gustavus Vasa were worthy models, consistent with the definitions of true greatness provided by Pope and Voltaire. But the most memorable eighteenth-century rulers were those who ruthlessly extended the reach of their power. It was upon them that public opinion bestowed the title *the Great*. Voltaire admired Peter and befriended Frederick and Catherine. They were not rulers of small peaceful states like Lorraine and, while one could argue that all sought to reform their countries, the principal aim of these reforms was military strength. They redrew the map of Europe and gave European history a new direction. The means they adopted was force. Voltaire was disturbed by the warlike nature of Frederick the Great, and that contributed to the tempestuous nature of their friendship. *Candide* was a bitter pill for the king to swallow. But Voltaire was capable of supporting war if it furthered his own idealistic goals. Accordingly, he urged Catherine, in the interests of civilization, to conduct a war of extermination against the Turks.[13] On paper, he could be more bloodthirsty than Frederick and Catherine were prepared to be in practice. Helvétius, for all his harsh words about Alexander and Cortez, dedicated his work to Frederick and Catherine, who "render themselves dear to humanity." As for France, "the nation is now so abased as to become the contempt of Europe. Conquest alone can afford a remedy proportioned to the virulence of her disease."[14] Voltaire and Helvétius turned blind eyes to the cynical acts of the so-called great if they advanced the cause of "humanity."

A WARLIKE AGE

The campaigns of Charles XII inaugurated a century dominated by war. The Great Northern War paralleled an even more destructive conflict in Western Europe, the War of the Spanish Succession (1701–1714), one of the first European wars to spill over into global conflict. Although the period 1700–1789 is sometimes portrayed as a period of relative peace between the seventeenth-century wars of religion and the wars of the French Revolution and Napoleon Bonaparte, contemporaries did not have the luxury of enjoying this calm. Periods of peace were frequently periods of truce by exhaustion, as in the period after 1714 when Britain and France joined in an uneasy alliance to maintain the settlements of Utrecht and Rastatt, which had divided the Spanish inheritance. Even the maintenance of peace might require violence, as when the British checked Spain's ambitions by destroying her fleet at Cape Passaro in 1718. The 1720s were stirred by rumors of renewed warfare, and every decade thereafter witnessed major European conflict, often with implications for other parts of the world:

The War of the Polish Succession, 1733–1735

The War of Jenkins' Ear (Anglo-Spanish), 1739

The War of the Austrian Succession, 1740–1748

The Seven Years' War, 1756–1763

The Russo-Turkish War, 1768–1774

The American War of Independence, 1775–1783

The War of the Bavarian Succession, 1778–1779

The Russo-Turkish War, 1787–1790

The Austro-Turkish War, 1788–1790

This is a list of the most-prominent conflicts between European states in the period. There were other forms of conflict, including such wars of national resistance as the Jacobite rebellions in Scotland in 1715 and 1745 and opposition to the French conquest of Corsica in 1768–1769. The Poles rose in revolt against the partition of their country by Russia, Prussia, and Austria in 1794. These were not the "cabinet wars" devised by eighteenth-century monarchs and their ministers for limited national gains—so often a stereotype of eighteenth-century warfare—but wars of peoples in which the line between civilian and combatant was blurred. When this occurred, war could be "total" for those involved.

Laurence Sterne claimed to have traveled from London to Paris before he became aware that Britain and France were at war. This must surely be taken with a grain of salt; one wonders if any Englishman could be so unaware. Still, Sterne's account is often mentioned to illustrate a more cosmopolitan age and a more civilized approach to war. Nostalgia pervades our view of the eighteenth century, especially when we turn to it as a symbol of order, restraint, and reason. This Popean image dissolves when one considers the restless forces, the dark passions, and the capacity for brutality of eighteenth-century life. Still, order, reason, and restraint are often considered to be prominent features of eighteenth-century warfare. It is the picture drawn by such older standard authorities as *The New Cam-*

bridge Modern History and *The Rise of Modern Europe,* and it continues to be shared by many experts.[15] Ironically, many aspects of eighteenth-century military life regarded as vices by contemporary observers have been pictured as virtues by a posterity that has experienced total war. Thus, eighteenth-century wars have been portrayed as fought for limited objectives by "absolute monarchs" at the head of dynastic (rather than national) states. Military operations were conducted by small armies of highly trained, long-serving mercenaries commanded by aristocrats who could be counted on to defend a hierarchical society from internal as well as external threats. Avoiding battle whenever possible, these armies engaged in wars of maneuver. Immobile (despite their propensity to maneuver), they were tied to supply depots. Because the troops did not live off the country and because they were strictly disciplined, looting and atrocities against civilians were kept to a minimum. It has also been suggested that cultural forces contributed to order and restraint. Religious zeal had ceased to inflame the combatants; the Enlightenment, with its cosmopolitanism and concern for humanity, had calmed the passions. Clausewitz, veteran of a later, more violent era, advanced a nostalgic view of the old regime: "It had ceased to be in harmony with the spirit of the times to plunder and lay waste the enemy's land."[16]

Compared to the conflicts of the twentieth century, eighteenth-century war does appear limited. However, this is very much a matter of perspective. The career of Charles XII serves to remind us that warfare was not limited in its objectives or in its practice. War claimed the lives of large numbers of soldiers and noncombatants during the period. One historian of the War of the Austrian Succession calculates that 100,000 soldiers and 400,000 civilians were killed. As a percentage of the European population of perhaps 100 to 120 million, this figure seems limited only from the perspective of later industrial-age conflict. The Seven Years' War was yet more destructive, with 500,000 combat deaths. The population of Prussia alone is estimated to have declined by at least a half million. Frederick the Great had no doubts about the effects of the war on his society: "Above 1,500 officers had fallen in the different actions which greatly diminished the number of the nobility; and those of that class who remained in the country were either old men or children."[17] Frederick emerged from the war a changed man. He was no longer a bold youth in search of glory, but a cautious cynic without the stomach for the horrors that he had witnessed. "Let us live and allow others to live," he replied to Voltaire's urgings that he join in a crusade against the Turks.[18] The war left even victorious Britain groaning under its public debt, and the regime in France was undermined financially and discredited by military defeat.

The historian Russell Weigley grants that much blood was spilled in eighteenth-century wars but finds them to have been indecisive for that very reason. Armies were too mutilated to follow up on victories in the field. The frequency of war in the eighteenth century suggests that there is truth in this view. Indecisive war often leads to more war. Nevertheless, the question of decisiveness also depends on one's point of view. Jeremy Black has observed that, since most eighteenth-century wars were fought by coalitions whose members did not necessarily share the same objectives, peace negotiations could leave even those on the winning side dissatisfied with the results. But European leaders did look to war as a means of gaining their political objectives, and their goals were not necessarily modest. Charles XII's invasion of Russia and Marshal Belle-Isle's plans to dismember the Austrian Empire in 1741 are examples of the ambition of men who sought definitive solutions through war. These plans failed, but they transformed the balance between European states during the century. French power was restrained while Britain rose to world-power status. Prussia arrived as a great power, "out of a cannonball," as sometimes has been suggested. Russia waxed and Sweden waned as a consequence of war. Contemporaries were aware that large issues were at stake. At the battle of Malplaquet in 1709, the Dutch army, although on the winning side, suffered a disaster that may have contributed to Holland's decline as a great power. However, the fate of Sweden and of Poland suggests that being on the losing side was worse. With war came revolution in Scotland, Corsica, Genoa, and America. Peasant insurrection, plague, and famine accompanied the course of the armies. Those who sought an enlightened society could not escape the challenge to their hopes and dreams.

THE ENLIGHTENMENT

The relationship between the Enlightenment and war confronts one with the problem of definition. What exactly was the Enlightenment? Does one focus on the philosophes or on the broader culture? Who were the philosophes? In a famous study, Peter Gay regards the philosophes as the party of the Enlightenment. They "were united on a vastly ambitious program, a program of secularism, humanity, cosmopolitanism, and freedom, above all, freedom in its many forms—freedom from arbitrary power, freedom of speech, freedom of trade, freedom to realize one's talents, freedom of aesthetic response, freedom, in a word, of a moral man to make his own world."[19] For Gay, the philosophes were a family, an army that shared a common experience from which it constructed a coherent philosophy. Gay does not give the problem of war much attention but does reflect on his subjects' relations with the "enlightened despots." He concludes that the philosophes were on the whole disappointed with rulers, who, in the end, were opponents of freedom. Thus one philosophe wrote of Joseph II of Austria that, although he accomplished much for his country, in foreign affairs—as a result of "his inclination to decide everything by force"—he appeared as a "terrible bird of prey."[20] One may conclude that war was foreign to the Enlightenment agenda as perceived by Peter Gay. Not all historians of the Enlightenment agree with Gay's definition, however. Ira O. Wade, for example, has rejected Gay's image of a philosophic army marching under a common banner and has offered a wider definition of the term *philosophe*. According to Wade, the term can apply to anyone, "provided that he live in society, that he take an active interest in it, and that he accept some sort of responsibility for its welfare, its coherence, and in its continuity." Wade's definition can apply to a rather broad group not normally thought of as philosophes, ranging from Samuel Johnson to John Adams. Wade's philosophes do not share an agenda, but rather an *esprit philosophique*.[21]

As we shall see, a philosophic spirit could lead one into paths uncharted by members of Gay's army. Each historian of Enlightenment thought approaches the subject from a different angle; it is not the purpose of this work to resolve their differences. Rather, the Enlightenment will be examined as one of a number of contributors to a culture of force that motivated war during the eighteenth century, influenced military operations, and established certain limits to violence. This suggests that the cultural movement known as the Enlightenment was more complex and diffuse than Gay has suggested. If we speak of an Enlightenment agenda, there was surely more than one. Gay's philosophes emphasized reforms that would deliver man from cruelty, ignorance, and superstition. As far as war was concerned, these adherents advocated peace or, if that was unrealistic, practical limits to the horrors of war. It was this group that has led some historians to conclude that the Enlightenment was a cultural force that contributed to humanity in war.[22]

A rational analysis of political and social institutions was fundamental to this process of reform. However, this method was not confined to the party of peace and humanity. Military writers seeking to overcome the obstacles to military decisiveness employed similar methodologies. In this respect, Wade's philosophic spirit or a spirit of scientific inquiry could be placed at the service of war as well as of peace. This "military Enlightenment" is the subject of chapter 2. It is important to note, however, that Diderot and d'Alembert's *Encyclopédie,* first published in the 1750s, combined these two approaches. It condemned war as a crime against humanity yet discussed the rules and laws that limited the conduct of war and incorporated the most-current thought on military tactics.[23]

Gay divides the Enlightenment into three generations but places Jean-Jacques Rousseau outside the party of the philosophes. Yet one cannot consider the late Enlightenment's relationship to war without placing Rousseau at the center. This late Enlightenment departed from the optimistic cosmopolitanism of the first decades. Reflecting the revolutionary movements of the time, a new emphasis was placed on patriotism, civic virtue, and republicanism. These republicans were not pacifists; their ideal was Sparta and the citizen soldier. This theme also influenced the military Enlightenment as military writers turned away from the harsh discipline and rigid maneuvers of contemporary armies and sought to tap new sources of psychological energy in order to promote self-motivation and self-reliance on the part of the troops. This required that the common soldier be treated as a human being rather than a robot, but, for all of this new concern with humanity, the principal focus of these writers was military effectiveness.

The Enlightenment was not the only contributor to the culture of force. Indeed, its impact may have been distorted by hindsight. Modern historians' sense of compatibility with Enlightenment thought may lead to an exaggerated view of its significance for contemporaries. European culture remained that of the Old Regime, dominated by the institutions of monarchy, aristocracy, and established churches. The historian J. C. D. Clark has contended that the Old Regime was alive and well in England after the Glorious Revolution of 1688. He also argues that religion was the central link between the revolutions of 1688 and 1776, with religion serving as the catalyst for both rebellions. According to Clark, the ideals of the reform movements were often drawn from theological premises.[24] Although kings and their ministers may no longer have considered religion to be a primary reason for armed conflict, it continued to provide a reservoir of popular support for war. For example, sermons preached in support of the Anglo-American invasion of Canada during the Seven Years' War placed the events firmly within providential history. The ongoing struggle with Antichrist that commenced with the Reformation remained very much alive for these clergymen and, one presumes, for many of their listeners.[25] Massachusetts soldiers embarking on the 1759 campaign were assured that the very art of war itself was a gift of God. Silvanus Conant wrote, "David was a Man after God's Hand, yet he was a Man of War, skill'd in the bloody Art, and furnished above the common Standard with the Qualifications of War: in this Art, terrible as it is, he informs us that he was taught of God: and we know that the holy God teaches nothing that is in itself sinful, nor any Thing which is not lawful and right, therefore seeing God taught him the Art of War, it is Evidence that the Art is lawful in itself."[26] The Old Testament continued to provide plenty of fuel for those who sought to justify war. Although most eighteenth-century military treatises looked to ancient Greece and Rome for inspiration, one early writer argued that Old Testament generals were clearly superior on the grounds of the great carnage they inflicted. He concluded that the Old Testament justified war and that the New Testament did not disallow it.[27] Such attitudes would continue to bear weight in a society that remained fundamentally Christian throughout the century.

Habits and attitudes developed within the traditional, hierarchical culture of the Old Regime retained deep roots in eighteenth-century life. This was certainly so in the case of army officers who embraced aristocratic values. These values taught them that a soldier's profession was an honorable one and an officer's career one befitting a gentleman. For them the chivalric tradition of the Middle Ages retained its power and provided them with a culture of honor. This culture at times found itself in tension with the military regulations developed by the powerful new centralized states. However, it also provided at least some observers with the confidence that warfare was more polite and the world safer when the troops were commanded by gentlemen rather than the mercenary chieftains of earlier centuries. Aristocratic restraint could thus inspire Enlightenment optimism. This culture of honor is the subject of chapter 3. Nevertheless, despite the continuing power of traditional cultural forces, the Enlightenment provided formidable instruments for an analysis of the problems of war and peace. It is to that analysis that we must turn.

PEACE PROJECTORS

Was war inevitable? Philosophers and social scientists grapple with this issue today and differ according to whether they believe war to be a product of human nature or of society. This is a debate inspired by the Enlightenment that opened new paths to the study of human nature and society. John Locke's tabula rasa raised the prospect of a world made anew, of an escape from the burden of original sin. Some philosophes were inspired by this prospect; others retained a "realistic" view of human affairs. The period of protracted war 1688–1697 (the Nine Years' War) and the renewed conflict of the War of the Spanish Succession and the Great Northern War, 1700–1721, stimulated a desire to escape from a condition of perpetual bloodshed. Throughout the century, intellectuals considered the prospects for peace. As with so many things in the modern world, eighteenth-century peace proposals provide the basis for modern peace studies and efforts to construct institutions for world peace. These eighteenth-century peace proposals are sometimes considered to have been utopian, but they provide an ideal that many continue to prefer to current realities. Three eighteenth-century figures stand out as the architects of designs for world peace: the Abbé de Saint-Pierre (Charles-Irénée Castel), Rousseau, and Immanuel Kant. They defined the theoretical limits of force for the eighteenth century.

Charles-Irénée Castel de Saint-Pierre (1648–1743) was representative of the early Enlightenment's optimism that human reason would lead man to conform to a rational, divinely ordered society in which war would no longer have a place. Saint-Pierre was dismissed by Voltaire as a naive dreamer, but others, including Rousseau, took his proposals seriously. His *Projet pour rendre la paix perpétuelle en Europe* first appeared in 1713 and went through many revisions. Seventeen thirteen was an auspicious year for such a treatise, coming as it did at a time of war exhaustion and peace-making. Saint-Pierre was near the center of these events. Since 1688 he had served at court as first almoner to the Duchess of Orleans, wife of the future regent. Chosen as secretary by the abbé and future cardinal Melchior de Polignac, a delegate at the peace conference at Utrecht, Saint-Pierre observed European politics firsthand. At Louis XIV's court, he was associated with Vauban, Fenelon, and Saint-Simon, critics of the king's military adventurism. In later years he continued to offer advice to such ministers as Cardinals Dubois and Fleury. One scholar believes that, in effect, Fleury adopted many of Saint-Pierre's ideas as the policy of the French government. Indeed, Saint-Pierre had many good ideas—perhaps too many. He was a tireless projector of new schemes to reform the administration, as well as education, medicine, and the nobility. His peace proposal may have influenced Fleury, although the latter came to regard him as a tiresome, disturbing agitator. Many of Saint-Pierre's ideas have been realized, but the very scope of his imagination exposed him to caricature as an impractical dreamer in his own time.

The treaties of Utrecht and Rastatt (1713) appeared to offer respite from war, and even former enemies had a stake in maintaining the settlements. Britain and France, each with debt-ridden, unstable regimes, entered into an alliance in 1716 to maintain order in Europe. James Stanhope, the British minister who negotiated the alliance, may not have been directly influenced by Saint-Pierre, but he thought along similar lines. He "produced grand peace plans based on mutual guarantees and the concept of collective security."[28] By 1718, Britain, France, the Netherlands, and Austria had formed a triple alliance aimed at a settlement of Austrian and Spanish claims in Italy and security for the Hanoverian succession in Britain and the regime of the regent duke of Orleans in France. In 1718–1719, the allies imposed such a settlement on Spain. Saint-Pierre was so encouraged by these developments that he provided Cardinal Dubois with a copy of his peace plan in hopes that the Quadruple Alliance could be extended to all European states. He proposed a union of European states with the authority to enforce the status quo as defined by current treaties. Princes would be expected to join because their domestic and international rights would be guaranteed by an international organization representing all of the states of Europe. This organization would have the power to arbitrate disputes and enforce its decisions by military means.

Saint-Pierre derived many of his ideas from the Grand Design of the duc de Sully that had appeared in 1638. Sully's proposals reflected the aspirations of his master Henry IV for a European league that would expel the Turks from Europe while conveniently reducing Habsburg power. Saint-Pierre differed from Sully in that his specific objective was peace. He was not so naive as to think that peace would break out in an era of reason and good feeling; rather he hoped that the warlike instincts of the princes would be restrained by a kind of Popean universal order in which self-love served social ends. European princes would find it in their interest to abide by this order. In the second edition of *Paix perpétuelle* (1738), Saint-Pierre argued the advantage for Britain in the guarantee of the Protestant Succession and for Austria in security for the Pragmatic Sanction. As Frederick the Great would later observe, the only problem with this scheme was to convince princes to join in the first place. Rousseau agreed that the weakness of Saint-Pierre's proposal lay in the fact that "The whole life of kings, or of those on whom they shuffle off their duties, is devoted solely to two objects: to extend their rule beyond their frontiers and to make it absolute within them."[29]

Yet perhaps Saint-Pierre's plan was not as chimerical as some have suggested. As we have seen, there was wide interest in the restoration of peace. Even Cardinal Alberoni, the minister of Philip V and Elizabeth Farnese of Spain, who sought by force to revise the Utrecht settlement in Italy in 1717–1718, wrote peace proposals after his dismissal from office. Sovereignty was a rather new concept in 1713, and there were those such as the philosopher Leibniz who, though he scorned Saint-Pierre's proposal, still dreamed of a European Christian republic under the pope and the emperor. Compared to Leibniz, Saint-Pierre seems strikingly modern. His views reflected a world not unlike that of 1815 or even 1918 and 1945, when the great powers found themselves shaken and exhausted. International organizations, whether the Concert of Europe, the League of Nations, or the United Nations, were not unreasonable to statesmen grappling with postwar dilemmas. Security for the established social order and international stability were valuable prizes. Saint-Pierre's substitution of international cooperation for traditional balance-of-power politics had appeal for those who had experienced their results. Perhaps twentieth-century events have redeemed Saint-Pierre's reputation for many writers do not find his ideas to be at all unreasonable.[30]

While the European powers did not adopt Saint-Pierre's system during the period 1713–1745, his ideas at least reflected to some degree the policies of leading statesmen. It is doubtful that a guarantee of the status quo would have satisfied the next generation of leaders as Cardinal Fleury gave way to Marshal Belle-Isle and Frederick the Great burst upon the scene in search of glory. This new generation launched Europe into another period of destructive war. It also provided the context in which Rousseau explored Saint-Pierre's ideas of peace. Although Rousseau was interested in Saint-Pierre's project, his own ideas on war and peace reflected his break with what had been heretofore Enlightenment thought. Rousseau did not believe that war was a product of human nature, but rather of society. War existed not among men but among states that were motivated by greed and the desire for power. He recognized, as did others, that Europe was the product of a social bond formed by religion, commerce, manners, and laws, and that a kind of equilibrium resulted from all of these influences. But these very qualities contributed to a warlike state of affairs. Commercial competition led to the materialism and inequality that lay at the heart of conflict in society. The laws only perpetuated the existence of this corruption.

According to Rousseau, the public law of Europe or what we today would call international law, rested not on general principles but varied incessantly according to time and place. It was full of contradictions that could only lead to war. In his essay "Projet de paix perpétuelle" he concluded that universal peace was possible granting three premises: that in Europe, excluding Turkey, there was the consciousness of a general social bond among the races; that the corruption of society that has made these ties a source of evil could be eliminated; and that, by strengthening these ties, society could be improved so that *war* and *peace* would become meaningless terms.[31] Unlike Saint-Pierre, Rousseau believed that the preservation of the status quo was not a means for the preservation of perpetual peace. But he also recognized that the radical reform of society that he considered to be a necessary condition was as difficult as persuading the princes to surrender their warlike ambitions. Most commentators on Rousseau conclude that he was pessimistic about the prospects for peace. He believed that the virtuous society he sought could only be achieved in small, autarkic, agricultural republics. Such republics should eschew conventional commerce and diplomacy and defend their rights by citizen militias and loose federations with other republics. This was essentially the advice he gave to the Corsicans and the Poles as they struggled to win national independence. Nevertheless, he did not believe that Europe was ripe for social reform; he believed that the prospect of a Europe organized in federative leagues of small republics was remote. He concluded with prophetic insight: "No federation could ever be established except by a revolution. That being so, which of us would dare to say whether the league of Europe is a thing more to be desired or feared? It would perhaps do more harm in a moment than it would guard against for ages."[32] Rousseau was more committed to freedom than to peace, but he had no illusions that either could be achieved without great sacrifice.

Immanuel Kant wrote his *Perpetual Peace* (1795) at the beginning of just such a revolutionary era. Although he considered war to be engrafted on human nature, he believed that nature had provided a powerful countervailing force that would eventually lead man to the condition of peace. "She unites nations whom the principle of a cosmopolitan right would not have secured against violence and war. And this union she brings about through an appeal to their mutual interests. The commercial spirit cannot co-exist with war, and sooner or later it takes possession of every nation."[33] Kant thus differed from Rousseau by joining the tradition ranging from Adam Smith to modern free-trade enthusiasts, who link peace and commerce. He agreed with Montesquieu, who wrote that "The natural effect of commerce is to lead to peace.... all unions are founded on mutual needs."[34] Still it is clear from Kant's essay that, although he thought that perpetual peace was eventually possible, he did not believe it to be imminent. His "preliminary" and "definitive" articles for a perpetual peace between states required a set of conditions not supplied by the Old Regime. His second definitive article: "The law of nations shall be founded upon a federation of free states" recalls Saint-Pierre's vision of an international organization and Rousseau's of a federation of republics. His first definitive article suggests the influence of Rousseau: "The civil constitution of each state shall be republican." By republican Kant did not necessarily mean democratic, for he believed that aristocracies and some monarchies embodied the spirit of republican government. But he did believe that a state in which the majority of the citizens determined questions of peace and war was likely to incline to peace. The preliminary articles also required conditions not present in the Old Regime. The second article would prevent wars of succession, the most common cause of eighteenth-century warfare: "No state having an independent existence— whether it is great or small shall be acquired by another through inheritance, exchange, purchase or donation." The third article provided that "standing armies (in this case mercenary or professional, rather than citizen, armies)...shall be abolished in the course of time." In 1795, Kant's Prussia had yet to contemplate changes such as these, but Europe was confronted by the dynamic alternative presented by the republican government and the citizen armies of France. Europe had given birth to a new era. Whether it would meet the expectations of the philosophes was yet to be seen.[35]

   We see an evolution in the thought of these projectors of peace. Saint-Pierre seems to have had little faith that human nature was pacific or could be improved. His plan for perpetual peace relied on positive law and force. His hopes were founded on war exhaustion, the self-interest of princes, and the maintenance of the status quo. Although he was dismissed by some as a dreamer, his plan was the most practical of the three in the context of his time. Portions of it may have influenced the foreign policies of senior statesmen of the early Enlightenment. Rousseau's *Extrait du projet de paix perpétuelle* appeared during the most destructive war of the Old Regime. The times were not propitious for a peace project that relied on the cooperation of the great powers, and this suggested that an alternative to the existing system was required. Rousseau's ideas on peace drew upon attitudes consistent in all of his work, but what one writer refers to as his "reluctant realism"[36] may be at least partially explained by the horrors of the Seven Years' War. Perpetual peace seemed possible only by means of a revolutionary change in society. Kant was living in revolutionary times when he wrote *Perpetual Peace.* He agreed that fundamental changes in European society were necessary but was more optimistic that this would occur. Both Saint-Pierre and Rousseau believed that perpetual peace would probably require the use of force. One should not regard these men as dogmatic pacifists. The theoretical alternatives to war thus included a reliance on force.

LIMITATIONS

If the elimination of war lay far in a misty future, there was widespread confidence among Europeans that war would not be "total," that it would be fought within certain recognized limits. These limits were defined by the relatively homogenous culture of Europe and the sense of equipoise provided by the balance of power. Voltaire's description of the European state system on the succession of Louis XIV suggests that the concept of balance had deep roots:

Already for a long time one could regard Christian Europe (except Russia) as a sort of great republic divided into several states, some monarchical, others of a mixed character; the former aristocratic, the latter popular, but all in harmony with each other, all having the same substratum of religion, although divided into various sects; all possessing the same principles of public and political law, unknown in other parts of the world. In obedience to these principles the European nations do not make their prisoners slaves, they respect their enemies' ambassadors, they agree as to the pre-eminence and rights of certain princes, such as the Emperor, kings and lesser potentates, and, above all, they are at one on the wise policy of maintaining among themselves so far as possible an equal balance of power, cease-lessly carrying on negotiations, even in wartime, and sending each to the other ambassadors or less honourable spies, who can acquaint every court with the designs of any one of them, give in a moment the alarm to Europe, and defend the weakest from invasions which the strongest is ready to attempt.[37]

There was widespread agreement that such a balance of power existed. Saint-Pierre acknowledged it but believed that it was inadequate to protect sovereigns and their subjects from foreign and civil war.[38] Rousseau observed that "the present (1756) balance of Europe is just firm enough to remain in perpetual oscillation without losing itself altogether; and if our troubles cannot increase, still less can we put an end to them seeing that any sweeping revolution is, henceforth, an impossibility."[39] Helvétius, as had Thucydides and Thomas Hobbes, cynically believed that states only treated one another justly as long as a balance of power existed between them. "Power," he observed, "is the only object of man's pursuit.... The much boasted respect of man for justice is never anything more than a respect for power."[40] Yet self-love, the pursuit of power, could in a Newtonian sense contribute to a universal—or at least a European—order. It was generally agreed that the balance of power arose from the inherent aggressiveness of European states.[41] The balance did not eliminate war, but it did prevent one state or coalition of states from exercising hegemony. Jean François, Marquis de Saint-Lambert believed that there would always be war in Europe, but that the balance protected from conquest small monarchies and large republics such as Poland.[42] That he was mistaken in the latter case reveals the uncertainties about the nature of the system. Was it the product of the evolution of European states from at least the time of the Renaissance? Was it a natural occurrence, a microcosm of the mechanical Newtonian universe, allowing, as Prince von Kaunitz-Rietberg claimed, diplomacy to be conducted with mathematical precision? Or was it something that statesmen should strive for? Did it represent a moral norm? David Hume did not think so. He concluded that Britain had engaged in wars to maintain the balance against France, but that these wars "begun with justice, and even perhaps from necessity,...have always been too far pushed, from obstinacy and passion...we see, that above half of all our wars with France, and all our public debts, are owing to our own imprudent vehemence, than to the ambitions of our neighbors."[43] Then there was the question of how the balance could be measured. It could certainly change, for as Voltaire observed, it had favored the House of Austria until the reign of Louis XIV. Rousseau believed that lack of German unity in the eighteenth century was a unique but central feature of the system. In the eighteenth century the emergence of Russia and the eclipse of Sweden required new assumptions on the part of those engaged in diplomacy. This suggested that maintenance of the balance required continual vigilance on the part of all parties. In the second half of the eighteenth century, commercial wealth began to play an increasing part in the calculation of state power, suggesting that colonialism and imperial competition had transformed the question of the balance into world, rather than European, terms. The nature of the balance depended on one's perspective. It could be argued that the "balance of Europe" allowed Britain to assume predominance in the scheme of world power. Prussia and Austria were more likely to focus exclusively on Europe or even Germany. M. S. Anderson concludes his discussion of balance-of-power theories by observing that, whatever their defects, they "also reflected the most constructive aspect of the Enlightenment—its faith in science and in the ability of man ultimately to control his own environment and future."[44] But one should add that these theories recognized war as a legitimate means to achieve that end.

THE LEGAL CONTEXT

One enthusiast of the balance of power was the Swiss diplomat and lawyer Emmerich von Vattel, author of *The Law of Nations* (1758) and the most-important eighteenth-century expert on international law. Vattel offered a guide to two critical questions: (1) Are there legitimate causes for war? and (2) Could war be regulated by rules or laws that limit the severity of its impact on humanity? He may be seen as a disciple of the seventeenth-century legal authority Hugo Grotius. Grotius adapted a traditional Christian theoretical framework, established by St. Augustine and Thomas Aquinas, to a world experiencing the breakdown of religious unity and the development of sovereign states. Vattel had little new to say about the objectives of lawful war: "1. To recover what belongs, or is due, to us. 2. To provide for our future safety by punishing the aggressor or offender. 3. To defend ourselves from injury, by repelling unjust violence. The first two are the objects of an offensive, the third of a defensive war." He considered self-defense a natural human right: "We have shown that nature gives men a right to employ force, when it is necessary for their defense, and for the preservation of their right. This principle is generally acknowledged: reason demonstrates it; and nature herself has engraved it on the heart of man. Some fanatics indeed, taking in a literal sense the moderation recommended in the gospel, have adopted the strange fancy of suffering themselves to be massacred or plundered rather than oppose force to violence. But we need not fear this error will make any great progress. The generality of mankind will of themselves guard against this contagion—happy, if they as well knew how to keep within the just bounds which nature has set to a right that is granted only through necessity."[45]

Vattel moved on to give attention to the bounds provided by nature. Here too he drew upon centuries of theoretical writing and practice that pre-dated the Enlightenment. Geoffrey Parker has concluded that the laws of war in Europe have rested since the Middle Ages on the same five foundations: (1) prescriptive texts—the Bible, Roman law, canon law, the writings of Augustine and Aquinas; (2) efforts by the medieval church to protect the weak by instituting the Peace of God and the Truce of God; (3) the enactment by armies of legal codes and articles of war that governed the behavior of the troops; (4) precedents created by the conduct of war itself; and (5) the acceptance by participants in armed conflict of the advantages of mutual restraint. Parker concludes that this powerful combination of natural and divine law, ecclesiastical precept, military law, and common custom coalesced to impart a new and enduring consistency to both *jus ad bellum* (just war theory) and *jus in bello* (the law of war) in the period between 1550 and 1700.[46] All of these factors were thus in place before the age of the Enlightenment, and one might conclude that Vattel had little to add. Although he claimed to have revealed the natural laws regulating human conflict, he was in fact providing a new gloss on old authorities. Nevertheless, his work reflects a new context shaped by two influences: (1) the increased power of the state over its armed forces and (2) the decline of religion as a motive for war. This led Vattel to conclude that war was being conducted with a new moderation that raised hopes, if not for the elimination of war, then at least for its humane conduct: "At present, " he observed, "the European nations generally carry on their wars with great moderation and generosity."[47] There was much to praise, he thought, in the treatment of prisoners and in the practice of paroles and exchanges. The capitulation, the arrangement for the honorable surrender and evacuation of a city, had relieved the worst horrors of the sack. Orderly contributions imposed on occupied territories were preferable to pillaging. If soldiers were sometimes carried away in the heat of action, the officers could be counted on to intervene. "Let us never forget that our enemies are men," he wrote, praising, of all people, the duke of Cumberland, "the butcher of Scotland," who, when seriously wounded at the battle of Dettingen, ordered his surgeon to treat first a more seriously wounded French officer.[48]

What standard should govern those who pursue lawful objectives in war? Vattel concluded that it is whatever is necessary to bring one's opponent to reason and to obtain "security and justice from him."[49] He wrote that sovereigns should not exceed those limits, and no doubt his belief in the moderation of the age gave him confidence that they would not. But necessity is frequently a compelling force, and reason and justice are fragile boundaries. Vattel left wide discretion to a sovereign on the question of what is necessary. With regard to noncombatants he revealed what Geoffrey Best has called Vattel's realism.[50] He had no illusions that they could be protected from the horrors of war. All subjects of an enemy state, including women and children, were to be considered enemies. If they contributed in any way to opposing one's just objectives, they should expect to suffer the consequences. His only qualification is that women, children, the elderly, and the sick should be spared, provided they make no resistance. As one scholar, Karma Nabulsi, has recently observed, resistance can come in many forms, both active and passive.[51] Vattel gives no direction to guide soldiers in these circumstances. Noncombatants have no resistance rights at all. The law, according to Vattel, exclusively favors the occupying army. As we shall see, eighteenth-century civilians did oppose occupying forces, but Vattel offered them little encouragement. Furthermore, his appeal to moderation applied only to the treatment of "civilized" people. "When we are at war with a savage nation, who observe no rules, we may punish them in the person of any of their people whom we take."[52] The harsh actions of the great powers in Corsica, the Scottish Highlands, and on the American frontier thus find justification in Vattel's rules. If a sovereign pursuing an unjust war is guilty of a criminal act, what of his officers and soldiers? Vattel insists that they are bound to follow orders "except in a case of a war so palpably and indisputably unjust, as not to permit a presumption of any secret reason of state that is capable of justifying it—a case in politics that is nearly impossible."[53] Vattel thus followed Aquinas in requiring that just wars be waged by legitimate sovereigns and in giving them considerable latitude to determine how to wage them.

Vattel was the principal keeper of the Grotian tradition in the eighteenth century, but that tradition was also reflected in the Enlightenment's great authoritative work, the *Encyclopédie*. Jaucourt, in a brief article "Guerre (Droit naturel et politique)," was more pessimistic about the conduct of eighteenth-century war for, as he noted, he wrote under the influence of the horrors of the Seven Years' War as reported by the gazettes of 1757. He believed that there were occasions for just war: "[A]ny war, says Cicero, that is not for defense, for the safety of the state, or for the established faith, is an illegitimate war." Sovereigns recognized the importance of asserting the justice of military action but frequently veiled their true and unjust motives. Jaucourt cited the example of Alexander the Great in this regard, but Frederick the Great seems his more likely target. Thus his view of contemporary politics was more pessimistic than that of Vattel. In his discussion of the law of war, he summarized Grotius's realistic position that exposed civilians to the effects of war. Those caught in its midst could expect what has come to be called collateral damage. The law of nature should encourage men to act with the greatest concern for humanity, "but war stifles the voice of nature, of justice, of religion, and of humanity." Legal restrictions had little force when war transformed men into beasts.[54]

Others argued for optimism. The British lawyer James Marriot, in an opinion concerning the status of the Anglo-French commercial treaty of 1686, concluded that even in wartime one retains one's investment in the public funds of the enemy. War, he concluded, suspends but does not abrogate public obligations. "In the present Age, as War is commenced on different Principles from the wars of Antiquity, so it ends with different Principles, in both more to the Honour of Humanity. The public law of Europe abhors the sanguinary object of antient [sic] Wars, universal Slavery, or Extirpation—Every war in these Times is considered but an Appeal to the rest of the Powers of Europe, and is but a temporary Exertion of Force to decide a Point of Interest which no human Tribunal can determine, thus it is in its nature but a *Suspense* of other Rights not in contest which existed between the belligerent powers reciprocally before the War...." The present era, he concluded was the "Age of Negotiation."[55]

Whether they viewed the international scene with optimism or pessimism, the philosophes could agree that the existing political system was warlike at heart. Montesquieu's dictum that "the spirit of monarchy is war and expansion; the spirit of republics is peace and moderation" is well known.[56] Saint-Lambert agreed that the spirit of republics was peaceful, but observed that love of liberty and fear of its loss drove republics to war against monarchical states.[57] The veteran officer Antoine de Pas de Feuquières ascribed no such high motives to republics. He wrote, "Those very Republics, who from the frame of their Constitution, should appear desirous of Tranquility, have, in my time, been all agitated by the Emotions of Jealousy, Ambition, or Interest, so that the Result, I may venture to declare, that this Character of a pacific Prince has never been exerted by any Power, with an Air of Unconstraint, since I have had any knowledge of the World."[58] Those philosophes who idealized ancient republics such as Sparta and Rome had to agree. In addition, it was recognized that war was not simply the hobby of kings or the product of reason of state. There were other, deeper emotional forces that made war a part of the European condition. The Scottish philosopher Adam Ferguson, who saw combat with the Highland regiment at the battle of Fontenoy in 1745, observed that "the statesman may explain his conduct on the motives of national jealousy and caution, but the people have dislikes and antipathies for which they cannot account."[59] War might have been a product of the social political system or part of human nature, but it was a fact of life. Nevertheless, most philosophes seem to have believed that enlightenment contributed to humane conduct in war. The French philosopher Paul-Henri-Dietrich d'Holbach, for example, concluded that "the more the peoples are enlightened, the more they demonstrate moderation in war." Voltaire, who scoffed at systems whether they were conceived by Saint-Pierre or Vattel, nevertheless believed that the Enlightenment had contributed to a gradual improvement in military conduct: "The letters have at last softened the mores."[60] These satisfied statements raise an interesting question of causation. Had the philosophes contributed to a new context that led to moderation in war or were they merely describing particular developments in the warfare of their time that were the result of other traditions and influences? As we have seen, many of the restraints on Western war were in place before 1700.

MEN OF WAR

Enlightenment writers relied on the aristocratic officer's culture of honor to provide a code of correct behavior. This code was defined by Lieutenant General Comte de Tressan in the *Encyclopédie* article "Homme de guerre." He observed that if through necessity an officer acted as the "rigorous minister of the vengeance of kings," he would "distinguish between the necessary evil and the unnecessary and the brigandage that he ought never to tolerate; that amid the cruel spectacles and chaos of war, pity should always have easy access to his heart; and that nothing should ever banish from it justice, disinterestedness, and the love of humanity."[61] Montesquieu believed that honor was the principle of monarchical government. It was also the essence of a military culture that combined obedience to the sovereign with a concern for status and self-respect. "For the nobility, honor prescribes nothing more than serving the prince in war;

indeed, this is the preeminent profession because its risks, successes, and even misfortunes lead to greatness. But honor wants to be the arbiter in imposing this law; and if honor has been offended it permits or requires one to withdraw to one's home."[62] The eighteenth century witnessed considerable tension between the formal rules of military discipline, recently enhanced by increased state power, and this culture of honor. As we shall see, the latter led to individual acts of disobedience that would be inconceivable to a modern military professional but were perfectly compatible with the chivalric traditions of earlier ages. But there seemed to be no alternative to society as it existed. Aristocrats remained the natural leaders of society and of men in time of war. Honor insured that officers would act bravely and set an example for their men. Honor provided that officers would act as the guardians of the traditional values and institutions of society. A soldier-king such as Frederick the Great accepted middle-class officers only out of necessity. The Seven Years' War bled white his aristocratic officer corps and required him to accept bourgeois candidates. When peace was restored, he proceeded to purge the corps of all but aristocrats. This bias continued in Britain through the nineteenth century. When the Victorian commentator Charles M. Clode discussed the 1749 British military code that limited a soldier's obedience to "any lawful command of his superior officer," he warned that such a provision was of little value "should the officers who give commands be desperadoes instead of gentlemen."[63] Any optimism about the nature of eighteenth-century warfare rested on the conduct of these men. Their values determined what actually happened in wartime. Only by evaluating the influence of the Enlightenment upon the officer culture can one truly determine the relationship between the Enlightenment and the conduct of war.

Few expected the common soldiers to behave as gentlemen. The rank and file were recruited from the peasantry and from the lower orders in the towns. They had a rather undeserved reputation as criminals and brigands who lived for loot but, when confronted by danger, would run away if given a chance. For this reason they required the harsh discipline associated with the Prussians. For good or bad, Frederick the Great's army was the model for the period: a standing army of disciplined robots led by aristocratic officers under a philosopher-king. The philosophes deplored these expensive armies of hirelings as economically ruinous and as causes of war in themselves. Kant believed that standing armies caused states to commit acts of aggression in order to relieve themselves of the financial burden of their upkeep. He wrote, "the practice of hiring men to kill or be killed seems to imply a use of them more as machines and instruments in the hands of another (namely the state) which cannot easily be reconciled with the right of humanity in our own person."[64] Rousseau argued that mercenaries had been one of the chief causes of the ruin of the Roman

Empire.[65] The answer to these "regiments of murderers" (Voltaire's term) was the citizen-soldier, or militiaman. "For this," wrote Montesquieu, "one must make use of the new invention of the militia established in almost all of Europe and push them to the same excess as the regular troops."[66] The idea of citizen-soldiers appealed to neoclassical admirers of Sparta and Rome. But they were, in a sense, an anachronism. The musket fire and linear tactics at the heart of the eighteenth-century military system required strict discipline and prolonged training if they were to be employed effectively. Militiamen were part-time soldiers, sometimes more of a social club than a military force. They were useful for garrisons, internal security, and as manpower reservoirs in emergencies. However, they could not easily replace battlefield soldiers. When Frederick the Great's armies were reduced by casualties during the midcentury wars, they declined in effectiveness as inexperienced replacements joined the ranks. The volunteer citizen-soldier envisaged by Rousseau was another matter. These volunteers committed to the defense of their country might overcome the disadvantages of lack of training. American forces deployed against Britain during the American War of Independence relied on such soldiers, although Continental regulars were trained in European techniques. British regulars usually retained the advantage on the battlefield. French revolutionary regimes would employ large numbers of volunteers and conscripts to overwhelm armies of the Old Regime. Such revolutions unleashed passions unforeseen by men of the early Enlightenment. John Adams, for example, cast moderation aside in his prescription for the conduct of the American War of Independence. "I have but one Piece of Advice to give," he wrote in reference to his enemies, "You must kill, starve or take them all."[67]

Inspired by the ideal of Sparta, Rousseau recommended the militia system to the Corsicans and the Poles, two European peoples struggling for independence. He cautioned the Poles not to invest in extensive fortifications, for he recognized that artillery and modern fortification required regular troops who, as in the case of Rome, ruin a free people. Moral qualities, patriotism, and virtue, he argued, provided the best shield against the predatory powers that surrounded them. Like the Spartans they should shun foreign contact and educate their citizens to love their country. Luxury and wealth were to be shunned and agriculture and self-sufficiency prized: "Tilling the soil makes men patient and robust which is needed to make good soldiers. Those recruited from the cities are flabby and mutinous; they cannot bear the fatigues of war; they break down under the strain of marching; they are consumed by illnesses; they fight among themselves and fly before the enemy. Trained militia are the best and most reliable troops; the true education of a soldier is to work on a farm."[68]

Such advice might been appropriate for a poor island such as Corsica, but Rousseau's discussion of the military system in his "Considerations on the Government of Poland" (1772), although consistent with his political thought, revealed the tension between his ideals and Polish realities. There, the institution of serfdom seemed to prohibit the formation of a peasant militia, which would have been like arming the helots. The infantry would have to be conscripted from the towns. Although townsmen were poor military material, Rousseau argued that they could be transformed into citizen-soldiers by a program of patriotic education. The Polish people should come to look upon their soldiers not as mercenary bandits, but as citizens performing their duty in the service of their country. This could be achieved only if the officers themselves were chosen on merit, rather than on birth. But here he encountered a problem similar to that of serfdom. His proposal concerning officers was at odds with the continuing powerful role of the nobility in Poland. His solution was to place them in the cavalry, a swift-moving, light force consistent with the horse-soldier traditions of Eastern Europe. Indeed, he pronounced the cavalry as the foundation of Poland's defense. It seems questionable that the nobility making up such a force would have adopted Rousseau's recipe of equality, simplicity, and virtue.

Perhaps no issue separated Rousseau and Voltaire so clearly as their attitudes toward Poland. Voltaire supported Catherine the Great's acquisitive designs on Poland—partly out of hatred of the strong, continuing influence of the Catholic Church in that country—and urged her to make war on the Turks. Rousseau warmed to a people's fight for independence and made a single exception to his recommendation of diplomatic isolation: alliance with the Turks, who, in contrast with Christian powers, fulfilled their obligations and respected treaties.[69]

Rousseau believed that his military values produced soldiers who were unsuited for wars of conquest but were formidable in the defense of their country. His military thought was exclusively defensive, consistent with his view that free republics should be isolationist. Could this have worked? In practice, revolutionary regimes in Corsica and Poland could not prevail against the regular troops of the great powers. The militia played only a secondary role in America's successful war for independence. Perhaps the leader who most closely realized Rousseau's idea of a virtuous republic was Thomas Jefferson, who became president of the United States in 1801. He preferred isolationism and a "passive defense" policy of reliance on militia and shallow-draft coastal gunboats. It was a policy as cheap as it was virtuous, but it left the United States woefully unprepared for any sort of war, whether against Europeans or Native Americans.[70] One must conclude that the philosophes' interest in citizen-soldiers was either naive or a means of advancing a revolutionary program.

Although the philosophes expressed concern about the right of humanity when soldiers were converted to machines, there is something rather abstract in their references to the rank and file. The latter appeared more as a symbol of some ill in society than as men and thus became subjects of caricature. In his *Encyclopédie* articles on recruitment and desertion, Jaucourt criticized the death penalty inflicted upon deserters, because it failed to remedy the problem. Desertion was the result of forcing men to serve and then spending them like money. The nations of Europe recruited the vilest of their subjects into their armies and therefore could not expect them to act as had the citizen-soldiers of Rome.[71] Desertion was a serious concern in all eighteenth-century armies, but Jaucourt's discussion of recruitment was simplistic. Recruitment of armies varied across the continent, with peasants constituting the bulk of eastern armies and townsmen those of the west. The soldiers were not isolated from society. In peacetime, the majority of the Prussian infantry, recruited under the cantonal system, spent part of each year in agricultural labor on their home farms. The encyclopedist Saint-Lambert advocated adoption of this practice in France as a means of reducing desertion.[72] Armies grew more national in character over the course of the century, with a subsequent decline in the number of foreign mercenaries. The German regiments in the French service, for example, increasingly came to be recruited from the French-ruled provinces of Alsace and Lorraine. Military writers were aware of this trend; as will be described in chapter 2, there was much discussion of the national character of armies. When a country was invaded, patriotism seems to have played a greater role in recruitment than the philosophes would have us believe. André Corvisier, a leading historian of the eighteenth-century French army, has concluded that "there is no doubt that patriotism played a part. It very likely influenced as many enlistees in the year 1709 as it unquestionably did in 1792."[73] Modern scholarship has also disposed of the notion that the British and Hessian soldiers who fought in the American War of Independence were a band of impressed criminals. Rather, the majority of the rank and file were poor-but-respectable men, similar in many respects to the social profile of their opponents, the citizen-soldiers of the Continental army.[74]

There were, of course, instances of crime, rioting, rape, and pillage committed by troops of all nations during the period. Civil authorities might claim with some justice that military officers failed to deliver up soldiers for punishment, but military codes provided harsh sanctions for these abuses. They were enforced by punishments that seem barbarous by modern standards. For example, in 1775 British soldiers in the Boston garrison who were convicted of robbery faced sentences ranging from 300 to 1,000 lashes to death.[75] Extreme as they may appear to the modern observer, these punishments mirrored those administered by civilian courts. It was a cruel age, one in which public executions and corporal punishment were commonplace. On my office wall are three William Hogarth prints, titled *The Three Stages of Cruelty*. They serve as a vivid reminder of the callous indifference of many contemporaries to scenes of man's inhumanity to animals and to his fellow men. One would be surprised if military justice departed from the standards of the period. In practice, as was true of the punishment of criminals in general, execution of these sentences was sporadic. One study of eighteenth-century British courts-martial finds that the severity of punishment depended on the reputation and character of the soldier and that the rank and file probably did not look upon the system as unfair.[76] In some respects, military justice may have been more humane than its civil counterpart. As Cesare Beccaria observed: "Torture is not considered necessary in military law, though armies, for the most part composed of the dregs of humanity, might be held on that account to be more in need of it than any other class of men. Strange if one forgets for a moment the tyrannical power of custom that, law and peace should have to learn from minds hardened in blood and slaughter, the most humane methods of adjudication."[77] Beccaria sought to ameliorate the cruelty of the age, and in doing so left an indelible mark on the subject of criminal justice. As is discussed in chapter 2, he won an audience among contemporary army officers who sought to apply his ideas to the military-justice system.

The second half of the eighteenth century saw a rising concern for the plight of the common soldier. There were expressions of pity for the ruined veteran and for the hapless deserter. Among the philosophes this concern was fueled by an increased interest in the common man and a hatred for war that intensified as a result of the brutal conflicts of the midcentury.[78] But humane sentiments were not limited to the philosophes. Samuel Johnson and John Wesley, not normally considered to be philosophes, intervened on behalf of captive French soldiers imprisoned in England. They were staunch patriots, deeply religious men, and servants of humanity. Of the French prisoners, Johnson wrote in 1760: "That charity is best, of which the consequences are the most extensive: the relief of enemies has a tendency to unite mankind in fraternal affection; to soften the acrimony of adverse nations, and dispose them to peace and amity: in the mean time, it alleviates captivity, and takes away something from the miseries of war. The rage of war, however mitigated, will always fill the world with calamity and horror: let it not then be unnecessarily extended; let animosity and hostility cease together; and no man be longer deemed an enemy, than while his sword is drawn against us."[79]

The public was well aware of the hard lot of the common soldier. Readers of Tobias Smollett's autobiographical novel *Roderick Random,* about the ill-fated British attack on Cartagena in 1741, understood that a soldier was as likely to be a victim of his own service as that of the enemy. Midcentury wars overwhelmed primitive state resources for military veterans and invalids. The wreckage of the armies was a common sight in eighteenth-century towns, and pity for the soldier's lot was undoubtedly provoked in many hearts, even among the illiterate. British poets of "sensibility," such as Oliver Goldsmith, took up the theme of the broken soldier. None did so more poignantly, however, than an anonymous Irish street song of the 1760s that reflected the lot of disabled veterans forced into beggary:

> "You haven't an arm and you haven't a leg
> You're an eyeless, noseless, chickenless egg;
> You'll have to be put with a bowl to beg;
> Och Johnny, I hardly knew ye!
> With drums and guns, and drums and guns,
> The enemy nearly slew ye;
> My darling dear, you look so queer.
> Och Johnny, I hardly knew ye!"[80]

Horror of war and compassion for its victims was widespread during the eighteenth century. The philosophes of Gay's army of humanity shared this sentiment with members of a broader culture. The Enlightenment provided the advocates of peace with intellectual tools to advance their cause, but those tools could be placed at the service of others. Soldiers were part of the culture of the Enlightenment as well. Military intellectuals were familiar with the works of Enlightenment authors and sometimes knew them personally. They were not unaffected by the concerns expressed by the philosophes, but in their profession they applied the scientific and rational elements that underpinned the Enlightenment to their primary mission: military success. This gave rise to an extensive military literature during the eighteenth century that I term the military Enlightenment. In this field, Mars clearly prevailed over Socrates.

NOTES

1. R.M. Hatton, *Charles XII of Sweden* (London: Weidenfeld and Nicolson, 1968). For a review of modern German assessments, see Jorg-Peter Findeison, "Karl XII von Schweden: Gekronter soldat oder genialer feldherr? Zum bild Karl XII in der Deutschen historiographie," *Zeitschrift fur Geschichtswissenschaft* 42, no. 11 (1994): 983–98. Charles has often been praised as a tactician and scorned as a strategist, but he is now perceived as responding to the realities of Sweden's strategic position. See Robert L. Frost, *The Northern Wars: War, State and Society in Northeastern Europe, 1558–1721* (Harlow, U.K.: Pearson Education Ltd., 2000), 279–318.

2. Essay on Man, Essay IV, lines 217–224.

3. Essay on Man, Essay IV, lines 230–236.

4. Thomas Gray, "Elegy Written in a Country Churchyard," lines 33–36, in Patricia Meyer Spacks, ed., *Eighteenth Century Poetry* (Englewood Cliffs, NJ: Prentice Hall, 1964), 252.

5. Samuel Johnson, "The Vanity of Human Wishes," in *Johnson Prose and Poetry* (Cambridge: Harvard University Press, 1963), 167.

6. James Barwell, Boswell, *Life of Johnson* (London: Oxford University Press, 1961), 926–927.

7. Henry Fielding, *The History of the Life of the Late Mr. Jonathan Wild the Great* (London: Hamish Hamilton, 1947); Claude-Adrien Helvétius, *A Treatise of Man; His Intellectual Faculties and His Education,* trans. W. Hooper, 2 vols. (London: Verner, Hood, and Sharpe, 1810), 1:316.

8. Voltaire, *History of Charles XII* (1731; reprint, London and New York: Dutton, 1925), 170 (page citation is to the reprint edition).

9. Ibid., 334.

10. Theodore Besterman, *Voltaire* (Chicago: University of Chicago Press, 1976), 563.

11. Voltaire, *The Age of Louis XIV,* trans. Martyn P. Pollack (London: J. M. Dent; New York: E. P. Dutton, 1961), 166.

12. Francesco Algarotti, *Letters Military and Political from the Italian of Count Algarotti* (London: T. Egerton, 1782), 48, 56–57.

13. Voltaire and Catherine the Great, *Voltaire and Catherine the Great: Selected Correspondence,* trans. A. Lentin (Cambridge: Oriental Research Partners, 1974), 52, 56, 66–67, 124.

14. Helvétius, *Treatise,* I vii.

15. Walter Dorn, "Eighteenth Century Militarism," *Competition for Empire, 1740–1763, The Rise of Modern Europe,* ed. William Langer (New York: Harper Turchbooks, 1963); Eric Robson, "The Armed Forces and the Art of War," in Peter Paret, ed., *The New Cambridge Modern History,* vol. 7, *The Old Regime* (Princeton, 1986). Important discussions of eighteenth-century warfare include: Michael Howard, *War in European History* (Oxford University Press, 1976); Gunther Rothenburg, *The Art of Warfare in the Age of Napoleon* (Bloomington: University of Indiana Press, 1978); J.P. Gooch, *Armies in Europe* (London: Routledge & Keesaw Paul, 1980); David Chandler, *The Art of Warfare in the Age of Marlborough* (New York: Sarpedon, 1995); André Corvisier, *Armies and Societies in Europe, 1494–1789* (Bloomington: Indiana University Press, 1979); Russell Weigley, *The Age of Battles: The Quest Warfare from Breitenfield to Waterloo* (Bloomington: Indiana University Press, 1991). Jeremy Black, *European Warfare 1660–1815* (London: UCL Press, 1994) should now be regarded as the standard authority on the military history of this period. Also of great value is Jean Chagniot, *Guerre et société à l'époque moderne* (Paris: Presses Universitaires de France, 2001).

16. Carl von Clausewitz, *On War,* trans. and ed. Michael Howard and Peter Paret (Princeton: Princeton University Press, 1976), 605.

17. Frederick II, the Great, *Frederick the Great on the Art of War,* ed. and trans. Jay Luvaas (New York: Free Press, 1966), 89; Reed Browning, *The War of the Austrian Succession* (New York: St. Martin's Press, 1993), 377; Christopher Duffy, *The Army of Frederick the Great* (New York: Hippocrene Books, 1974), 199.

18. Frederick II to Voltaire, 18 August 1770, *Letters of Voltaire and Frederick the Great,* trans. Richard Addington (London: Routledge, 1927), 309.

19. Peter Gay, *The Enlightenment,* 2 vols. (New York: Knopf, 1969), 1:3.

20. Ibid., 2:493.

21. Ira O. Wade, *The Structure and Form of the French Enlightenment,* 2 vols. (Princeton: Princeton University Press, 1977), 1:3, 24–34. For a survey of recent scholarship on the Enlightenment, see Roy Porter, *The Enlightenment,* 2d ed. (New York: Palgrave, 2001). One of the best brief surveys of the history of the Enlightenment remains Norman Hampson, *The Enlightenment* (Hammondsworth, U.K.: Penguin, 1968; reprint, 1976).

22. Geoffrey Best, *Humanity in Warfare* (New York: Columbia University Press, 1980), 35–36.

23. See John A. Lynn, "The Treatment of Military Subjects in Diderot's *Encyclopédie*," *The Journal of Military History* 65 (January 2001), 131–65.

24. J. C. D. Clark, "Revolution in the English Atlantic Empire, 1660–1780," in *Revolution and Counter-Revolution*, ed. E. E. Rice (Oxford: Oxford University Press, 1990), 27–93. See also Henry F. May, *The Enlightenment in America* (New York: Oxford University Press, 1976), 159–60.

25. Examples of such sermons include Andrew Eliot, "A Sermon Preached October 25th, 1759, Being a Day of Public Thanksgiving Appointed by Authority for the Success of British Arms This Year.... " (Boston, 1759) and "Mr. Appleton's Sermon Occasioned by the Surrender of Montreal, and All Canada to His Britannic Majesty" (Boston, 1760).

26. Silvanus Conant, "The Art of War, the Gift of God.... " (Boston, 1759), 4–5.

27. Anonymous, *The Ancient Policy of War: A Glorious Precedent to a Modern Way of Fighting* (1704), 7, 13–14. See also Fred Anderson, *Crucible of War* (New York: Knopf, 2000), 373–76.

28. Jeremy Black, *British Foreign Policy in the Age of Walpole* (Edinburgh: John Donald, 1985), 3.

29. Jean-Jacques Rousseau, "Abstract and Judgement of Saint-Pierre's *Project for Perpetual Peace*" (1756) in *Rousseau on International Relations*, ed. Stanley Hoffman (Oxford: Clarendon Press, 1991), 93.

30. Saint-Pierre's works went through many revisions, and I have relied upon "Selections from the second edition of the *Abrégé du projet de paix perpétuelle* by C.-I. Castel de Saint-Pierre, Abbot of Tiron, 1738," trans. H. Hale Bellot in *Peace Projects of the Eighteenth Century* (New York and London: Garland, 1974). His ideas are discussed in Christine Jane Carter, *Rousseau and the Problem of War* (New York: Garland, 1987), 21–25; Paul Hazard, *European Thought in the Eighteenth Century from Montesquieu to Lessing* (New Haven: Yale University Press, 1954), 184–85; F. H. Hinsley, Chapter 2: "Penn, Bellers, and Saint Pierre;" Chapter 3: "Rousseau;" Chapter 4: "Kant," *Power and the Pursuit of Peace* (Cambridge: Cambridge University Press, 1963); and Wade, *Structure and Form of the French Enlightenment*, 1:318–33. For Cardinal Alberoni's ideas on peace see Mil. R. Vesnitch, "Le Cardinal Alberoni pacifiste," *Revue d'histoire diplomatique* 26 (1912): 352–88. For Leibniz, see *The Political Writings of Leibniz*, trans. Patrick Riley (Cambridge: Cambridge University Press, 1972), 111–17. Voltaire's dismissal of Saint-Pierre is discussed by M. L. Perkins, "Voltaire and the Abbé de Saint-Pierre on World Peace," *Studies on Voltaire and the Eighteenth Century* 17 (1961): 9-34. See also Herbert Lamm, "Voltaire et l'idée de paix a l'occasion du bicentenaire de la mort de Voltaire," *Revue d'histoire diplomatique* 92, no. 3 (1978): 262-74. Scholars who dismiss Saint-Pierre's influence on statesmen include Derek McKay and H. M. Scott. See their *The Rise of the Great Powers* (London and New York: Longman, 1983), 101.

31. J.-J. Rousseau, "Extrail du Projet de paix perpétuelle," in *"L'état de guerre" and "Projet de paix perpétuelle," Two Essays by Jean-Jacques Rousseau*, ed. Shirley D. Patterson (New York and London: G.P. Putnam, 1920), 3, 26, 39.

32. Rousseau, "Abstract and Judgement of Saint-Pierre," 100.

33. Immanuel Kant, *Perpetual Peace*, trans. M. Campbell Smith, ed. A. Robert Caponagi (New York: Liberal Arts Press, 1948), 29–30.

34. Montesquieu (Charles-Louis de Secondat), *The Spirit of the Laws*, trans. Anne M. Cohler, Basia Carolyn Miller, Harold Samuel Stone (1748; reprint, Cambridge: Cambridge University Press, 1989), 338 (page citation is to the reprint edition).

35. Kant, Perpetual Peace, 3–6.

36. Christine Jane Carter, *Rousseau and the Problem of War* (NY & London: Garland Publishing, 1987), 205.

37. Voltaire, *Age of Louis XIV*, 5–6.

38. Saint-Pierre, *Abrégé du projet de paix perpétuelle*, 59.

39. Rousseau, "Abstract and Judgement of Saint-Pierre," 62.

40. Helvétius, *Treatise*, 1:290, 307.

41. M.S. Anderson, "Eighteenth-Century Theories of the Balance of Power," in *Studies in Diplomatic History: Essays in Memory of David Bayne Horn*, ed. Ragnhild Hatton and M.S. Anderson (Archon Books, 1970), 188. My discussion of balance of power theories owes much to this essay. See also Edward Vose Gulick, *Europe's Classical Balance of Power: A Case History of the Theory and Practice of One of the Great Concepts of European Statecraft* (New York: Norton, 1967) and McKay and Scott, *The Rise of the Great Powers*, 211–14. Jeremy Black provides an illuminating discussion of Edward Gibbon's views of the balance of power in *War and the World: Military Power and the Fate of Continents 1450–2000* (New Haven: Yale University Press, 2000).

42. Jean François, Marquis de Saint-Lambert, "Législateur," in *L'Encyclopédie, ou Dictionnaire raisonné des sciences, des arts et des métiers*, ed. Denis Diderot and Jean Le Rond d'Alembert, 28 vols. (1751-72; facsimile of the first edition, Stuttgart-Bad Cannstatt: Frommann, 1969), 9:363-64.

43. David Hume, "Of the Balance of Power," *The Philosophical Works of David Hume*, 4 vols. (Boston: Little, Brown, 1854), 3:371.

44. Anderson, "Eighteenth-Century Theories of the Balance of Power," 197.

45. Emmerich von Vattel, "Of War," in *The Law of Nations, or, the Principles of the Law of Nature, Applied to the Conduct and Affairs of Nations and Sovereigns*, ed. Joseph Chitty (Philadelphia: T. and J.W. Johnson, 1861), 296, 302.

46. Geoffrey Parker, "Early Modern Europe," in *The Laws of War: Constraints on War in the Western World*, ed. Michael Howard, George Andreopoulos, and Mark Shulman (New Haven: Yale University Press, 1994), 41–42.

47. Vattel, "Of War," 362.

48. Ibid.

49. Ibid., 346.

50. Geoffrey Best, *Humanity in War* (NY: Columbia University Press, 1980), 54–55.

51. Karma Nabulsi, *Traditions of War: Occupation, Resistance, and the Law* (Oxford: Oxford University Press, 1999), 36–55.

52. Vattel, "Of War," 348.

53. Ibid., 379.

54. Louis de Jaucourt, "Guerre (Droit naturel et politique)," in *Encyclopédie*, 7:995–98.

55. James Marriot, Advocate General, to John Pownall, Secretary to the Lords Commissioners of Trade and Plantations, 15 February 1765, Great Britain, Public Record Office, CO/5/66, f35.

56. Montesquieu, *The Spirit of the Laws*, 132.

57. Saint-Lambert, "Législateur," *Encyclopédie*, 9:364.

58. Antoine de Pas de Feuquières, *Memoirs Historical and Military*, 2 vols. (London: T. Woodward and C. Davis, 1736; reprint, New York: Greenwood Press, 1968), 1:13 (page citation is to the reprint edition).

59. Adam Ferguson, *An Essay on Civil Society* (1767), ed. Duncan Ferber (Edinburgh, 1966), 23.

60. Jaucourt, "Guerre," *Encyclopédie*, 7:995.

61. Counte de Tressan, "Homme de Guerre," Ibid., 995.

62. Montesquieu, *The Spirit of the Laws*, 33–34.

63. Charles M. Clode, *The Administration of Justice under Military and Martial Law* (London: John Murray, 1872), 57–58.

64. Kant, *Perpetual Peace*, 4.

65. Rousseau, "Économie," *Encyclopédie*, 5:346.

66. Montesquieu, *The Spirit of the Laws*, 224.

67. John Adams to Benjamin Rush, 6 December 1778, *The Papers of John Adams*, ed. Gregg Lint, Robert Taylor, Richard Alan Riverson, Celeste Walker, Joanna Revelas, 10 vols. (Cambridge, Mass., and London: Belknap Press, 1989), 7:254.

68. Rousseau, "Constitutional Project for Corsica" (1765), in *Rousseau on International Relations*, 145.

69. Rousseau, "Considerations on the Government of Poland," (1772), Ibid., 182–91.

70. Russell Weigley, *The American Way of War: A History of United States Military Strategy and Policy* (Bloomington: Indiana University Press, 1973), 45–46. To be fair to Jefferson, more recent studies recognize that he appreciated the importance of limited numbers of regular soldiers and ocean-going warships as part of a national defense policy. His own congressional followers refused to fund them. See Theodore J. Crackel, *Mr. Jefferson's Army: Political and Social Reform of the Military Establishment, 1801–1808* (New York: New York University Press, 1987) and Gene A. Smith, *The Politics of the Jeffersonian Gunboat Program* (Newark: University of Delaware Press and London: Associated University Presses, 1995).

71. Jaucourt, "Déserteur," *Encyclopédie*, 4:881; "Enrolement," Ibid., 5:706.

72. Saint-Lambert, "Transfuge," *Encyclopédie*, 17:835.

73. André Corvisier, *Armies and Societies in Europe, 1494–1789*, trans. Abigail T. Siddall (Bloomington: Indiana University Press, 1979), 134.

74. Sylvia Frey, *The British Soldier in America: A Social History of Military Life in the Revolutionary Period* (Austin: University of Texas Press, 1981), 21; Rodney Atwood, *The Hessians: Mercenaries from Hessen-Kassel in the American Revolution* (Cambridge: Cambridge University Press, 1980), 45.

75. William Howe, *General Sir William Howe's Orderly Book at Charleston, Boston and Halifax, June 1775 to 26 May 1776*, ed. Benjamin Franklin Stevens (London, 1890; reprint New York: Kennikat Press, 1970), 46, 69, 97, 101, 118, 132, 151, 187–88 (page citations are to the reprint edition).

76. Arthur N. Gilbert, "Military and Civilian Justice in Eighteenth-Century England: An Assessment," *The Journal of British Studies* 17 (spring 1978), 41–65; G. A. Steppler, "British Military Law, Discipline, and the Conduct of Courts-Martial in the Later Eighteenth Century," *The English Historical Review* 102 (October 1987): 854–86.

77. Cesare Beccaria, *Of Crimes and Punishment,* trans. Jane Grigson (New York: Marsilio Publishers, 1996), 42.

78. Adrienne Hytier, "The Decline of Military Values: The Theme of the Deserter in Eighteenth-Century French Literature," in *Studies in Eighteenth-Century Culture,* vol. 11, ed. Henry C. Payne (Madison: University of Wisconsin Press, 1982), 157.

79. Samuel Johnson, "French Prisoners of War," in *Johnson: Prose and Poetry* (Cambridge: Harvard University Press, 1963), 486. See also Samuel J. Rogal, "John Wesley on War and Peace," in *Studies in Eighteenth-Century Culture,* vol. 7, ed. Roseanne Runte (Madison: University of Wisconsin Press, 1978), 332.

80. See J. Walter Nelson, "War and Peace and the British Poets of Sensibility," in *Studies in Eighteenth-Century Culture,* vol. 7, 357.

CHAPTER 2

The Military Enlightenment

"War has been called, like modern medicine, an art conjectural and homicidal."
—Francesco Algarotti

"I was mad for heroism. Charles XII and Condé kept me from sleeping; I even fancied I could do better than they. I gasped over Polybius; I commented the commentaries of Folard. I longed to be off to the wars. But what can one do at fifteen?"[1] It was thus that Prince Charles-Joseph de Ligne (1735–1814) recalled his early enthusiasm for a military career. It remained a passion throughout his life as he achieved high rank in the Austrian service. He was a classic figure of the ancien régime, elegant, witty, and cosmopolitan. He participated in the great events of the Seven Years' War as a devoted soldier of the Habsburg state, but moved with ease among almost all European court circles. He was an intimate friend and a chivalrous defender of the French queen Marie-Antoinette. He was at home with the "enlightened despots" Frederick the Great, Catherine II, and Joseph II. He traded witticisms with Voltaire at the latter's retreat at Ferney and sought out the acquaintance of Rousseau. The outbreak of the French Revolution and the death of his patron Joseph II cut him off from the society and the profession that he loved. Sidelined during the great events of the succeeding years, he made a brief and fitting reappearance before his death, as master of ceremonies at the Congress of Vienna, which sought to restore the lost world.

Charles XII of Sweden was a worthy example for a boy dreaming of heroism. The 15-year-old Prince de Ligne had already begun to study seriously his intended profession by reading the works of one of the century's most-influential military writers, Jean-Charles, chevalier de Folard (1669–1752). He was not alone, for Folard influenced many of the most-creative military minds of the era, including Maurice de Saxe (1696–1750), France's outstanding commander during the War of the Austrian Succession, and Frederick the Great. Folard had served with distinction during the War of the Spanish Succession, but his subsequent career as an author was in reaction to passivity of the French armies during that conflict. Critics of the French war effort cited excessive control exercised by the royal court over its generals in the field, reliance on fortresses to protect the frontier, lack of professionalism among the officers, and a general decline of military spirit.[2] Following the Peace of Utrecht, Folard briefly served the Knights Hospitalers as an engineer in defense of the citadel of Malta and in 1715 entered the service of Charles XII. Here he found his ideal soldier. His admiration for the king was boundless: "Mr. Folard regards this hero as one of the greatest men who has ever lived. He compares him to Alexander the Great, or perhaps it would be better to say, he considers him to have been superior to that conqueror."[3] It was under this king that he found the inspiration for his subsequent work, the advocacy of shock tactics as a means to overcome the apparent stalemate produced by the linear fire tactics of the time. It was more than a tactical program, for Folard believed that an aggressive offensive would restore France's lagging military spirit. Folard's work provided the most-important vehicle by which Charles XII exercised a powerful indirect influence on the military thought and practice of the eighteenth century.

Three principal themes characteristic of the Military Enlightenment were evident in Folard's military treatises, which consisted of two major works: *Nouvelles découvertes sur la guerre* (1724) and the seven-volume *Histoire de Polybe* (known also as *Commentaires sur Polybe*; 1727–1730). These themes were (1) classicism, admiration of ancient Greek and Roman military practice, which might serve as a model for modern military institutions; (2) war as a science, the attempt to identify rational and universal principles governing the conduct of war; and (3) the military spirit, what might be called the psychological foundations of war. In *Nouvelles découvertes*, Folard declared that war should be subjected to reflection and rational analysis. "It is wrong to think that war is understood by routine. It is a science, more speculative than experimental."[4] Folard was among the first of the military philosophes to apply *l'esprit philosophique* to war.[5] There was a speculative element in his doctrine, particularly in his famous advocacy of a massive column partially armed with pikes that was intended to rupture the enemy line and thus restore the offensive to its proper place in war.[6] His classicism was evident in his interest in the ancient historian Polybius (c. 200–c. 118 B.C.), "of all historians the most capable of giving us the most profound lessons on war."[7] Polybius was one of the best authorities on Roman military practice, and Folard invoked that respected model in favor of his own system. One eighteenth-century critic commented that Folard had chosen Polybius as the subject of his historical study rather than Caesar because the latter did not provide support for his system.[8] From a modern perspective, Folard's column seems quaintly anachronistic in its attempt to assert shock tactics against firepower. Indeed, Folard seems to have suggested a reversal of the "military revolution," a phenomenon connected with the introduction of gunpowder weapons into European warfare. Nevertheless, Folard's ideas were incorporated into advanced French tactical doctrines that at the end of the eighteenth century culminated in Napoleonic methods.[9]

The term *military revolution* has become a subject of debate among military historians of early modern Europe.[10] Although they disagree about the specific time and place, they concur that Europe witnessed a profound period of military innovation from approximately 1500 to 1800. One of the central issues in this debate is the relationship between war and early modern state formation. The concept of a military revolution also involves technology and, in this case, its place in the European military experience in the period 1500–1800. The introduction of gunpowder was fundamental to this revolution, which included the introduction of cannon, artillery fortification, and big-gun sailing vessels. These developments allowed European states to achieve global reach, if not military dominance, in other areas of the world, where indigenous societies often adopted gunpowder weapons themselves. European battlefields were also altered by the introduction of field artillery and individual firearms. The latter in company with the pike (replaced by the bayonet at the end of the seventeenth century) restored the infantry to a place of primacy on the battlefield. Proper use of these weapons required a new emphasis on discipline and drill. Thus, lines of musketeers firing in unison had become standard battlefield tactics in Europe by the time of Marlborough.[11] Eighteenth-century military writers were well aware that a profound change had occurred. Although the issues in the debate over the military revolution among modern historians are somewhat different from those that concerned their eighteenth-century predecessors, the term *revolution* is not an anachronism. "Suppose that the Greeks or the Romans had discovered powder; would that invention in their hands have produced the same revolution in the military art that we have seen in our times?" asked a writer in 1788.[12] "It is incontestable," wrote another, "that all these successive wars have occasioned advantageous revolutions in several branches of the art."[13] This writer contended that modern and ancient tactics were entirely different because of the differences in the nature of weapons.[14] As today, however, eighteenth-century writers could not agree on the significance of the new weapons. Contended another, "It is a popular prejudice that the change in weapons has altered the system of war, and...that a very good general among the ancients would now be foiled by a very bad general among the moderns," but "that the great principles of war can be altered by a casual change of weapons, I own staggers my belief."[15]

One is tempted to see an ancient versus modern struggle among the military authors of the period and to place Folard, the commentator on Polybius, on the side of the ancients. However, this would be an oversimplification of Folard's thought and of eighteenth-century military writing in general. As noted, he sought to overcome the paralysis that had seized the French army by a rational analysis of tactical doctrine. Folard was not alone in believing that a reliance on firearms had sapped the natural offensive spirit of French soldiers. He was well aware of the successful application of the shock techniques mastered by the king of Sweden. The Roman example taught him that decisive victory was gained by armies that came to grips in hand-to-hand combat instead of relying on missile weapons. He had good reason to question the effectiveness of the inaccurate, single-shot muskets of his day. His proposed column offered greater mobility and flexibility than was found in the linear formations of the era. It offered a freedom of movement and the prospect of breaking free from predictable linear tactics. There was also reason to think that an attack with cold steel would reanimate the troops and revive the offensive in war. Modern military technology may suggest that Folard was swimming against a tide. However, French military doctrine continued to emphasize the military spirit on the eve of World War I. Even today, officers wish to maintain a military spirit among their troops, and Folard's ideas are not irrelevant in this regard. Despite modern reliance on massive firepower, bayonet training continues to be prized in the United States Army as a means of fostering a martial spirit among the troops. One officer recalls that American soldiers assigned to the protection of nuclear weapons became alert to the significance of this duty only when they began to train with bayonets.[16]

Many eighteenth-century soldiers were interested in Folard's proposals. Maurice de Saxe and Frederick the Great expressed interest in his work and sought to implement shock tactics. Later in the century other French writers sought to revive his system. Some thought that the reliance on gunpowder was reversible. The British writer Campbell Dalrymple concluded that battles fought with firearms were less bloody but more humane than those waged with edged weapons. The effectiveness of the latter might "produce another military revolution, and send us back to the arms in use before the invention of gunpowder."[17] Enlightened military thought might take one in directions other than those associated with technological progress. Enlightenment military writers were at least as concerned with military spirit as with technology, and this concern has not vanished from military affairs even today.

The French historian Émile Léonard believed that Folard's most important contribution was in his attempt to restore the military spirit and that too much attention has been focused on his proposal for shock tactics administered by a deep column of pikemen. There was much reason to find this scheme impractical. Folard had too lightly dismissed the significance of musketry and, more important, that of the artillery. Both experienced steady technical improvement during the eighteenth century. The introduction of iron ramrods and the development of platoon fire made musketry more rapid, if not more accurate. The number and mobility of field pieces increased in every major army. Folard's column provided the ideal target for the latter, and its flanks were clearly vulnerable. A neoclassicist might have remembered Cannae, or a more recent example, Agincourt, where a massed force was slaughtered by attacks on its flanks. Moreover, one can argue that Folard misread the lessons of the War of the Spanish Succession, in which the duke of Marlborough prevailed by means of aggressive tactics that combined shock and disciplined firepower. Folard believed that French soldiers were incapable of the necessary discipline and cited French successes with bayonet attacks to support his case. He contended that his phalanx would succeed against fire because it would be moving rather than stationary and that its flexibility and mobility would enable it to exploit weaknesses in the enemy position. This was particularly true if the army were divided into independent columns rather than acting as a massive phalanx. His ideas appealed to officers seeking to restore the offensive; they became the subject of experiments, and elements of Folard's thought were included in the French Regulations of 1753 and 1754 and the Ordinance of 1755.[18]

Frederick the Great and Maurice de Saxe believed that Folard's ideas were interesting but extreme. The Italian philosopher Francesco Algarotti recalled their discussion of the British column at the battle of Fontenoy, 1745, Saxe's greatest victory (see chap. 4). Although the duke of Cumberland's force penetrated the French line and rendered the outcome doubtful, the column was compressed by obstacles such as woods, villages, and ditches and raked by the French artillery, "from all of which the Count concluded that his friend Folard was wrong in thinking the column the most perfect and successful military order in all cases, and in every situation."[19] (To be fair, Folard himself doubted that his column would work in all circumstances.)[20] Frederick was an avid reader of military treatises and invited Folard to Berlin to experiment with his system, but ill health prevented the visit. He recommended Folard's *Commentaires sur Polybe* to his officers, observing that "the visions and ravings of this illustrious soldier contain treasures."[21] It was the spirit of Folard's work rather than the letter that inspired these commanders.

Folard's column had no relevance for "siegecraft," a central preoccupation of eighteenth-century commanders. Assault and defense of numerous fortifications that dominated the strategic points of Europe was a much more common military experience than battle. Folard believed that

France's reliance on fortresses was a bad thing because it had sapped the nation's offensive spirit. He was also critical of time-consuming sieges and argued that fortresses should be taken by assault. However, there was much about the nature of siege warfare that ran parallel to Folard's thought. His contemporary Marshal Puységur, whose *Art de la guerre* was published in 1748, shared Folard's wish to treat war as a rational science. He dismissed most contemporary military writing as concerned with *"l'exercise,"* the proper drill and care of the troops, and argued for a geometrical theory of war to provide sound principles for the guidance of commanders. He was more open than was Folard to the employment of modern weapons. The latter, an enthusiast for the restoration of pikes, claimed that he had never seen an instance of the successful use of a bayonet, but Puységur accepted its value and advocated the replacement of standard-issue muskets with lightweight fusils. Although more open to technological innovation, Puységur shared Folard's method of extracting axioms, definitions, and principles from ancient and modern military history as a means of constructing a theory of war. He wished to bring to the battlefield the mathematical certainty found in siege warfare.[22] This search for what was perceived to be a rational order was shared by all of the military theorists of the early Enlightenment and linked them to the larger culture.[23]

VAUBAN

Those seeking a general theory of war could benefit from specialized studies. Preeminent among these was the work of Louis XIV's master engineer, Sébastien Le Prestre de Vauban, whose fortresses shielded France from invasion throughout the century and whose treatise on siege-craft and fortification, written between 1667 and 1672, was published in 1740.[24] Folard considered Vauban's fortress system at least partly responsible for the decline of military spirit in the French army during the reign of Louis XIV and dedicated his work to a restoration of a commander's freedom of maneuver and offensive action. The commitment to fortresses was the result of a conscious royal strategy, however. The modern expert John Lynn finds that 1675 marked a turning point for Louis XIV's armies as the aggressive commanders Turenne and Condé departed from the scene and François Le Tellier, the marquis de Louvois, became the principal military adviser. Louis became more concerned with protecting his gains than with seeking further conquests, and greater emphasis was placed on Vauban's approach to warfare.[25] Initially, Vauban's treatise focused on the attack of fortresses, but a revision of 1706, perhaps reflecting his growing disenchantment with the prolonged period of destructive war, placed greater emphasis on defense. Vauban had little regard for battles: "I might also remark that whatever precautions the greatest commanders have taken on the day of battle to best dispose their forces and to take every advantage of the position and terrain, they have never been able to prevent the reverses of Dame Fortune, who is fickle and often decides against them; but in the attack and defense of fortifications fortune plays a far lesser role than do prudence and dexterity."[26]

Siege warfare, he maintained, offered the only sure means of taking and holding the country. A recent study of the duke of Marlborough's greatest battlefield victory in Flanders, Ramillies in 1706, supports Vauban's assertion. Marlborough inflicted a severe defeat on the French army and swept up important towns and cities across western Flanders until he came upon well-maintained and well-defended fortresses designed by Vauban. Although he was within 150 miles of Paris, Marlborough was compelled to revert to the slow business of siege warfare. Moreover, the allies found to their dismay that poorly designed and maintained fortresses provided them with no safe hold on newly conquered territory.[27] Vauban had provided France with an early modern version of the Maginot Line, and a successful one. Vauban's influence on later French military thought has, perhaps, been insufficiently appreciated.

Vauban did not suggest that fortresses alone could protect France from invasion. His treatise offered the certainty that no unrelieved fortress was impregnable from a properly conducted siege operation. He described in detail the methods of siegecraft: the steady advance of the besiegers by means of parallel and communication trenches, the establishment of batteries and protective redoubts, the crossing of the ditch or moat, the mining of the wall, and the exploitation of the breech.[28] Most of this was not new, but Lynn credits Vauban with three innovations: parallel trenches that gave greater protection to the besiegers and created uncertainty about their point of attack; the *tir a ricochet,* the lobbing of cannonballs from artillery sited parallel to the ramparts to drive the enemy from the walls; and the *cavaliers de tranchée,* raised platforms that allowed besiegers to fire down upon the enemy.

Siege warfare was a costly and dangerous undertaking for the troops and full of hardship for the civilians caught in its midst, who could expect hunger and fire resulting from enemy mortar bombs. Soldiers defending the city of Bergen op Zoom in 1747 began to pillage the houses of the inhabitants they were supposed to defend when they came under such fire.[29] The civilians would suffer a worse fate when the French troops sacked the city. However, Vauban and the method that he perfected—if he did not create—brought a level of certainty to these operations that usually prevented the worst consequences. The inevitability of the besiegers' success provided a formula by which the defenders could honorably concede before the final assault. The result was the capitulation, a procedure praised by Vattel, by which the defenders were allowed to depart under arms with the honors of war. This was war at its most reasonable. Of course, not all defending commanders were "reasonable," or they might disagree with their besiegers on the definition of the term, and a defense maintained too long might result in a surrender at the victors' "discretion," an altogether different matter.

Vauban contended, with good reason, that "there is no fortress to which this method is not applicable, but it is more advantageous with some than with others, depending upon the geography and the composition of the terrain."[30] However, he insisted that he had no real system and that his fortresses were adapted to local conditions. They were intended to achieve the maximum utilization of cross fire and flanking fire along with defense in depth. This was not new. Indeed, Vauban's success always owed much to others. Jean Chagniot observes that innovations attributed by Lynn to Vauban had already been practiced by others.[31] He had thus perfected an art of artillery fortification and siegecraft under steady development from the sixteenth century. Battlefield tactics had also evolved since the sixteenth century, but they resisted the level of perfection achieved by the engineers. The battlefield remained shrouded in obscurity and unpredictability.

Vauban's career demonstrates that the battlefield was not necessarily the chief preoccupation of eighteenth-century commanders. In a study of generals in the Habsburg service in the period 1680–1740, Erik Lund described the great technical knowledge required by commanders to manage the enlarged armies that appeared in the late seventeenth century. Armies had always utilized such knowledge if they were to feed themselves and their animals and build the roads, bridges, camps, and field fortifications necessary for the army's everyday operations. Commanders now worked within a new context. The period 1681–1683 marked a divide between the 40,000–70,000-man Habsburg armies and the 100,000–150,000 numbers of the eighteenth century. Similarly, the French army expanded to the enormous paper strength of 420,000 in the 1690s. Such numbers imposed new challenges on the logistical and engineering skills of the generals. According to Lund, the commanders responded with technical knowledge enhanced by the "scientific revolution": "They were well educated, alert to the possibilities of a scientific study of their work and of the 'art of war'; ... among them a substantial minority were accustomed to the work of the chief of staff, technical staff or engineering corps.... Moreover, the idea that a prejudice against technical officers kept them from reaching the highest ranks of the army is completely in error."[32]

These armies allowed states to conduct warfare on a far greater scale than ever before in the early modern period. French armies during the eighteenth century often fought on three or four major fronts at the same time, in the Netherlands, Germany, Italy, or Spain and, from the 1740s in other parts of the world. At the same time, the Habsburgs fought on fronts in the Netherlands, Italy, the Balkans, and Germany. Maintaining and directing armies fighting over great distances in different environments strained the capacity of European states. Far-flung armies created a centrifugal force that tested central control, but such control was essential to the realization of state strategy. French military critics in the eighteenth century complained that Louis XIV had stifled his commanders' initiative by detailed instructions that today would be called micromanagement. There was more than one reason for this *guerre de cabinet*. Louis's experience in the *Fronde,* the aristocratic rebellion of 1648–1649, gave him cause to limit the independence of aristocratic generals. His growing distaste for risking his soldiers' lives on the battlefield led him to restrain his generals' enthusiasm. Even had this not been the case, Versailles had to maintain a grip if there was to be a coordinated effort to apply properly the available force. Furthermore, political and diplomatic considerations properly led the court to occasionally restrain the freedom of action of generals in the field.[33]

Although Louis commanded at a number of sieges, he was more a war administrator than soldier and was assisted by another great administrator, Louvois, until the latter's death in 1690. Without taking a position on the debate of whether armed forces were the cause or the result of state formation, it may be said that the task of raising, arming, and providing for these forces became the central preoccupation of states, a fact frequently lamented by philosophes and peace projectors. This preoccupation fostered a bureaucratic culture that drew upon the best available financial, technical, and administrative talent, a development of enormous consequence: "If the first phase in the establishment of a state monopoly on armed forces may be termed the 'gunpowder revolution,' the second may be called with equal right the 'bureaucratic revolution.' "[34] In Britain the navy and its supporting infrastructure became the nation's largest industry and the greatest consumer of technical ability. Battle fleets had emerged as instruments of state power during the last quarter of the seventeenth century, but the eighteenth century witnessed an evolution in infrastructure development such as dockyard facilities and in technical innovation, ship design, and naval doctrine.[35] Admiralties obviously had difficulty in directing the decisions of commanders who were sometimes thousands of miles from home, but great fleets brought into being powerful bureaucracies to sustain them. One is tempted to link the scientific revolution to this new technical and administrative culture, but causation is difficult to establish. Trial and error is not exactly science, and the Royal Navy's search for the solutions to such problems as the prevention of scurvy and the determination of longitude seems to have been guided as much by one as by the other. The British approach to ship design was empirical, improving on what seemed to work, whereas French and Swedish shipbuilders drew more extensively on the physical sciences.[36] Despite the significance of sea power for Britain, there is a dearth of eighteenth-century theoretical writing about its use when one considers the enormous outpouring of military treatises during the period. There is no "Art of Naval Warfare" to draw upon. British naval doctrine developed slowly as a reflection of experience. Ironically, one of the most important papers on naval strategy was submitted by Vauban, who provided the rationale for France's reduction of its battle fleet in favor of commerce raiding, the *guerre de course.* To a modern observer, the British Admiralty and its complex of boards and authorities appears to be something of an administrative nightmare, but it was arguably the most effective military bureaucracy in Europe, one that meshed with its political and social environment. It had the advantage of a solid financial base, for, as one scholar observed, "One of the great strengths of the British Navy in the eighteenth century, arguably its decisive advantage over its rivals, was that in wartime money was never really lacking."[37] British administrative success appears to have been founded on evolving experience and continuity. There was no need for an "enlightened reform" of the system.

In Prussia the bureaucracy of a small and peaceful state was suddenly challenged after 1740 by the great power aspirations of its king. Some reformers, usually referred to as the *cameralists,* attempted to rationalize the bureaucracy and to increase the country's economic base. Prussia is sometimes seen as a model of administrative "science" harnessed for war, but the reformers found themselves limited by a lack of skilled administrators and technicians. According to historian Hubert C. Johnson, "Obstacles in the way of administrative reform included the presence of conservative-minded officials in the bureaucracy, the stultifying effect of the army, the opposition of the judiciary, and Frederick's own beliefs."[38] A recent study of Old Regime warfare argues that no state was able to master the financial and technical challenges to provide armies with essential supply, transportation, and medical services. This failure in itself led to the indecisive nature of war in the period.[39]

Britain may have taken better care of its men because of superior financial resources.[40] The Royal Navy, of course, did master its supply problems. The navy was its own transportation system, carrying its supplies with it. Even though ground transportation in Europe was so primitive that armies might go hungry only a few miles from well-stocked depots, Britain managed to supply its army in America directly from the British Isles during the War of Independence.[41] The bureaucracies of "enlightened absolutism" could not overcome the material limits imposed on the power of their states. By contrast, Britain's unique political, financial, and strategic circumstances allowed it freedom of action unmatched by any other state. Bureaucratic cultures differed distinctly across societies and did not necessarily serve as inhibitors to action. For instance, whereas bureaucracy may have stifled French military initiative under Louis XIV, the British Admiralty under the leadership of an experienced commander, such as Lord Anson during the Seven Years' War, cultivated a spirit of aggressive enterprise throughout the service. Anson combined the technical accomplishment and military spirit idealized by Folard.

Siege warfare and unique campaign environments required armies to develop specialized knowledge. French campaigns in Italy were imperiled if the House of Savoy, which controlled communications through the maritime Alps, was in the enemy's camp. The narrow Alpine passes, furnished with mule tracks rather than roads, could be blocked by small numbers of troops. A barren countryside and inadequate transportation made this theater of operations a logistical nightmare for commanders. The Nine Years' War, 1688–1697, demonstrated that a small state such as Savoy-Piedmont could resist French power. Despite winning two major battles, the French army was unable to overcome an enemy whose very territory formed a great fortress. Fortunately for Savoy-Piedmont, Louis XIV chose to concentrate on Germany. Lack of money and supplies prevented the French marshal Catinat from exploiting battlefield victories and forced him on the defensive. His troops, dispersed over a wide area, were exposed to defeat in detail. The collapse of French finances in the 1690s undermined the war effort, and Louis was compelled to sign an almost-humiliating peace with Savoy-Piedmont to neutralize Italy. Clearly, more was involved in France's defeat than a decline in military spirit.[42]

BOURCET

The maritime Alps remained a strategic problem for French commanders as long as France retained an interest in Italy. As the preceding makes clear, no campaign could succeed without sufficient resources. But how were they to be employed? Savoy-Piedmont's strategic asset was its geography, which rendered it a natural fortress. Vauban had established that no fortress was foolproof against a master engineer, and such a master was the engineer and staff officer Pierre-Joseph de Bourcet (1700–1780), who achieved fame as a mountain-warfare expert. Bourcet began his military education at the age of nine, serving with his father in the Alps. In 1719 he was a volunteer (an unpaid soldier in the ranks, a common apprenticeship for young officers) in the artillery in Spain. During a long career in which he rose to the rank of lieutenant general, he served in Germany, Italy, and Corsica. As chief of staff to French commanders in Savoy-Piedmont and northern Italy during the War of the Austrian Succession, he won renown by his plans that enabled Franco-Spanish forces to turn enemy positions in the mountains. His most-notable success was the almost-bloodless capture of the formidable Savoyard position the Barricades in 1744. In many respects he may be seen as the heir to Vauban, one who successfully applied engineering principles to offensive operations in the mountains. Bourcet believed that an offensive commander could exploit mountainous terrain to conceal his intentions from the enemy.

Whereas the concentration of armies was desirable in flat countryside, mountains required that the army be divided to threaten every passage into the enemy's country. Such a division would leave the enemy in doubt as to the invader's intentions and force a dispersal of the defender's forces. An offensive commander with detailed knowledge of the country and good lateral communications with his detachments had the opportunity to concentrate against a single point and turn the enemy's entire defensive line. This was similar to Vauban's method of approaching defensive works by means of parallel trenches, thereby stretching the defenders and leaving them uncertain of the point of attack. Bourcet proved the value of his plans in practice and wrote a treatise on mountain warfare that influenced succeeding generations of commanders, including Napoleon. According to Robert Quimby, not only did Napoleon conduct operations in similar conditions but also Bourcet's division of the mountain army into self-contained but mutually supporting units anticipated Napoleon's divisional and corps organization, which enabled him to advance on a wide front and to quickly concentrate on his opponent.[43]

Bourcet's treatise is of interest because it addressed questions beyond the specific subject of mountain warfare. As did many eighteenth-century French officers, Bourcet called for greater freedom of action for the commander in the field to determine the strategy of a campaign. Excessive interference by the court stifled the general's initiative, and decisions in the field also required specialized knowledge not available to planners at Versailles. Bourcet observed that the science of war consisted of two parts. First was the training and discipline of the troops, which in the eighteenth century was so much a matter of drill and routine. Second was the science of general officers, which Bourcet concluded was "totally speculative." Bourcet's use of the term speculative has a rather different meaning from that of Folard. He believed that generals could be successful only if they formed their plans with exact knowledge of specific circumstances. His approach was therefore more empirical than Folard's. He believed that choosing the correct position was the key to military success and offered principles drawn from his own experience as a guide. He dismissed writers who expounded on the general principles of war but lacked detailed knowledge of the country and the technical ability to make camps, conduct marches, organize forage parties, and supply convoys, to effect combinations, and to overcome obstacles. Only through tireless study and long experience could an officer acquire the talent of coup d'oeil, by which he meant the proper choice of positions. (This term may be interpreted in different ways but is best understood to mean that a commander understands the tactical situation and knows what to do.) He deemed it a rare quality; if a commander did not have it, he required a quartermaster general who did.

Both Folard and Bourcet sought to restore military initiative and decisiveness on the battlefield, but the latter was a proponent of positional warfare. Such an approach was appealing to the technical mind and offered a relatively safe and bloodless way of making war. It also conformed to the realities of eighteenth-century operations, in which opportunities for battle were few and their decisiveness questionable. According to Jurgen Luh, armies were paralyzed by their logistical problems and eighteenth-century infantry firearms, on which conventional, ineffective tactics were based. Warfare was dominated by sieges. The duke of Marlborough, who won fame as Britain's greatest battlefield commander, fought only four major battles but conducted 30 sieges. Luh also found that by the second half of the eighteenth century modern fortification had spread to central and eastern Europe and played a greater role in the outcome of wars there than has been traditionally understood. Frederick the Great found his conquest of Silesia during the War of the Austrian Succession complicated even by poorly maintained and garrisoned Austrian fortresses. Although initially scornful of siege warfare, the king realized the value of fortresses if he was to keep his gains. "During the Seven Years' War, the possession of Silesia was decided by fortresses and not by battles," writes Luh.[44] The Seven Years' War also saw improvement in the quality and quantity of artillery in both the Prussian and Austrian armies, which was responsible for the terrible battlefield casualties on both sides. Military writers, including Clausewitz, have since heaped scorn on the Austrian commander Daun, who was known for his delaying tactics. Daun's reliance on positional warfare, field fortifications, and maneuver against the enemy's supply system had much to recommend it in the conditions of the time, however. He well understood that his army was not equal to Frederick's on the battlefield.

FREDERICK THE GREAT

Frederick the Great's military thought evolved as follows. During his reign (1740–1786), Prussia emerged from second rank to great-power status through war. This was an extraordinary achievement for a thinly populated agricultural state, 12th in population in 1740. It was an artificial state, geographically splintered, ranging from small duchies in the Rhineland to Prussia itself, isolated in the great territorial sea of Poland. Frederick's father, Frederick William I, had made this state viable by creating a standing army out of proportion in size to the number of his subjects and by establishing a bureaucracy that proved capable of extracting resources to sustain it. Frederick William had pursued a cautious foreign policy in which this army served primarily as a deterrent. Nevertheless, Frederick II inherited the most-highly disciplined and best-trained infantry in Europe, capable of quickly and efficiently executing the complex maneuvers demanded by the linear tactics of the day. Although its effectiveness in battle has been questioned, on the parade ground the

Prussian infantry achieved a higher rate of fire than most troops. This instrument was at Frederick's hand when he learned of the death of Emperor Charles VI. "His death alters all my pacific ideas," he wrote Voltaire in October 1740, "and I think that in June it will be rather a matter of cannon-powder, soldiers and trenches than of actresses, of balls and stages.... now is the moment for a complete change in the old political system; 'tis that falling rock striking the idol of four metals seen by Nebuchadnezzar, which destroyed them all."[45]

The apparent equilibrium of Europe was overturned when Frederick sought to wrest the valuable province of Silesia from the Habsburg heir Maria Theresa. His two Silesian wars in the 1740s, in retrospect part of the War of the Austrian Succession, gained him the glory that he sought, the title "the Great," and possession of the province. His title to the latter was not secure, however, and in the Seven Years' War he would be forced to fight a desperate struggle against a seemingly overwhelming combination of Austria, Russia, and France, not only to preserve Silesia but also to prevent the dismemberment of Prussia itself. In this war his military success was mixed, but his durability and resiliency enabled him to prevail against the loose and ill-coordinated coalition. Circumstances gave Frederick no choice but to act boldly, just as Daun adopted Fabian tactics. By 1763, both Silesia and his fame were secure, but at a horrible cost. Thenceforth, his foreign policy began to resemble that of his father, but soldiers throughout Europe continued to look upon the Prussian army as a model.[46]

Frederick was an Enlightenment figure in his own right, the composer of music, poetry, and philosophic pieces as well as the friend and patron of philosophes. Since war consumed his attention for much of his career, he turned the same rational, critical, and penetrating eye on its science and art as on any of his other intellectual pursuits. Over the course of his career, he wrote numerous confidential treatises for the instruction of his officers and histories to explain and justify his actions. Many of these documents fell into enemy hands and, published in France, were intensely studied by officers throughout Europe. These works demonstrate Frederick's development from an aggressive young leader in pursuit of fame into a great commander and military thinker whose prudence had been forged in the hard school of experience. His treatises seek to define the underlying principles by which war was fought in his day, and they range from practical advice on such matters as how to defend a river line to a hypothetical war against France by Prussia in league with equally hypothetical allies. As far as tactical advice is concerned, the early writings emphasize the offensive. He was an avid reader of other military treatises, including those of Turenne, Montecuccoli, and Folard. He was a student of the campaigns of the Imperial general Prince Eugène of Savoy, whom he greatly admired, and, although he did not adopt it, he was interested in Folard's tactical doctrine. These writers whetted his early instinct for the offensive. He shared

Folard's distrust of firearms. In 1747 he wrote that morale factors determine the outcome of battles: "As for rapid step by the infantry and attack, rifle on shoulder, I have some good reason to prefer it to any other. It is not the greater or lesser number of dead that decides an action, but the ground you gain. It is not fire but bearing that defeats an enemy."[47] Frederick's victories in the Silesian wars had come at the expense of a weak and unprepared Austria that was also beset by other powerful enemies. Even so, Luh demonstrates that in the course of these wars, Frederick learned the necessity of increasing his cavalry and artillery and to recognize the importance of fortifications. The Seven Years' War, in which he was faced by a coalition led by a regenerate Austria, confirmed that it took more than bearing to prevail against his enemies.

Frederick's later treatises on war conclude that its practice had changed over the course of the century and that his army should adapt to new circumstances. His earlier *Instructions* no longer sufficed to guide his officers to meet these new threats. War had become more refined, more murderous, and required greater caution. Dismissing military practice of the French because of their inconsistency and indiscretion, and the Russians, unfairly, because they were "as savage as they were inept," he now recommended a war of positions rather than the search for decisive battle. He wrote favorably of the Austrians, who were masters of this kind of war with their new and deadly field artillery, their field fortifications and powerful encampments, and their shrewd use of the terrain. His treatises of 1758 and 1770 recommended that generals approach this form of warfare as if it were siegecraft. Frederick had joined the technicians.[48]

Although his military thought evolved through experience, he never ceased to search for its underlying principles. In recommending Folard to his officers, he wrote: "Every art has its rules and maxims. One must study them: theory facilitates practice. The lifetime of one man is not long enough to enable him to acquire perfect knowledge and experience. Theory helps to supplement it, it provides youth with premature experience and makes him skillful also through the mistakes of others. In the profession of war the rules of the art never are violated without drawing some punishment from the enemy, who is delighted to find us at fault."[49] Nevertheless, it would be wrong to view him as the creator of a system. The famous oblique order by which he struck the enemy with one reinforced wing while refusing the other was the result of circumstances. It allowed him to attack an enemy with superior forces, but it depended on favorable ground and surprise. The oblique order did lead to battlefield victory, once, at the battle of Leuthen in 1757. Nevertheless, it made a powerful impression on contemporaries. "This order is the most scientific, the most artful, the most perfect of all," enthused one commentator. "Fredrick the Great, has, of all the moderns, best studied the principles and properties of the oblique order. In his grand encampments and reviews, in time of peace, he showed the mechanism of his order to his generals.... The Prussian tactics form an æra in military history."[50] Frederick was a creative military thinker and challenged his senior commanders to think for themselves. His works were studied as dogma, but, when his dynamic spirit was removed, the result was an ossified institution, one that would be swept away by the Napoleonic hurricane.

Frederick echoed other writers when he wrote that coup d'oeil was necessary for a successful general. This talent, which he surely possessed, he believed consisted of two points: the ability to judge how many troops a position could hold and exploiting the terrain. "The foundation of this coup d'oeil without doubt is fortification, which has rules that must be applied to the positions of the army."[51] His summary of campaign maxims reflects the broad nature of a soldier-king's responsibilities, which went far beyond tactics:

He must have an accurate idea of politics in order to be informed of the intention of princes and the forces of states and of their communications; to know the number of troops that princes and their allies can put into the field; and to judge the condition of their finances. Knowledge of the country where he must wage war serves as the basis for all strategy. He must be able to imagine himself in the enemy's shoes in order to anticipate all the obstacles that are likely to be placed in his way. Above all, he must train his mind to furnish him with a multitude of expedients, ways, and means in case of need. For those who are destined for the military profession, peace must be a time of meditation, and war the period where one puts his ideas into practice.[52]

Frederick's role as warlord confirms the complexity of the Enlightenment. He disappointed those philosophes who looked to him to inaugurate a new age of enlightened, peaceful, and humane government. Although he stood for religious toleration, his deep social conservatism marked him as a defender of the ancien régime. The skepticism and ironic wit that enliven his published work reflect an increasingly bitter cynicism. Nevertheless, one can only reject Frederick as an Enlightenment figure if one accepts the idea that there was only one Enlightenment agenda. Frederick did care about enlightened opinion and did his best to influence it. He was concerned to demonstrate that his wars were fought justly. "The Art of War," he wrote, "is just like any other art: used correctly it can be profitable; abused it is fatal. A prince who wages war from unrest, frivolity, or wanton ambition deserves to be punished as much as a judge who murders an innocent man with the sword of justice. That war is virtuous which is waged in order to maintain the authority of the state, preserve its allies, or check an ambitious prince who plots conquests contrary to your interests.... There is no finer and more useful art than the art of war when practiced by decent men. Under the protection of the noble defenders of the fatherland the peasant tills his fields, commerce thrives, and all business proceeds peacefully."[53] Thus, he justified his conquest of Silesia as a defense of a legitimate right, no matter how much others might consider it piracy, and he argued that his preemptive invasion of Saxony in 1756 was a defense against threatening danger.[54]

Frederick's worldview was that of the early Enlightenment. He praised its scientific and intellectual achievements: "Perfected physics has carried the flame of truth into the shadows of metaphysics."[55] This attitude was also reflected in his understanding of the European state system; he observed that he operated within the context of a balance of power that limited ambition and freedom of action. "The ambitious ought never to forget that arms and military discipline are much the same throughout Europe, and that alliances have the general effect of producing equality between the forces of the belligerents. In these times, therefore, all that princes may hope to acquire, after accumulated success, is some small frontier town or some suburb, neither of which will pay interest on the debt incurred by war or contain nearly as many people who have perished in the field."[56]

Was Silesia worth the desperate wars that he waged for it? Frederick's final conclusion is unknown. The conquest added to Prussia's great power status, but it is doubtful that his subjects benefited much. It has been argued that Frederick's preoccupation with the army and the rigid bureaucracy that supported it set back any attempts at reform in Prussia. "The overriding conservatism of the king and of his subjects really retarded the modernization of Prussia. Both the judiciary and the army acted as protectors of the old society and neither supported economic reform."[57] With the exception of the indecisive War of the Bavarian Succession, Frederick pursued a policy of peace in the period following the Seven Years' War. He contented himself with digesting portions of Poland during its "peaceful" partitions by the great eastern powers. Gerhard Ritter, describing the peaceful world of late-Enlightenment Germany, says he believes that Frederick gained followers as a "sovereign of peace."[58]

Frederick's military treatises were considered confidential documents and, except for his *Instructions to His Generals of 1747*, had limited circulation until the nineteenth century. His contemporaries studied and imitated his battlefield techniques and the severe Prussian discipline without fully comprehending the creative and skeptical genius that produced them. There was good reason to choose him as a model, for he had perfected warfare within the eighteenth-century social system. As he himself admitted, that system imposed limits on a war leader, but Frederick was not the man to envisage a change in the context. It was his great contemporary Maurice de Saxe who suggested something new.

MAURICE DE SAXE

The illegitimate son of Augustus II of Saxony-Poland, Hermann Moritz, comte de Saxe (known as Maurice de Saxe; 1698–1750) commanded the

French army in Flanders during the War of the Austrian Succession There he achieved a series of remarkable victories, including Fontenoy (1745), Roucoux (1746), and Lawfeldt (1747), that appeared to confirm France's military supremacy in Europe, a myth that was dispelled within a few years of his death. Like the Prince de Ligne, Saxe was one of the cosmopolitan members of the eighteenth-century European officer corps. Having enrolled in the Saxon army, he participated in the murderous battle of Malplaquet in 1709 and fought against the Swedes in Pomerania in 1711–1712. He then joined the Austrian army and served under Prince Eugene against the Turks in 1717–1718. In 1719 he transferred to the French service and fought against Prince Eugene during the War of the Polish Succession. In 1741 he won fame by leading French troops in a successful nighttime attack that resulted in the capture of Prague. By 1743 he was a marshal of France and on the verge of greatness as a military commander. He brought to the task one of the boldest and most creative minds of the period.

Even before he achieved fame as a general, Saxe had contributed an imaginative and stimulating treatise to eighteenth-century military literature. In 1732 he collected his thoughts in his *Mes Rêveries*, written for a small circle, including his father and Folard. He subsequently made revisions in the manuscript; published in 1757, it became one of the most influential military essays of the century. Unlike Folard, Saxe did not offer a new system of war, but rather a collection of ideas that sought to liberate commanders from the restraints imposed by eighteenth-century conditions and to suggest new sources of energy. Saxe claimed to have written his *Rêveries* in three days, while suffering from a fever; Thomas Carlyle suggested that he was under the influence of opium at the time. However, the manuscript probably was revised before publication, and the *Rêveries* should be considered to be the serious, if at times whimsical, reflections of an experienced and insightful officer.[59]

Saxe has been criticized as conventional or even backward-looking in some respects. He observed that a good general could prevail by maneuver without ever having to fight a battle; he believed that edged weapons were preferable to firearms; and he considered the fortification of cities to be an unnecessary expense. Robert Quimby points out that Saxe was present on the day of Malplaquet, during which firearms were responsible for most of the 25,000–30,000 casualties, thus rendering curious his rejection of these weapons. Nevertheless, the question of the efficacy of firearms remains subject to debate. Two more-recent works dismiss the destructive effect of infantry firearms in eighteenth-century battle.[60] Even today the realities of infantry combat in the eighteenth century seem shrouded in a black-powder fog. David Chandler, the leading writer on eighteenth-century battlefield tactics, concludes that the British became committed to infantry firepower under the victorious Marlborough and never looked back. For all the instances of surprisingly few casualties resulting from battlefield musket volleys, there is the example of Bunker Hill, where troops advancing on determined defenders were slaughtered. Despite predictions by Saxe and others that infantry firearms might be discarded, they were not. Historians have also puzzled over the Native American abandonment of bows, which they deem superior, in favor of seventeenth- and eighteenth-century firearms. Jacques Antoine Hippolyte de Guibert, a distinguished military writer of the latter half of the century, pointed this out when he defended the usefulness of firearms. Native Americans pre- ferred firearms to other missile weapons, "such as slings, bows, javelins lanced from the hand, etc. Look with what eagerness the savages in Amer- ica have, in spite of the inconveniences of noise, quitted these last to adopt our muskets; for men who exist by hunting and which exercise is alone their occupation, this is no fictitious inconvenience."[61]

In 1732, Saxe was attracted to Folard's argument that the restoration of the offensive spirit required the troops to rely on edged weapons in the attack. He concluded that "if the previous war had lasted a little longer indubitably everyone would have fought hand to hand. This was because the abuse of firing began to be appreciated; it causes more noise than dam- age, and those who depend on it are always beaten."[62] As we have seen, Frederick the Great began his career with similar views, but neither he nor Saxe were prisoners of doctrine. They were practical commanders who adapted to the exigencies of war. Fontenoy, Saxe's most famous victory, was a defensive action. He employed field fortifications similar to those used by Peter the Great at Poltava, skirmishers in the woods, concentrated artillery fire, and cavalry charges to repel the advance of the duke of Cum- berland's great column.

Like Folard, Saxe was inspired by classical models. Unlike his mentor, whose tactics were based on the Macedonian phalanx, Saxe proposed that the army be organized along the lines of the Roman legion. Of course no one knew exactly how the Roman legion had been organized and, indeed, that organization had changed over time. What Saxe had in mind was a flexible, self-contained force of infantry, cavalry, and light artillery capable of sus- taining itself in both offensive and defensive action. The legion would allow commanders greater freedom of maneuver and provide a prospect of more decisive results. Saxe's proposal aroused great interest during the period. Many armies adapted Saxe's legion as a model for their light troops. It also had relevance for the organization of the army as a whole. According to Jur- gen Luh, the large unitary armies of the eighteenth century could not be kept together for long periods because of logistical difficulties. The result was their division into ad hoc corps. Saxe looked ahead to a permanent divi- sional and corps structure, the hallmark of the Napoleonic army. Comman- ders experimented with the idea before Napoleon arrived on the scene, most notably Marshal Broglie, who introduced the scheme in French maneuvers in the 1760s. The legion idea reached its culmination in 1792 when the small U.S. army was reorganized for a brief period into four legions and renamed the Legion of the United States.

Although Saxe's *Rêveries* is perhaps the least systematic of all eighteenth-century military treatises, none bears a greater imprint of Enlightenment thought. Saxe was one of the first eighteenth-century commanders to give serious thought to the kind of men who should be recruited as soldiers, and this led him to conclusions that were radical for his time. Most armies and navies filled their wartime ranks by some form of conscription, as in Prussia's use of the cantonal system and the French practice of drafting from the provincial militia. Saxe, however, proposed a form of universal service. "Would it not be better to prescribe by law that every man, whatever his condition in life, should be obliged to serve his prince and his country for five years? This law should not be objected to, because it is natural and just that all citizens should participate in the defense of the nation."[63] Perhaps he was not fully aware of the implications of an idea that had the potential to change the relationship of the people to their government, but he seems to have been serious in calling for a body of trained citizen-soldiers as preferable to the scorned mercenaries who composed contemporary armies. It is evident that he believed that soldiers should be treated as human beings rather than as disposable robots. He called for moderation of military punishments and argued that they should be proportionate to the offense. Saxe preferred to rely on motivation and morale rather than fear as the principle of his leadership.

Saxe's views on citizen-soldiers appear to anticipate the ideas of Montesquieu and Rousseau on this subject. His call for moderation of military punishments came long before the publication of the Italian jurist Cesare Beccaria's work on criminal punishment in 1764. Montesquieu's *The Spirit of the Laws* was published in 1748, two years before Saxe's death. Although Saxe's 1732 manuscript of *Rêveries* was probably revised before its publication in 1757, he seems to have arrived at his conclusions independently of these writers. According to one of Saxe's biographers, Jean-Pierre Bois, Saxe's idea of a national army was the result of isolated reflection. One cannot know what was said in his conversations with others or what ideas were au courant. The climate of opinion was shifting in the direction pointed out by Saxe. The philosophes did not ignore the military literature of the time and were as likely to be familiar with Saxe's ideas as he with theirs. His *Rêveries* suggests that military thought was not an independent department, something to be influenced by the Enlightenment, but rather a robust and creative contributor to the intellectual ferment of the age.

THE LATE MILITARY ENLIGHTENMENT

Military writers of the early Enlightenment, 1700–1740, wrote about war within the context of a particular experience, the War of the Spanish

Succession and the parallel Northern War. Victorious Britons, content with the linear fire tactics associated with the duke of Marlborough, contributed little to military thought in this period. The French, although saved by Vauban's fortresses, knew that something had gone badly wrong with their military institutions. As noted, Folard responded by seeking to capture the offensive spirit of Charles XII of Sweden by creating offensive infantry tactics using a phalanx that relied on edged weapons rather than firearms. He was one of many eighteenth-century writers who concluded that firearms did little damage and served only to sap the aggressive spirit. Many were attracted to Folard's ideas even though, like Saxe, they thought them too extreme. Folard was influenced by classical models and by a desire to establish war on scientific principles. He continued to have disciples throughout the century, most notably Baron Mesnil-Durand, the advocate for the *ordre profonde,* the attack by columns rather than line. Despite the contempt Folard and Saxe displayed for fortresses, fortification offered the prospect of war being conducted on scientific principles. During the War of the Austrian Succession, Bourcet demonstrated how the rules of fortification could be applied to an entire campaign. Technical knowledge became more diffuse within the armies, and Frederick the Great, who initially appears to have been moved by the spirit of Folard, found it necessary to adapt to new conditions.

After 1740, military thought was influenced by new developments that Geoffrey Parker has called the military post revolutions of the eighteenth century: the extensive use of light troops and skirmishers, the introduction of divisional organizations (a development envisaged by Saxe), and the creation of a swift and mobile field artillery.[64] Two of these innovations were Austrian. During the War of the Austrian Succession, the Habsburg government raised large numbers of Hungarian light cavalry and tough irregulars from their military border with the Ottoman Empire. These hussars, Croats, and Pandours, as they were known, played havoc with Frederick's vulnerable communications and logistics and played no small part in the preservation of the monarchy. They were in the field again during the Seven Years' War, forcing Frederick to seek countermeasures against what was known as *petite guerre,* or partisan war. By the time of the latter conflict, the Prussian cavalry was so improved that it was able establish a margin of superiority over the pesky Austrians. Partisan warfare was not limited to central Europe, but one that European soldiers would encounter in Scotland, Corsica, and North America.

This form of warfare inspired a new branch of military literature. One may contrast it with Humphrey Bland's *A Treatise of Military Discipline,* first published in 1727 and running to nine editions by 1762, a work that was relied upon by British and American officers as their introduction to the military profession. Bland provided a distillation of the military experience as seen through the eyes of Marlborough's veterans. He had little to say about *petite guerre;* indeed, he found the subject distasteful. He admitted that armies sometimes had to forage, exact contributions, and even lay waste to the countryside, but he thought it did more harm than good by wearing out one's men and horses. "Formerly," he wrote, "these sorts of exploits were much in vogue, particularly by the French, who call it *La Petite Guerre;* but of late they are very much left off, since they only serve to render the poor inhabitants more miserable, or particular officers, whose horses and baggage they take, uneasy in their affairs..., which reason is sufficient in my opinion, to discontinue the practice, or at least not use it on particular occasions."[65] The marquis de Feuquières agreed. In his memoirs, published in 1736, he dismissed the entire subject of ambushes as not worthy of reflection.[66] How dated was this view in 1750! The Austrian irregulars had certainly inconvenienced Frederick, going so far as to carry off his silver service in one raid on his camp.[67]

This dimension of war now attracted much attention. (Peter Paret has counted 50 military treatises dealing with this subject, beginning in 1752.[68] On one level these treatises are technical in nature, providing handbooks for the partisan officer.) As armies began to incorporate their own specialized light forces, however, questions arose about the kind of officers and men required for this service. Partisan warfare required a level of independence and self-reliance not seen in line battalions. Issues of recruitment, leadership, and training of these men coincided with a belief that soldiers should be looked upon as human beings rather than mindless instruments of war. Furthermore, many officers encountered this form of warfare in unconventional situations, in revolutionary America, for example. Count de Guibert, author of the most celebrated military treatise of the late Enlightenment, had seen service in Corsica, a very different environment from the Flanders plains so familiar to Humphrey Bland. Changing conditions required officers to view war in a new way.

A second change, already mentioned above, was the introduction of powerful new field artillery that rendered the battlefield a more murderous place. In France the early-eighteenth-century artillery system developed by Jean-Florent de Valliére, which focused on siege warfare and thus heavy, but immobile guns, was outdated by 1750. Technical developments originating in Holland allowed the casting of lighter and more maneuverable field guns and a closer integration of the artillery with battlefield tactics. Prince Joseph Wenzel von Liechtenstein had exploited these new techniques and was responsible for providing Austria with the dominant field artillery of the Seven Years' War. He was also mentor to Jean-Baptiste Vaquette de Gribeauval, a French engineer attached to the Austrian army during the Seven Years' War, who helped to upgrade that army's technical branch. Gribeauval was a critic of Valliére's system and drew upon his experience with Liechtenstein to reorganize the French artillery after 1763. Gribeauval introduced technical innovations such as the elevating screw to raise or lower the breech and graduated rear sights. He standardized the calibers of French pieces while emphasizing mobility and striking power. These developments made possible the introduction of horse artillery as an offensive arm of the cavalry and allowed generals to mass artillery against particular points in the enemy line in order to puncture it.[69] Luh argues persuasively that artillery developments served the cause of the defense and positional warfare. They certainly had that effect on Frederick the Great. One eighteenth-century writer concluded that the new field artillery would simply make mincemeat of the phalanxes proposed by Folard and his later disciples Baron Mesnil-Durand and Joly de Maizeroy.[70] This was demonstrated in practice. A Hessian officer at the siege of Savannah during the War of American Independence observed a French attack in column, "a favorite method with the French." They rushed forward heedless of a battery on their flank. "The battery sent such a murderous fire of grapeshot into the column that, instead of the mere 250 to 300 which the enemy had lost in the attack, their retreat made losses mount to between 1,200 and 1,300 killed and wounded."[71] Nevertheless, the new artillery did not stop officers from considering means to reassert the offensive in warfare.

GUIBERT

The first major military treatise to appear in the wake of Gribeauval's artillery reform was Jacques de Guibert's *A General Essay on Tactics*, published in 1772. Because his essay contained a preliminary discourse on politics couched in Rousseauan rhetoric, it gained an audience far beyond professional military readers and made Guibert a celebrated figure in salon culture. Nevertheless, this was a serious military work in which Guibert developed the tactical ideas fostered by his father, who had served as a senior staff officer during the Seven Years' War. He stressed mobile warfare, flexibility rather than doctrinaire systems, the supremacy of firepower, and the coordination of infantry, cavalry, and artillery. Robert Quimby regards Guibert along with Bourcet as the most important influence on Napoleon's military ideas. Although Guibert believed European armies were encumbered with too much artillery, he understood its offensive potential: "The main object of artillery should not consist in destroying men on the totality of the enemy's front; but to effectively rout, or...to make a breach in a part of it; whether towards those points from points from whence an advantageous attack can be made or proximate to those where it can be attacked with greatest success."[72] Such an employment of artillery pointed to the Napoleonic use of columns to exploit gaps in the enemy line already produced by cannon fire. Guibert had not hesitated to grasp the significance of technical developments as a basis for his new theory of war.

On the one hand Guibert sought to understand the principles that lay behind Frederick the Great's success. However, he wrote in an intellectual climate no longer dominated by that king and his friend Voltaire. Guibert's celebrity was inspired by the vogue for Rousseau and the idea of the citizen-soldier. He shared his contemporaries' enthusiasm for Roman virtue in contrast to the current age. "Where is there a warlike people, enemies to luxury, friends to labor, and animated by their laws to a love of glory?"[73] He shared the view of many philosophes that the constitution of a state determined national character. At that time he believed that the military constitutions of all European states were similar. The "genius" of a nation was no longer the basis for war-making, because all depended on mercenaries. This created a stalemate, which was not without benefit, because no nation needed to fear conquest and enslavement as a result of defeat. Guibert wrote, "At this day, all Europe is civilized. War is become less barbarous and cruel. When battles are finished, no longer is any blood shed; prisoners are well treated, towns are not sacked, countries are not ravaged and laid waste.... the military line is looked upon as fatiguing and despised by every class of citizens; hence the extinction of patriotism, and the epidemical falling away of national bravery.... Nothing is more obvious than the fate of countries now depends on despicable and ill constituted mercenary troops."[74]

The answer to this sad state of affairs was the military education of the whole people, which would restore honor and respect to the military profession. "How easy it is to have armies invincible, in a state where its subjects are citizens, where they cherish the government, where they are fond of glory, where they are not intimidated at the idea of toiling for the general good!" Guibert concluded.[75] The influence of the late Enlightenment is evident in these passages. Constitutional reform could liberate energies that would transform the European situation. Yet, like Rousseau, Guibert was ambivalent as to whether this would be a good thing or even possible. The primary focus of his *General Essay on Tactics* was the development of a tactical system that would allow Old Regime armies to perform at their best. He saw at firsthand the limitations of citizen-soldiers in Corsica and was not impressed by what he heard about the performance of such troops in America. In the end, he would prefer the professional to the amateur and as an officer regarded himself as a defender of the established order. In a later work, he defended his military proposals but distanced himself from the radical political ideas expressed in his essay. Robert Quimby concludes that "Guibert's real influence lay in the military ideas which he propounded. These ideas were embodied in the Ordinance of 1791 in so far as they concerned elementary tactics. They were the basis for the best practice in the great wars that followed."[76]

LLOYD

Guibert had succeeded in establishing himself as a military philosophe. He not only moved freely among the intellectual elite but also offered creative solutions to military problems. He was not the only writer to bear the imprint of the later Enlightenment. Henry Lloyd (1720–1783), the son of a Welsh clergyman, participated in the Jacobite uprising of 1745 and, as a result, spent the rest of his military career abroad, in the service of the French, Prussian, and Austrian armies, in the last of which he attained the rank of major general. Although he was eventually reconciled to the British establishment, he never acquired military rank in that service. So dominant were the duke of Marlborough's tactical ideas that the British army produced few writers who reflected deeply on the fundamentals of the military system. Lloyd's career as a "wild goose" provided him with an acquaintance and a perspective that few British officers could match. To this he added a serious study of contemporary military thought and practice coupled with a wide reading of Enlightenment literature. As a result, he was one of the few British writers to discuss large operations and major military issues within the context of late-Enlightenment thought. Christopher Duffy views Lloyd as a "highly unstable individual," a chatterbox, and possibly a British spy while serving with the Austrian army during the Seven Years' War. Duffy is critical of Lloyd's history of that war: "It is impersonal in tone, geometrical in content, and tells us nothing about that conflict that cannot be derived from other sources, and can in no way be considered as representative of an Austrian body of thought on the conduct of warfare as a whole."[77] However, although Lloyd's history is not a good source for Austrian military thought, it does reflect trends in what might be called the Military Enlightenment. His military principles combine the influence of Helvétius and Rousseau with that of Saxe and Frederick the Great.

Lloyd's work represents a tension between themes in enlightened military thought. The Seven Years' War led him to the conclusion that a war of position was preferable to battle. The exact knowledge of the country, the science of position, camps, and marches were the essential disciplines to be mastered by a general. They allowed him to "reduce military operations to geometrical precision, and may for ever make war without being obliged to fight. Marshal Saxe calls battles the resource of ignorant generals; when they do not know what to do they give battle."[78] Lloyd's introduction to his principles describes war as a branch of Newtonian mechanics: "War is a state of action. An army is the instrument with which every species of military action is performed; like all machines it is composed of various parts, and its perfection will depend, first on that of its several parts; and second, on the manner in which they are arranged; so that the whole may have the following properties, viz., strength, agility, and universality; if these are properly combined the machine is perfect."[79]

Along with many contemporaries, Lloyd concluded from the Seven Years' War that battles were inconclusive and that infantry firepower was limited in effect. Because armies no longer had to come to grips to engage and because musket fire was so ineffective, battles were seldom decisive, nor were wars. "No kingdom is overturned—no nation is enslaved. The subject alone feels the weight and calamities of war."[80] He calculated that even good marksmen hit their targets one time in 10. This was a conservative view when one considers the murderous nature of that war, even if it was the result of the new artillery. Although Guibert believed that the answer to ineffective fire was better training, Lloyd remained a disciple of Folard and Saxe. He contended that firepower was useful only for defense and advocated the reintroduction of pikes and leather armor along with the development of a new kind of lance in place of the bayonet.

At this point, one might expect Lloyd to have entered into the camp of the advocates of the *ordre profonde,* those such as Baron Mesnil-Durand and Joly de Maizeroy, who continued to propose tactical solutions to what seemed to be a military impasse. Although their ideas varied in detail and emphasis, they produced new versions of Folard's attack by massed columns meant to penetrate the enemy line, the *ordre mince.*[81] Lloyd, however, looked for solutions in a different way, turning to a social and psychological analysis of military institutions. In one sense it may be said that he was true to the legacy of Folard, who had sought to revive the military spirit, but Lloyd's approach was consistent with the concerns of the late Enlightenment. This is most evident in his discussion of human passions as motivating factors, including fear, honor, shame, and desire for riches. Most powerful of all, he concluded, were love of liberty and religion. Although a knowledge of positions was important to a general, still more essential was the ability to channel and master the passions of his soldiers. A general should lead by example by demonstrating exemplary personal qualities. Victory lay not with the disciplinarian, but with one who could inspire the men. Lloyd recognized that not all armies were the same.

Although there was a multinational dimension in most eighteenth-century European armies, Lloyd joined many military observers who alluded to national character as the basis on which armies should be understood and organized. Thus, there was a widespread belief that French national character was too emotional and individualistic to undergo Prussian discipline and that its strength lay in the attack rather than the defensive. In keeping with most Enlightenment thought, Lloyd believed that national character was a reflection of a country's "constitution," He admired the Austrian and Russian soldiers, whom he had observed as naturally obedient, uncomplaining, and brave. Of course, there was really no such thing as an Austrian army; there was a Habsburg army of many different nationalities. The national character of this army was the product of military institutions, some of recent date, rather than the result of a national culture in the nineteenth-century sense. Lloyd's concept of national character was thus superficial but consistent with eighteenth-century political and social thought. Lloyd believed that an average general could prosper with manpower such as the Austrian and Russian soldiers but that the Prussians, an army of "strangers" consisting of at least one-half mercenaries, were a different matter. They lacked national identity and could only be held together by the iron discipline and genius of the king. Soldiers of a despotic prince were better-disciplined than those of a republic and better-suited for foreign conquest. Love of liberty clashed with the subordination required by a good army, but a despotic prince might arouse his troops through religion, if not liberty. However, Lloyd regarded love of liberty as the most powerful of all motivating forces; soldiers so inspired would be invincible if properly led. This was especially true if the love of liberty and religion were combined.[82] These latter thoughts were perhaps more influenced by events in America than in Germany, for Lloyd wrote in a revolutionary age: "A people reduced to the necessity of taking up arms against their sovereign, is obliged to exert itself by fear of a revengeful master, death and slavery, and by hopes of independency, and all the advantages which attend it; such powerful motives generally render their efforts successful." Lloyd had George III in mind when he advised that "the sovereign conducting such a war should, by moderate conduct, diminish the idea of danger, and leave room to a solid and hearty reconciliation."[83]

Lloyd was reconciled to the British government at the time he wrote his history but was critical of British military institutions. He regarded Britain's limited monarchy as a kind of aristocratic republic in which faction and intrigue prevailed. Only clear and pressing danger could provide the unity required for success in war. The century saw many aristocratic republics in decline as a result of these very causes, and contemporary critics lamented the corruption of the British political system. From a modern perspective, British corruption seems modest compared to that encountered in other states, and Britain may be regarded as the most efficient and successful military power of the era. But Britain's Hanoverian monarchs who strove to increase professionalism in the army, would have agreed with Lloyd's prescription for reform: "If the nature of the English constitution permitted some more degree of discipline, a more equal distribution of favours, and the total abolishment of buying and selling commissions, I think they would surpass, at least equal, any troops in the world."[84]

Lloyd's work was a provocative mix of old and new. He sought to revive the military spirit on which the offense depended, but he remained committed to the tactics rendered obsolete by the technical changes of the midcentury. Criticism of the British practice of selling army commissions was not new. The venerable Humphrey Bland believed that it was the chief obstacle to the professionalism essential to modern armies.[85] However, his work was enriched by contemporary political and social thought. The ideas of Montesquieu, Helvétius, and Rousseau emerge from his pages as guides to a new approach to war. There is a new concern with the human element of the armies and an emphasis on leadership and motivation. Lloyd believed that armies, like societies, were the result of their constitutions and that real improvement lay at that fundamental level. His ideal army was one inspired by liberty and one in which careers were open to merit. In this sense, he pointed toward a new era in warfare.

A striking feature of the military writing of the late Enlightenment is a concern with the proper treatment of the rank and file. Maurice de Saxe was father of this new approach. Lloyd sought to introduce sources of motivation beyond the harsh discipline of the times. This coincided with increased public sensitivity to the hard conditions of military service, with particular regard to prisoners and invalids. The late-Enlightenment concern with the humane treatment of individuals extended to military thought as well. The increased interest in the military practices of ancient republics pointed in this direction. There was much interest in the work of the late Roman military authority Vegetius whose *Military Institutions* was translated and published in 1767 by John Clarke, a lieutenant of the marines, who later wrote a firsthand account of the battle of Bunker Hill. Clarke believed that the principles of war "always have been and always will be, the same invariably, notwithstanding the Alteration of particular Modes or Weapons; and many of these ancient institutions are even applicable to these."[86] In many ways, Clarke's translation of Vegetius echoed Bland's description of the rules of proper military discipline, the "military manner" that young recruits are taught even today. The focus is on the troops. They "should, if possible, be of reputable families, and unexceptional in their Manners. Such sentiments as may be expected in these men will make good Soldiers; a Sense of Honor, by preventing them from behaving ill, will make them victorious."[87] Rome provided an ideal of citizen-soldiers self-motivated by a sense of honor. Could such qualities be nurtured in the rank and file of eighteenth-century European armies?

The modern image of the eighteenth-century army remains the long lines of mercenary soldiers and impressed men advancing on one another to exchange almost point-blank fire. To maneuver such an army and to ensure that it stood up to the enemy's volleys required the endless drill and harsh discipline associated with the Prussians. However, many writers agreed with Lloyd that the Prussian system was unsuited for other nationalities. Edward Drewe, for example, maintained that the Prussian discipline was inappropriate for "the high-born spirit of the British soldier."[88] Furthermore, there were forms of eighteenth-century warfare that called for greater self-sufficiency on the part of the soldier. This was the theme of much of the writing on partisan warfare, or *petite guerre*. Armies needed soldiers who could counter the threats posed by Austrian light troops while not committing the brigandage associated with the pandours. British regulars fighting in North America found it necessary to adopt a more open order of combat than was typical in Europe. The high

rate of desertion was offered as one reason for strict discipline and keeping armies in close order. What would induce soldiers to fight and not run
away if they were under looser control? "The great point for an officer that
often goes on parties [i.e. scouting, ambushes, or foraging]," wrote one
officer, "is to establish an implicit obedience, without which, he can never
act to good purpose even in the easiest or best concerted enterprises; on
the contrary, he is detested by the people of the country on the account of
the disorders committed by his men; this gives the enemy the opportunity
of attacking him, possibly when least prepared to receive them."[89]

The significant words in the foregoing sentence are "implicit obedience." How was this to be earned? Writers on this form of warfare placed
much emphasis on the example of the officer whose bravery, professionalism, and humanity would inspire obedience. In other words, officers
should lead their men. During the American War of Independence, officers such as Johann Ewald and J. G. Simcoe lived up to the standard established by these treatises. Ewald led the Hessian jaegers recruited from
respectable woodsmen, and Simcoe commanded the loyalist Queen's
Rangers, who were committed to the British cause. The light service
required particular types of officers and men. Could this standard be
extended to an entire army?

The citizen-soldier was an ideal for writers in ancien régime states, but
there was interest in improving the manpower of existing armies. The
British military essayist Campbell Dalrymple lamented recruiting conditions in his country. On the one hand, volunteers were attracted by the
"levity, accident, and dexterity of recruiting officers for them; by the second plan, the country gets clear of their banditti, and the ranks are filled
up with the scum of every country, the refuse of mankind."[90] As an alternative, he argued that by raising regiments on a county basis and by
appealing to the common soldiers' concern for reputation and honor, one
could enhance the quality of the troops and reduce the necessity for harsh
discipline and punishment. "Many officers consider their men as mere
machines, and treat them accordingly, but that system is erroneous, as
well as derogatory to them as intelligent beings: we ought therefore to
apply first to their senses, and by making them understand, enable them
to execute any evolution."[91]

This enlightened attitude, which Dalrymple attributed to Caesar, was
shared by other authors. Bennet Cuthbertson urged that brothers and
kinsmen be placed in the same company, because nothing could bind men
more closely to the service. He shared Dalrymple's distaste for the current
system of punishment and observed that officers had many means to
inspire good behavior in the troops. Before resorting to corporal punishment, an officer should be certain that he had taken every other step for a
soldier's reformation. Corporal punishment eliminated the soldier's sense
of shame, and he would become more profligate than before. Cuthbertson

recommended religious instruction and observance as a better method of suppressing immorality among the troops and urged that every effort should be made to appeal to a soldier's sense of honor. An order of merit for noncommissioned officers (NCOs), drummers, and privates would encourage good conduct and competition for the approval of their officers. This was a radical proposal in an age in which honor was usually regarded as the quality that defined the aristocratic officer class.[92]

These themes were echoed by Laissac on the eve of the French Revolution. "Men, says the philosopher of Geneva, are what governments make them: citizens, warriors when it wishes; a rabble and riffraff when it pleases." Laissac believed that the military spirit could not be recaptured without a reform of the political system. "Europe is covered with soldiers, nearly all governments are military, yet I do not see a warrior people. The safety of nations is confided to a mob of vagabonds, foreigners, and fugitives, instead of men." The best troops were volunteer citizen soldiers on the Roman model.[93] All of these writers acknowledged their debt to Saxe but spoke to the concerns of the late Enlightenment. Proper recruitment and a concern for a system of just rewards and punishments as an appeal to a soldier's sense of honor and duty were a common theme.[94]

Particularly eloquent was the legal expert Stephen Payne Adye, who served as judge advocate in the British army in America during the War of Independence. Adye set out to write a treatise to instruct young officers sitting on regimental courts-martial in the basic elements of English common law. However, he concluded this handbook with a remarkable essay on punishments and rewards that was inspired by the great legal reformer Beccaria. As did Dalrymple and Cuthbertson, Adye believed that punishment should be inflicted as a last resort. Officers should appeal first to the soldier's sense of honor and shame. Punishment had three purposes: (1) to induce reform, (2) to deprive criminals of the capacity to do harm, and (3) to serve as an example to reduce crime. If reformation was the object, the punishment should produce only temporary pain and anxiety, not carry lasting infamy. Although the death penalty seemed to do little to decrease French desertion rates, the Spartans had used shame effectively to punish cowardice. "The reason," argued Montesquieu, "is very natural. A soldier accustomed to venture his life, despises, or affects to despise the danger of losing it."[95]

Adye praised the Romans for their rewards of spears, bracelets, and collars for those who had saved the life of a comrade in battle, but he lamented the cruelty of their punishments. As for the British soldiers, he admitted that it was true that they were recruited from a criminal class and were frequently guilty of crimes that disgraced their profession. He joined other reformers in calling for the recruitment of regiments on a county basis and advocated a military order for officers that could be extended to meritorious common soldiers. Adye found it ironic that the modern humane conduct of war had deprived soldiers of their customary plunder. A rational system of rewards would transform the troops from the brigands of old to honest and motivated soldiers. There can be no more compelling expression of the Enlightenment's "humane agenda" than Adye's conclusion: "Let us not forget that every soldier is a human creature, susceptible of the same feelings and passions as other men, and as such, every method should be taken to deter him from vice, rather than trust to a reformation by punishment; that punishment must sometimes be inflicted is most certain; in such cases let it be exemplary, for the sake of the multitude; but let there ever be shewn a greater desire to *reward* than to punish."[96]

As we have seen, the Enlightenment influenced eighteenth-century military thought in many ways. Military writers concerned themselves with many topics, ranging from the principles that underlay the art of war to the relationship between political and military institutions. Many treatises dealt with technical subjects that arose from the evolution of military practice in the period. Like the philosophes, military writers passionately disagreed with one another. Were the basic principles of war unchanging or had there been a military revolution? What were the best battlefield tactics—fire or shock? Should commanders seek decisive action or rely upon maneuver and fortification? To these questions writers applied analytic techniques and attitudes borrowed from the philosophes. They shared contemporary concerns about humane conduct in war and the proper treatment of soldiers. Some writers, such as Frederick the Great and, perhaps, Guibert, should be considered as philosophes in their own right. Maurice de Saxe may have actually paved the way for the philosophes. Military treatises covered every area of conceivable interest to an aspiring officer, even how to find the right woman.[97] They tell us much about the standards of officer duty, values, and professionalism. These standards are the subject of chapter 3.

NOTES

1. Charles-Joseph de Ligne, *His Memoirs, Letters, and Miscellaneous Papers,* 2 vols. (New York: P. F. Collier and Son, 1899), 1:60.

2. This indictment is spelled out by Émile Léonard, *L'Armée et ses problèmes au XVIIIe siècle* (Paris: Libraire Plon, 1958), 46–53. For a good discussion of Folard, see pp. 107–17.

3. Jean-Charles de Folard, *Histoire de Polybe...avec un commentaire ou un corps de science militaire....,* 7 vols. (Amsterdam: Arkstée et Merkus, 1753), 1:iii.

4. Jean-Charles de Folard, *Nouvelles découvertes sur la guerre* (Paris, 1726), 11.

5. For an excellent discussion of the influence of the Enlightenment on the development of military thought, see Azar Gat, *The Origins of Military Thought from the Enlightenment to Clausewitz* (Oxford: Clarendon Press, 1989).

6. The most-detailed description of Folard's famous column, "Traité de la colonne, la manière de la former et de combattre dans cet ordre," is in the *Histoire de Polybe*, 1:lij–xcix.

7. Folard, *Nouvelles découvertes*, 28.

8. Francesco Algarotti, *Letters Military and Political from the Italian of Count Algarotti* (London: T. Egerton, 1782), 25–26.

9. The best study of Folard's life and ideas is that of Jean Chagniot, *Le chevalier de Folard: La stratégie de l'incertitude* (Paris: Editions du Rocher, 1997).

10. A good introduction to the discussion of the military revolution is provided in Michael Roberts, *The Military Revolution 1560–1660: An Inaugural Lecture Delivered before the Queen's University of Belfast* (Belfast: Marjory Boyd, 1956); Geoffrey Parker, *The Military Revolution: Military Innovation and the Rise of the West* (Cambridge: Cambridge University Press, 1988); and Jeremy Black, *A Military Revolution? Military Change and European Society 1550–1800* (Atlantic Highlands, N.J.: Humanities Press International, 1991). An excellent recent discussion of the military revolution is provided by Jean Chagniot in *Guerre et société a l'époque moderne* (Paris: Presses Universitaires de France, 2001), 275–312.

11. Early-eighteenth-century infantry tactics are described in David Chandler, *The Art of Warfare in the Age of Marlborough* (New York: Sarpedon, 1995), 114–30.

12. M. de Laissac, *L'Esprit militaire*, new edition (The Hague, 1788), 132.

13. F. Nockern de Schorn, *Idées raisonnées sur un système général et suivi de toutes les connoisances militaires et une methode lumineuse pour etudier la science de la guerre avec ordre et discernement en trois partes* (Nuremberg and Altdorf, 1783), 30.

14. Ibid., 42–43.

15. Edward Drewe, *Military Sketches* (Exeter, England, 1784), 32–33.

16. I wish to thank Colonel Kenneth Hamburger of the United States Military Academy for this information.

17. Campbell Dalrymple, *A Military Essay Containing Reflections on the Raising, Arming, Cloathing, and Discipline of the British Infantry and Cavalry* (London, 1761), 57.

18. Chandler, *Art of Warfare in the Age of Marlborough*, 130–31.

19. Algarotti, *Letters*, 23.

20. Chagniot, *Folard*, 21.

21. *Frederick the Great on the Art of War* (hereinafter cited as *FGAW*), ed. Jay Luvaas (New York: Free Press, 1966), 51. Frederick's writings are published in *Oeuvres de Frédéric le Grand*, 31 vols. (Berlin: Rodolphe Decker, 1846). His historical works, including *Histoire de mon temps* and *Histoire de la Guerre de Sept-Ans*, are in vols. 1–5; his military works in French and, in some technical subjects, in German, are in vols. 28–30. His military writing is most accessible in the significant excerpts provided by Luvaas. See also, Frederick's *Instructions for His Generals*, trans. Thomas Phillips (Harrisburg: Stackpole Press, 1960).

22. Jacques François de Chastenet de Puységur, *Art de la guerre par principles et par règles*, 2 vols. (1748) 1:40–41, 69–72.

23. This point is most fully developed in Gat, *Origins of Military Thought*.

24. For Vauban, see Henry Guerlac, "Vauban: The Impact of Science on War," in *Makers of Modern Strategy: Military Thought from Machiavelli to the Nuclear Age*, ed. Peter Paret (Princeton: Princeton University Press, 1986).

25. John A. Lynn, *Giant of the Grand Siècle: The French Army 1610–1715* (Cambridge: Cambridge University Press, 1997). For Vauban's career, see pp. 556–578.

26. Sébastien Le Prestre de Vauban, *A Manual of Siegecraft and Fortification,* trans. George Rothrock (Ann Arbor: University of Michigan Press, 1981), 21. Eighteenth-century fortress and siege warfare is best described in Christopher Duffy, *Fire and Stone: The Science of Fortress Warfare 1660–1860* (London and Vancouver: David and Charles, 1975). For Vauban's life, see Reginald Blomfiels, *Sébastien Le Prestre de Vauban, 1603–1707* (New York: Barnes and Noble, 1938; London: Methuen, 1971).

27. James Ostwald, "The 'Decisive' Battle of Ramillies, 1706: Prerequisites for Decisiveness in Early Modern Warfare," *Journal of Military History,* 64 (July 2000): 649–77.

28. Vauban, *Manual,* 21–91.

29. Anonymous, "A Journal of the Works in the Trenches during the Siege of Bergen-Op-Zoom," in *Remarks on the Military Operations of the English and French Armies commanded by the Duke of Cumberland and Marshal Saxe During the Campaign of 1747 by an Officer* (London: T. Becker, 1760), xxviii.

30. Vauban, *Manual,* 93.

31. Chagniot, *Guerre et société,* 289.

32. Erik Lund, *War for the Every Day: Generals, Knowledge, and Warfare in Early Modern Europe, 1680–1740* (Westport, Conn.: Greenwood Press, 1999), 50–51. Lund perhaps overstates his case. Many of the skills that he describes had always been needed by generals and, as he points out, were available in the agricultural society. For an unfavorable assessment of Austrian technical competence, see Christopher Duffy, *Instrument of War,* vol. 1 of *The Austrian Army in the Seven Years' War* (Rosemont, Ill.: The Emperor's Press, 2000), 296.

33. The issue of cabinet war is discussed in Chagniot, *Guerre et société,* 307–9.

34. Jan Glete, *Navies and Nations: Warships, Navies and State Building in Europe and America, 1500–1860,* 2 vols. (Stockholm: Almquist and Wiksell International), 1:8.

35. See Richard Harding, *Seapower and Naval Warfare 1650–1830* (London: UCL Press, 1999), for a discussion of these developments.

36. Glete, *Navies and Nations,* 1:49.

37. N. A. M. Rodger, *The Wooden World: An Anatomy of the Georgian Navy* (Annapolis: Naval Institute Press, 1986), 321. For a description of the complicated workings of the navy administration, see pp. 29–36. Britain's advantages are made clear in John Brewer, *The Sinews of Power: War, Money and the English State, 1688–1763* (New York: Alfred A. Knopf, 1989).

38. Hubert C. Johnson, *Frederick the Great and His Officials* (New Haven and London: Yale University Press, 1975), 243.

39. Jurgen Luh, *Ancien Régime Warfare and the Military Revolution: A Study* (Groningen, The Netherlands: INOS, 2000), 9–77.

40. This is Luh's view, but Reginald Savory contrasts British supply and medical services unfavorably with Prussian and French practice. See Savory's *His Britannic Majesty's Army in Germany* (Oxford: Clarendon Press, 1966), 305–7.

41. R. Arthur Bowler, *Logistics and the Failure of the British Army in America, 1775–1783* (Princeton: Princeton University Press, 1975).

42. Guy Rowlands, "Louis XIV, Vittorio Amedeo II and French Military Failure in Italy, 1689–96," *The English Historical Review* 115 (2000): 534–69. See also, Christopher Storrs, *War, Diplomacy, and the Rise of Savoy, 1690–1720* (Cambridge: Cambridge University Press, 1999). The latter is particularly good on the issue of the military revolution and state formation in the case of Savoy-Piedmont.

43. Robert Quimby, *The Background of Napoleonic Warfare: The Theory of Military Tactics in Eighteenth Century France* (New York: Columbia University Press, 1957), 175–84. Bourcet's treatise, written in 1775, circulated in manuscript until its publication in 1888. See P. J. de Bourcet, *Principes de la guerre de montagnes* (Paris, 1888). Many excerpts from Bourcet's papers are published in Spencer Wilkinson, *The Defence of Piedmont, 1742–1748: A Prelude to the Study of Napoleon* (Oxford: Clarendon Press, 1927). See pp. 108–9 for Bourcet's plan for 1744.

44. Luh, *Ancien Régime Warfare*, 117.

45. *The Letters of Voltaire and Frederick the Great*, trans. Richard Addington (London: Routledge, 1927), 143.

46. Jeremy Black, *European Warfare, 1660–1815* (London: UCL Press, 1994), 119–36. Walter Dorn, *Competition for Empire, 1740–1763* (New York: Harper and Row, 1963), provides an excellent survey of this period. There are many good biographies of Frederick. I have relied most upon Gerhard Ritter, *Frederick the Great: A Historical Profile*, trans. Peter Paret (Berkeley: University of California Press, 1974), and the same author's *The Sword and the Scepter: The Problem of Militarism in Germany*, vol. 1, *The Prussian Military Tradition, 1740–1890*, trans. Henz Norden (Coral Gables: University of Miami Press, 1969). Indispensable for eighteenth-century central and eastern European military history is the work of Christopher Duffy. In particular, see his *Military Life of Frederick the Great* (New York: Atheneum, 1986) and *The Army of Frederick the Great* (New York: Hippocrene Books, 1974).

47. Frederick II, *Instructions for His Generals*, 99.

48. Luvaas, *FGAW*, 264, 276.

49. Ibid., 54.

50. *The Military Mentor: Being a Series of Letters recently written by a General Officer to his Son, on his entering the Army*, 2d ed., 2 vols. (Salem, Mass.: Cushing and Appleton, 1808), 2:83–85.

51. Luvaas, *FGAW*, 142.

52. Ibid., 337.

53. Ibid., 44.

54. Frederick the Great, *Histoire de mon temps*, 50–56. Duffy, *Military Life of Frederick the Great*, 19.

55. Frederick the Great, *Histoire de mon temps*, 36.

56. Luvaas, *FGAW*, 45.

57. Johnson, *Frederick the Great and his Officials*, 266.

58. Ritter, *The Sword and the Scepter*, 38.

59. Maurice de Saxe, *Reveries on the Art of War* (French title, *Mes Rêveries*), trans. Thomas R. Phillips (Harrisburg, Penn.: The Military Institute Publishing Co., 1944). See also, Jean-Pierre Bois, *Maurice de Saxe* (Paris: Fayard, 1992), especially pp. 177–237; Frederic Hulot, *Le Maréchal de Saxe* (Paris: Pymalion, 1989), especially pp. 85–99; Robert Quimby, *The Background of Napoleonic Warfare*, 41–62; and John Manchip White, *Marshal of France: The Life and Times of Maurice, Comte de Saxe* (Chicago, 1962).

60. According to Luh, *Ancien Régime Warfare* (137–78), bayonets and artillery were responsible for the majority of battlefield casualties. Lund, *War for the Every Day* (79–83) believes that the attack with the bayonet and morale factors determined the outcome of infantry combat.

61. Jacques Antoine Hippolyte de Guibert, *A General Essay on Tactics,* trans. by an officer (London, 1781), 157. For a discussion of how experts have explained the Native American adoption of firearms, see Armstrong Starkey, *European and Native American Warfare, 1675–1815* (London: UCL Press, and Norman: University of Oklahoma Press, 1998), 20–25.

62. Saxe, *Reveries,* 32.

63. Ibid., 21.

64. Parker, *Military Revolution,* 151. Parker's fourth military post revolution, the great increase in manpower, occurred after 1793 outside the period considered in this book.

65. Humphrey Bland, *A Treatise of Military Discipline: in which is laid down and explained the duty of the officer and soldier, through the several branches of the service,* 9th ed. (London: R. Baldwin, 1762), 283–84.

66. Antoine de Pas de Feuquières, *Memoirs Historical and Military,* 2 vols. (London: T. Woodward and C. Davis, 1736; reprint, New York: Greenwood Press, 1968), 1:384 (page citation is to the reprint edition).

67. See "History of Francis Baron Trenck, a partisan colonel, and Commander in Chief of the Pandours in the service of Her Majesty the Empress-Queen, written by Frederick Baron Trenck as a necessary supplement to his own history," in *The Life of Frederick Baron Trenck* (Boston, 1828).

68. Peter Paret, "Colonial Experience and European Military Reform at the End of the Eighteenth Century," *Bulletin of the Institute of Historical Research* 37 (1964): 57.

69. Bruce McConachy, "The Roots of Artillery Doctrine: Napoleonic Artillery Tactics Reconsidered," *Journal of Military History* 5 (July 2001): 517–640; Luh, *Ancien Régime Warfare,* 167–78.

70. Nockhern de Schorn, *Idées raisonnéesl,* 50.

71. Johann Hinrichs, "Diary of Captain Johann Hinrichs," in *The Siege of Charleston with an Account of the Province of South Carolina: Diaries and Letters of Hessian Officers from the von Jungken Papers in the William L. Clements Library,* trans. and ed. Bernhard Uhlendorf (Ann Arbor: University of Michigan Press, 1938; reprint, New York: Arno Press, 1968), 169 (page citation is to the reprint edition).

72. Quoted in McConachy, "The Roots of Artillery Doctrine," 625–26. For a full discussion of Guibert's ideas, see Quimby, *Background of Napoleonic Warfare,* 106–74.

73. Guibert, *Tactics,* vii.

74. Ibid., 103–5.

75. Ibid., xxiii.

76. Quimby, *Background of Napoleonic Warfare,* 267.

77. Duffy, *Instrument of War,* 380. On the other hand, a new officer arriving at the headquarters of the Austrian army found that Lloyd was only one of two staff officers who seemed to have any idea of what was going on. See p. 172.

78. Henry Lloyd, *The History of the Late War in Germany between the King of Prussia and the Empress of Germany and Her Allies,* 2 vols. (London, 1781), 2:xxxi.

79. Ibid., 1.

80. Ibid., 13–14.

81. The debate between advocates of these systems is best covered in Quimby, *Background of Napoleonic Warfare.*

82. Lloyd, *History of the Late War,* 2:xxxiii–xxxiv, 69–93, 114–21.

83. Ibid., 90–91.

84. Ibid., xxxviii, 121.

85. Bland, *Treatise,* 134.

86. John Clarke, *Military Institutions of Vegetius* (1767), vii.

87. Ibid., 14–15.

88. Drewe, *Military Sketches,* 45.

89. Hector de Grandmaison, *A Treatise on the Military Service of Light Horse and Light Infantry in the Field and in Fortified Places,* trans. Lewis Nicola (Philadelphia, 1777), 35–36. Other writers who explore this theme in a similar manner include Lancelot, Comte Turpin de Crissé, *Essai sur l'art de la guerre,* 2 vols. (Paris, 1754), and M. de Jeney, *Le Partisan ou l'art de faire la petite guerre* (1759).

90. Dalrymple, *Military Essay,* 8.

91. Ibid., 113.

92. Bennet Cuthbertson, *System for the Complete Interior Management and Oeconomy of a Battalion of Infantry* (1768; 2d ed., 1776).

93. De Laissac, *De l'esprit militaire,* 6–7, 22, 25–35.

94. For example, see James Anderson, *Essay on the Art of War* (London, 1761), 109; M de Zimmerman, *Essais de principes d'une morale militaire et autres objets* (Amsterdam, 1769), 33–34, 37; Nockhern de Schorn, *Idées raisonnées,* 106–9.

95. Stephen Payne Adye, *A Treatise on Courts Martial to which is added, An Essay on Military Punishments and Rewards,* 3d ed. (London, 1786), 251.

96. Ibid., 283–84.

97. Zimmerman, *Essais de principes d'une morale militaire,* 116 ff.

CHAPTER 3

A Culture of Honor

When a man chooses a calling, he must do everything that can be done in that he can never suffer reproach for having done half of his duty. On this account I keep the mottoes in my portfolio, to serve at times as a reminder, the following from Boileau: Honor is like an island, / Steep and without shore: / They who once leave / Can never return[1]

This was the code professed by Johann Ewald (1744–1813), captain of the Hessian jaegers during the American War of Independence. The son of a bookkeeper in Kassel, Germany, he followed a military career that led eventually to ennoblement and the rank of major general in the Danish service. Ewald was a veteran of the Seven Years' War in Germany and served with distinction as a leader of light troops in America. He later became noted as the author of treatises on *petite guerre.* His journal of his American experience reveals an officer motivated by his loyalty to his landgrave, his hope for professional advancement, and his concern for honor. The motto from Boileau captured his sense that his honor was a priceless possession, irredeemable if lost.

The British officer Major Robert Donkin cited the same lines from Boileau in his discussion of honor: "Many have wrote on this topic, but I find none that have compared it to the eye, which can't suffer the least moat in it, without being blemished! Honor may be called a precious stone, which the smallest speck makes less valuable! It is a treasure irrecoverable when once unfortunately lost! Honor is for this life what good works are for the other world! The first is preserved by the greatest delicacy; the latter by the greatest care."[2]

But what exactly was "honor"? The astute Campbell Dalrymple observed that although it was one of the most important engines of government, it was an imaginary thing. He supported the idea of a military order to recompense distinguished service or extraordinary bravery but cautioned that the distribution of honor could be easily corrupted.[3] Wealth and privilege might be seen as automatically conferring honor, but true honor was something to be earned. Honor represented the soldier's ethic of duty, bravery, and self-sacrifice. Another officer believed that honor guaranteed that a soldier would defend a post to the last man if ordered to do so. "It is then that a man of honour will never trouble himself about the consequences, but continue to defend his post, whatever may happen to the last extremity."[4] Honor, wrote another, was a prejudice rather than a virtue. "It is thus that I wish to distinguish it from virtue, a principle sometimes less powerful and less active than that of honour. The one has its foundation in the heart; the other is governed by public opinion, which is a judge not less severe."[5] Public opinion was thus the judge of honor. A disloyal or cowardly officer faced ostracism; his reputation would never recover. Honor, observed Laissac, "directs all human actions through fear of scorn and the desire for esteem."[6]

Lieutenant George Eid of the Coldstream Guards experienced the power of this axiom during an action in America in 1780. He was part of a rear guard withdrawing across a bridge while threatened by a superior American force. It was necessary to destroy the bridge, although it meant exposing his fellow soldiers to heavy enemy fire. Eid recalled that:

I volunteered the duty and promised Colonel Howard to destroy the bridge. I never professed myself a volunteer for any duty, but on this occasion I had two reasons for my conduct. The first reason arose from my having perceived that the enemy were bringing cannon and horse, the whole weight of which must have been sustained by the rear guard; the other was vanity,—the vanity of attempting that danger the whole army had avoided. I now called the light infantry, which composed the rear guard, to assist me; but so great was the panic, *that only* FOUR remained. Captain Dundass, hearing my voice, joined me, as did Captains Anstruther and Dennis, with one private of the 43d, and two privates of the 42d regiment. The Hessian detachment, perceiving our intentions, formed on a small rise and covered our attempt. Under a very heavy fire, we effected our design, by dislodging the planks, which effectually prevented the horse and field pieces from following our line of march. As this was done in the full view of the whole army, my vanity once more got ascendancy over my reason, inducing me to remain last on the bridge.[7]

Those who wrote on this topic often cited Montesquieu's observation that honor was the ruling principle of monarchies and virtue that of republics. The problem with this view, wrote the encyclopedist Saint-Lambert, was that although Montesquieu defined virtue as the love of country and its laws, he did not define honor. Saint-Lambert concluded that honor was based on self-esteem and one's desire for the esteem of others. "True honor" was gained by the individual who followed the principles of virtue and did not shrink from his obligations to his fellow citizens, to the laws, and to his country. There were countries in Europe where honor had been corrupted. Public opinion honored such false idols as riches and the possession of offices, which were often inherited rather than earned. Softness and luxury rotted the moral fiber. Honors, even glory, became separated from true honor, which existed in only a few enlightened men who had the courage to be poor. However, this situation could be remedied in a monarchy if the legislator rewarded true honor, the dedication to country and the common good. True honor thus mobilized public opinion in support of the principles of virtue. Saint-Lambert wrote, "When the prince ties the idea of honor and of virtue to the love and observation of all the laws; then the warrior who lacks discipline is as dishonored as one who flees before the enemy."[8] Military essayists pursued the themes of true and false honor. "Glory being attached to the most excellent and most difficult Actions," observed one writer, "the Profession of War is called the Profession of Honour." However, he wrote, "Men of indiscreet Bravery, whose valour consists in violent and brutal Actions, are always despised by the troops, while the Man of real Honour, who makes Religion, Humanity, and Justice, the rule of his Actions, is distinguished, honoured, recompensed, and applauded."[9]

Military essayists offered this concept of true honor as the code of the professional soldier, a man who followed a career of stoic self-sacrifice in the service of others. One author presented Charles XII as a model of true honor, for not only did he dedicate his life to his country, he did not hesitate to share the hardship borne by his soldiers. "Under such a monarch what officer would dare to neglect any of the duties of his station!"[10] This same writer argued that it was not enough for an officer to be brave. Bravery was an instinct natural to many soldiers, but it was not constant. Courage was a matter of resolve and, when combined with bravery, produced the valor required of officers.[11] This sense of valor was a hallmark of true honor. True honor in turn was an essential ingredient of the Caroline military spirit prized by François Folard. Honor was therefore a central subject of discussion during the Military Enlightenment.

Ideally, the code of honor represented an internalized ethic of devotion to duty. Military essayists were aware that, unfortunately, they did not define honor for most military men. Whatever their prescriptions, the court of public opinion ruled the conduct of the officer corps. Among officers, concerns with personal honor could undermine discipline and work against the development of military professionalism.

DUELS

On May 7, 1778, Lieutenant John Peebles of the 42d Highlanders, then stationed in North America, recorded the following in his diary: "Remember you had some words today at table which obliged you to take a step you did not like." His entry for the following day reveals the fortunate consequence of that step: "Went out and settled that affair better than I expected." Then, in broken French: "*Mais prendre garde in future, point....*" The remainder of the passage is firmly crossed out and is illegible. It is seldom that one may hold in one's hands today a manuscript that so cryptically and yet so powerfully catches the emotion of one who has been through the ordeal of a duel. We cannot know the circumstances, whether Peebles offered or received a challenge. He and his brother officers drank heavily while dining. The diary offers frequent tallies of copious consumption. The common pastime of winter quarters and garrison life was card playing. This could be an explosive mix. There was ample opportunity for an indiscreet word that might force an officer to defend his honor with pistol or sword. An argument over cards, over a woman, or an aspersion against one's courage was just the kind of thing that could swiftly transform a convivial evening into a life-threatening moment. At such a moment Peebles had no choice but to give or receive a challenge, for his behavior was under the scrutiny of his brother officers, who would ostracize him if he declined to fight. "To take a step you did not like" was an understatement of what he must have felt following the challenge, but his relief at the outcome was palpable. Things had been concluded in some satisfactory way. Perhaps, as sometimes happened, others had intervened and brought about an amicable understanding. He was alive and so probably was the other party, for there were consequences even for the winner of a duel, an action explicitly prohibited by the Articles of War. But Peebles had learned something, though he chose to erase his thoughts from the record. It is clear that he had determined to be more cautious in his future choice of words and to respect the deadly business of honor.[12]

What had private quarrels of this nature to do with the business of being a soldier? Such behavior seems anachronistic in an age of enlightenment. Peebles had violated military law and had undermined the discipline associated with true honor. Yet he could not have survived as an officer had his bravery been doubted by his peers or his subordinates. Indeed, there were those who believed that the duel was a means of establishing proper subordination in both military and civilian life. The anonymous author of *The Military Mentor* cited the view of Bernard Mandeville that duels supported polite manners. He also cited Dr. Johnson's comment that "he who fights a duel, does not fight from passion against his antagonist, but out of self defense; to avert the stigma of the world, and to prevent himself from being driven out of society." The author himself thought that dueling was prompted by false courage and false honor but concluded, "The principles of our conduct and character must in every situation be regulated in conformity with the opinions and prejudices of those among whom we are placed; and it is much to be regretted, that dueling is not yet universally looked upon in this light by the army at large."[13] There were others who believed that it served a constructive purpose. Donkin argued that: "Dueling should be either a manly decision of such differences between particulars, as come not within the cognizance of the state: or a generous punishment of injuries irreparable by the magistrate. Was a computation to be made of all that have fallen in duels for a series of years, the inconsiderableness of the number wou'd but ill justify the claim against them."[14] In 1762–1763, John Burgoyne, later to command at Saratoga, served in Portugal under the German general Count Schaumberg Lippe. The latter had opposed dueling in the Prussian army but found Portuguese officers to be so dispirited and cowardly that he threatened them with dismissal from the service if they did not defend their honor with sword or pistol.[15] In 1741, Admiral Edward Vernon sent home from the West Indies an officer who refused to fight a duel when challenged. He observed, "That officer that don't picque himself on supporting his own honour and the dignity of his commission may not be the likeliest to defend the honour of his Prince and the security of his country against the face of his enemies."[16] Others agreed that duels protected the honor of the officer corps in general and might weed out unsavory characters: "[F]irst Lieut. [Robert] Anderson (who was killed in a duel here) was promoted out of all line whatsoever, a man who cou'd neither boast of being an Officer or a Gentleman, but by being so sty'd in his Commission."[17]

These defenders of the duel associated it with the military spirit. Therefore, the practice might not stand in contradiction to a principal theme of the Military Enlightenment. It was, however, a brutal custom, and it is difficult to find much that was honorable about the drunkenness and hot temper that usually inspired it. Most quarrels were over trivial matters although, as Mark Odintz has demonstrated, they may have been motivated by more fundamental antagonisms. Every army had its bullies who delighted in violence and sought out prospective victims. Lieutenant Eid recalled that while on service in America in 1780 he was forced to fight a Lieutenant Callender of the 42d with whom he declined to share a glass of punch. Eid successfully defended himself and "afterwards was informed that Captain C., being an uncommon good swordsman, often insulted strangers in a similar manner."[18] The Hessian officer Lieutenant Joseph Charles Philip von Krafft was often depressed and irritable during his service in America, which was usually confined to garrison duty. He seems only to have been at ease during periods of active and dangerous service with the chasseurs. His diary mentions numerous quarrels and duels that seem to have provided an outlet for his pent-up aggression. He does not seem to have fought for any higher motive than that.[19]

Some officers were attracted to the "romance" of the duel, such as Lieutenant Colonel Hervey Aston of the 12th regiment, a polite and cultivated man who fought numerous duels until he was killed in one. Captain

George Elers, also of the 12th, revered Aston as a kind and fatherly man and denied that he possessed a quarrelsome nature. Yet Aston seems to have gone out of his way to provoke those who did not meet his high standards of gentility, and he brawled with social inferiors. He was killed after offering satisfaction over what appears today to be a very obscure point of honor. Indeed, on this occasion he offered to meet every officer in the regiment![20]

There were also irresponsible commanding officers who pressured unwilling young men into fighting. General Lord Harris recalled a duel forced upon him while a subaltern by his commanding officer, Captain Bell, who clearly seems to have been deranged.[21] Third parties could find themselves imperiled in affairs of honor. Elers once reported to a kinsman disparaging remarks spoken by a clergyman. The former appeared to seek satisfaction and required Elers to act as his second. Since Elers was on duty as a member of a court-martial, his participation would have caused him serious trouble. Fortunately, the offending cleric fled the town, but Elers's kinsman never spoke to him again due to his lack of enthusiasm for his role as second.[22]

A similar culture prevailed in the French officer corps. Relations between French officers in America during the War of Independence were not very good, and they quarreled over the same matters as did the British. Measures to prohibit dueling among them have been described as more theoretical than real. They were scarcely applied to those who did not kill their adversaries. One officer, condemned to death for having killed an opponent, was refused mercy by the king, but escaped punishment.[23] British officers could also hope for leniency. After an exchange of words between two British officers in Boston in 1775, one struck the other and both drew swords. Another officer fired off their pistols before they could be used in a duel. Both officers were arrested and tried by court-martial. Only one of the offenders was reprimanded, and he was briefly suspended.[24] In the British army, courts-martial reflected the military's ambivalence about duels. While these courts enforced military law that prohibited dueling, they also served as courts of honor. As such they offered a peaceful and public means of settling disputes concerning honor, but an officer who refused to issue or accept a challenge might find himself convicted of conduct "unbecoming an officer and a gentleman." These were grounds for expulsion from the service.[25]

Dueling was not limited to the military; it was part of a larger social problem. It was a means by which the privileged could assert their prestige and social status.[26] Some Enlightenment writers derided dueling as a barbaric vestige of the Middle Ages, one that barred the way to a new age of progress, enlightenment and improvement. The philosophes found allies in England among Evangelical Christians, who challenged the principle of pride and the value of social approbation. However, not until the nineteenth century were they able to effect a significant change in the culture. Donna Andrew wrote, "Only with the replacement of the code of honour by what might be called the code of Christian commerce, only with the determination that class privilege and immunity from the Law should give way to a strict and universal application of a law which recognized no superiors did the practice of dueling finally end."[27] Some eighteenth-century reformers hoped that the military might be brought in line with their vision of society: "Soldiers, like the rest of modern society must free themselves from the bondage of custom; those men who submit to the...*Yoke* of other Men's depraved opinions and unreasonable customs (in contradiction to *natural Knowledge* of *Good* and *Evil* which we inherit, in common with the rest of Mankind from our first Parents) cannot justly be deemed *Men of Honour;* and consequently are not worthy of rank in the honourable Profession of Arms."[28] These reformers sought to replace the ideal of the aristocratic warrior with that of the Christian citizen-soldier; their vision remained unfulfilled in the eighteenth century. Indeed it was contrary to the hopes of those officers who linked the revival of aristocratic privilege to that of the military spirit.

Equality was a concept foreign to most officers. For example, while serving in Bermuda in 1766, the British captain Nicholas Delacherois condemned the lack of wealthy men, resulting from the wide division of property among the inhabitants "which is the means of a general indistinction and level of the people, as their profession [merchants] all over the world is generally attended with great boorishness and rusticity."[29] Fraternizing with the rank and file was considered "conduct unbecoming" on the part of an eighteenth-century British officer. It was bad for discipline and undermined the principle of subordination. This subordination reflected the hierarchical nature of society; ideally former peasant-soldiers would feel comfortable with the authority of officers of the landowning aristocracy.

The reality was very different from the ideal. Western European armies drew large numbers of their recruits from the towns and, while the upper ranks of the officer corps were drawn from the nobility, subalterns and regimental officers represented a more-complex social mix. J. A. Houlding has identified four categories among the 4,100 officers serving in the British army in 1775: (1) the nobility and landed gentry, who made up 25 percent of the corps and more than half of the proprietary colonels and general officers; (2) the majority of regimental officers, drawn from cadet branches of the aristocracy, professional families, and from among yeomen farmers; (3) a wide spectrum of the well-enough educated and well-enough born, including foreigners and members of army families, the latter having developed a professional or service mentality by the end of the Seven Years' War; and (4) subaltern officers of advanced age and experience, promoted from among noncommissioned officers (NCOs).

About two-thirds of the corps held their commission by purchase.[30] One-fifth to one-third of the total were Scots. Thus the picture of the officer corps as a preserve of the warrior aristocracy was only partially true. Delacherois is a good example. He was a long-service company officer, the son of Huguenot immigrants. It was his position as an officer and his adherence to the values of the corps that confirmed his status. The same held true for other eighteenth-century European armies that experienced an increase in numbers and in regulation by the state. The Habsburg officer corps was extremely diverse, including grandees such as the Prince de Ligne as well as the sons of middle-class families. Many subalterns were promoted NCOs, and it was theoretically possible for an officer with such a background to achieve high rank. Maria Theresa of Austria believed that merit should be rewarded. After 1757, an officer with 30 years of distinguished service was eligible for ennoblement.[31] Frederick the Great disapproved of the "rabble" in the Habsburg service and could rely on a more homogeneous corps of officers drawn from the Junker nobility, but losses during the Seven Years' War forced him to rely on bourgeois officers as well. The much-lamented decline of military spirit among the French nobility left the French army short of officers during the Seven Years' War and led to the commissioning of men from the middle class or the recently ennobled. These men became a scapegoat for French military failure during the Seven Years' War and led to an aristocratic reaction in the officer corps.[32] Thus the link between the officer corps and the nobility remained strong throughout Europe; one study finds an increased militarization of noble life and culture in the period.[33] However, there were clearly many officers of non-noble or recent-noble status who shared this culture containing a mix of professional and aristocratic values.

The eighteenth-century code of honor was not simply an extension of medieval chivalry, although it contained many of its ingredients. Rather it represented a corporate culture that assimilated men of nonaristocratic background. The standards were aristocratic. Men had to be prepared to defend their personal honor with their lives. Failure to do so resulted in their exclusion. The officer corps provided social mobility for many of its members who accepted the culture of honor as an emblem of their new status. The rules of this culture were uniquely western European in character. Christopher Duffy has found that eighteenth-century Russian officers were almost entirely devoid of the Western code of honor. They treated trickery at cards as a joke rather than as a cause for a duel.[34] In the West, however, the culture of honor was central to an officer's growing sense of professionalism in the eighteenth century. Few eighteenth-century officers found their personal honor and their professional lives to be incompatible. As one modern writer put it: "The average Army officer of whatever rank or social degree was a diligent, painstaking man, very jealous of his personal reputation, with a simple rigid creed of honour, forthright and unself-conscious in his patriotism."[35]

A young officer arriving at his regiment for the first time might conclude that he had joined a family. Indeed, it was common to view the regiment as a family or a school in which young men learned their profession under the guidance of their seniors.[36] The officers' mess consisted of social equals, regardless of rank, and in some cases the colonel might become a surrogate father. But, as we have seen, it could be an unhappy family riven by factions and jealousy. The code of honor appeared to legitimize resistance to authority. In the British army, wrote Alan J. Guy, "beneath their veneer of technical professionalism the soldiers were often deeply insubordinate. They eagerly competed for royal grace and favour, but, as members of the warrior fraternity of the *ancien régime* and free-born Englishmen to boot, with the idea that no man, howsoever distinguished by lace or titles, had any greater merit than themselves, they were ready to criticize the throne itself if their pretensions to honour and performance were not gratified and even to withdraw their services."[37]

The eighteenth century was a period of transition from feudal noble and mercenary entrepreneur to officers whose total loyalty was claimed by the state and by their country. The code of honor allowed eighteenth-century officers, who were increasingly dependent upon the state for preferment, to retain a sense of independence. This attitude frustrated the efforts of monarchs who wished to modernize professional standards. In Prussia the creation of a service nobility and the force of Frederick the Great's personality curbed the independence of the officer corps and increased its competence. However, the attempt by Britain's Hanoverian monarchs to introduce Prussian discipline was very unpopular. The claims that Prussian discipline was contrary to the English or French national character undoubtedly were sometimes a defense of the officers' self-interest.

In Britain and elsewhere the independence of the officers was enhanced by the practice of commission purchases. An officer's commission was thus his property, and he could only lose it as the result of a court-martial offense. Commission purchase could be defended on more than one ground. It was a way by which financially strapped governments could staff their officer corps. Officers of sufficient means to buy a commission could be expected to bear some of the cost of their service. In England the memory of Cromwell's major generals provided a strong argument for retaining a connection between men of property and the officer corps. Still, purchase was no substitute for merit. Humphrey Bland expressed admiration for the discipline of the Dutch soldiers and the experience of their officers, with whom he had served. He attributed the quality of the Dutch officers to the fact that commissions were not sold in Holland.[38] He believed that young British officers had no incentive to learn the details of their profession. German officers had to spend a period in the ranks to acquire these skills, but in England "money and powerful relations will always procure them whatever they want; they have therefore no occasion to apply themselves to the knowledge of their duty. It is from this way of thinking that so many of them do little credit to their posts; not from want of genius, but application."[39] Britain's Hanoverian monarchs were unable to eliminate commission sales but succeeded in regulating them through an official tariff of prices. Alan Guy believes that their efforts did change the character of the officer corps, although the failure of pay to match the rate of inflation continued to limit the officer corps to men of private means. By the end of the century, officers gave less attention to the details of regimental duty, tending to leave them in the hands of the NCOs. On the other hand, the waning proprietary interest led officers to develop a more exalted ethic of service and sacrifice.[40]

SACRIFICE

Earlier in the century, Humphrey Bland had asserted that honor was gained by sacrifice. "The military profession has, in all ages, been esteemed the most honorable, from the danger that attends it. The motives that lead mankind into it, must proceed from a noble and generous inclination, since they sacrifice their ease, and their lives, in the defense of their country."[41] Where was one to find men who would sacrifice all for the knowledge that they had served king and country? Many writers believed that an age of luxury and commerce had led to moral rot. They arrived through moral analysis at the same conclusion drawn by some nineteenth-century Social Darwinists: war was a positive good. French critics believed that their nobility had been corrupted by softness and the love of pleasure. For example, Luc de Clapiers, marquis de Vauvenargues, a true eighteenth-century Spartan, argued that war produced virtue and peace produced vice. He lamented that patriotism had come to be considered an old-fashioned prejudice. He called for a new pursuit of glory by the nobility.[42]

There was regret that the pursuit of glory had given way to avarice and its attendant vices. Reformers advocated the rebirth of a military nobility inspired by an ethic of sacrifice and service. Voltaire's praise of the commercial interests of the English nobility drew a rejoinder from Philippe-Auguste de Saint Foix, chevalier d'Arc. In *Le noblesse militaire ou le Patriote français,* he argued for a Spartan military nobility, free of material corruption. Wealth acted as a corroding agent in the officer corps. Poor long-service officers of merit were pushed aside by the members of a new plutocratic nobility that monopolized the highest ranks in the army. Luxury, gambling, and pillage were pastimes of such people. This sad state of affairs was the result of the bad example set by a frivolous court. Indeed, the court had encouraged pillage as a means of avoiding proper payment of its soldiers, a circumstance that led to bad discipline and failure to pursue the enemy. It was imperative that the court honor men for whom money was not everything. Against the model of the new commercial economy, d'Arc offered an alternative "economy of function and of service." He did not oppose plebeian officers who served for the right reasons; his target was the new men who achieved privilege through wealth. But many noble officers believed that they alone, by family tradition, possessed the disinterest and sentiment of honor necessary for their function.[43] Reformers such as d'Arc looked to the legislator, in this case the monarchy, to initiate a program of reform and to restore the military nobility. They were to be disappointed. The monarchy's failure in this regard may be compared to its financial struggles. Both may have undermined the monarchy's legitimacy in the eyes of the elites, on whom its survival depended.

Nevertheless, the reform program was reflected in the Ségur Law of 1781, which required that officers possess four quarters of nobility. David Bien has discussed a committee of French general officers who met regularly from 1780 to 1784 and who supported the Ségur Law. They hoped to reverse the tide of French military failure by improving the quality of the officer corps. Consistent with the views of Vauvenargues and d'Arc, they stressed moral themes: hard work, duty, and professionalism. Like d'Arc, they wished to assure that men of merit were promoted without being pushed aside by wealthy arrivistes. These reformers were grounded in Enlightenment thought. They believed that the essentials of the military profession could be learned. The École militaire taught prospective young officers (recruited from the nobility since 1751) that honor consisted of duty and service to the king. According to Bien, the reformers hoped to create a military class motivated by this sense of honor, and they believed that it could best be recruited from the old nobility rather than from the sons of the wealthy bourgeoisie. Within this class, talent, merit, and self-sacrifice would be fostered and rewarded. However, Jean Chagniot has recently challenged Bien's conclusions, observing that the Ordinance of March 17, 1788, created two tracks for officer promotion. One track restricted promotion to the rank of general to officers admitted to court. The other track, for the poor provincial nobility, placed a ceiling on promotion. Rather than encouraging the latter, the "reform" became a source of grievance on the eve of the Revolution. A principal effect of the aristocratic reaction in France after 1758 was an increase in the production of fraudulent genealogies.[44]

One old officer, Mercoyral de Beaulieu (1725–1817), agreed that the poor provincial nobility were often ignored by the court, which promoted only wealthy courtiers to the highest posts. The latter were no better than poor gentlemen "who served from father to son, satisfied to retire after a long career, with the rank of captain, the cross of Saint Louis, and a pension of one hundred ecus." The provincial nobles provided the true soldiers, the men of true honor. In his memoirs, de Beaulieu suggested something like the revival of the military orders of the Middle Ages, particularly in his insistence of the value of chastity to a soldier: *Si vous voulez être guerrier, soyez chaste!"*[45] This may have set too high a standard, even for the poor nobility.[46]

Bien points out a paradox. The reformers embraced some Enlightenment ideas, such as Lockean environmentalism, merit, and moral reform, while appearing reactionary in their social exclusion of the middle class.[47] However, this is only a paradox when seen from a post-1789 perspective. Duty and self-sacrifice had been a constant theme of military writers throughout the century. These were the ingredients of "true honor." False honor was associated with luxury, gambling, insubordination, and inattention to duty. The king of Prussia and his poor Junker officers provided reformers with a concrete example of the relationship between true honor and military success. True honor was Spartan virtue. Rousseau's political writing would lead one to the same conclusion. There are many similarities between the outlook of those seeking to rekindle a military spirit in France and Rousseau's idea of the good citizen. Neither Rousseau nor the military reformers would have embraced the program of those Evangelicals who sought to reform the officer corps by means of a spirit of Christian commercialism.

The French reformers discussed above were secular in outlook. There were of course devout officers and those who denounced dueling and other officer vices as un-Christian. Lieutenant Colonel John Blackadder (1664–1729) was the son of a Presbyterian field preacher, a "sufferer" at the hands of the Stuart regime in Scotland. Blackadder entered the service as a cadet in the Cameronians, a regiment of psalm singers recruited from people whom most regarded as religious fanatics. He served with distinction under Marlborough but was shocked by vice "raging openly and impudently" in the army. "They speak just such a language as devils would do. I find this ill in our trade, that there is so much tyranny and knavery in the army, that it is a wonder how a man of a straight, generous, honest soul can live in it."[48] Blackadder saw the hand of providence at work in the great events of the War of the Spanish Succession. The British army's success was limited by its wickedness. On the other hand, while God had given strength to the French "tyrant who wasted God's church…while God was using him as a scourge to the earth," there was now a change. The French "are not like the men they were," he wrote. Corpses littering a battlefield provided a preaching from the dead: "The carcasses were very thick strewed upon the ground, naked and corrupting; yet all this works no impression or reformation upon us, seeing the bodies of our comrades and friends lying as dung upon the face of the earth. Lord make me humble and thankful!"[49] Blackadder was a devout and introspective man. The Cameronians were not representative of British officers, but they made excellent warriors. Leading his men into action at the siege of Lille, Blackadder shouted "Grenadiers, in the name of God attack!"[50]

The marquis de Valfons would have approved of Blackadder's brevity. He recalled that before the battle of Hastenbeck in 1757 that the chaplain of the Grenadiers of France, elite troops recruited from the Provincial Militia, addressed them in a crisp, military manner: "Children of war, in spite of the audacity in your spirits, humiliate yourselves before God, who alone gives victory." Valfons suggested that the chaplain's colleagues should adopt this style. "In general these gentlemen are always long winded at these moments and the soldiers are not allowed enough time to reflect."[51] Valfons lacked Blackadder's piety but recognized the value of religion if properly applied in military matters.

Many writers believed that religion contributed to a spirit of military subordination. One author observed that "an excellent divine, acknowledged by the whole corps as a man of probity and zeal, who by his conduct and discourse excites and supports the most solid sentiments of religion, upon which alone true honour is founded, would be of great use to support...justice and dependence in the corps."[52] Another agreed that religion was a necessary ingredient of military discipline. "It is the greatest error to think that religion is incompatible with the military state."[53] However, many officers found little room for religion in their lives. Frederick the Great's humorless, stoical, Protestant Junkers perhaps came closest to incorporating religion into their ethos. Other German soldiers shared this devotion. General Howe's secretary Ambrose Serle contrasted the evident piety of the Hessian troops with the blasphemies of their British brothers in arms.[54] On the other hand, the duke of Cumberland supported the spread of Methodism in the British army, a movement that attracted officers as well other ranks.[55] Religion was a delicate topic in the Habsburg army because the high command had to lead Catholic, Protestant, and Orthodox soldiers. The "men of style" among the Austrian officer corps held chaplains in low esteem, Duffy writes. "Few of them have religious belief, and they scorn those who harbor them."[56] French soldiers were also known for irreligion in contrast to the pious Spaniards.[57] The eighteenth-century British officer corps was notoriously irreligious. The author of the satirical *Advice to the Officers of the British Army* offered this advice about duels to chaplains: "If any one offends you by rivaling you in your amours, or debauching your girl, call him out to give you the satisfaction of a gentleman: for though the Christian religion and the articles of war both forbid dueling, yet these restraints are not regarded by men of spirit."[58] No doubt many officers were less merry on the day of battle, but there seems to have been a great gap between the everyday religious observance of officers and that called for by those who wished to improve the moral quality of the military culture.

EDUCATION

Those who wished to assimilate new officers into military culture and to encourage serious study of war inevitably turned to the issue of education. Military academies had appeared in Italy in the sixteenth century and had spread throughout western Europe. These academies were originally dedicated to the training of cavalry officers, but the importance of fortress warfare led to the establishment of schools providing scientific knowledge and technical training. The state had an interest in fostering a common military education for its officers, but as so often in the early modern period, lack of money hindered efforts in many countries. Some, such as Great Britain through the Royal Academy at Woolwich, provided an education only for technical officers of the engineers and artillery. States with larger armies and a desperate need for qualified officers extended education to infantry officers as well. Cadet companies or service in the household troops provided prospective officers with preparation in France, Prussia, and Russia. All founded state military academies during this period, but the majority of officers began their career without any formal military education.[59] Denmark seems to have led the way in the professionalization of its officer corps. Danish absolutism limited aristocratic influence and the sale of commissions. Officer candidates were expected to come from good families, to have an inclination for the service, and to demonstrate theoretical knowledge of their profession. The state placed an emphasis on officer schools, the first of which was founded in 1713. Many officers were products of these schools; foreigners with expert knowledge were recruited to fill out deficiencies. By 1799 all new officers were required to pass a professional examination.[60]

About one third of the Prussian officer corps was trained in the Berlin Cadet Corps. During Frederick the Great's reign 2,987 cadets were trained, of whom 41 became generals. Frederick eased the harsh regime imposed by his father and insisted that the cadets be treated as noblemen. He also placed greater emphasis on academic instruction, particularly addressing the technical knowledge required by his officers. Each year, 12 cadets were chosen to attend the Academy of Nobles, where they studied a variety of subjects that prepared them for high careers in the army or the diplomatic service.[61] Austria responded to the shortcomings revealed in its officer corps during the War of the Austrian Succession by the establishment of the Military Academy at Wiener-Neustadt, chartered in 1751 and opened in 1752. The students were chosen from the children of the nobility and deserving officers so that they "will have the assurance that, if they put their lives and fortunes at risk for the common good, their descendants will be preserved from poverty, and maintained and educated under the protection of our most gracious monarch as children of the state for the service and good of the fatherland."[62] The curriculum included fortification and mathematics, riding, fencing, and dancing, and instruction in Bohemian, Italian, and French. Language study was particularly important in an army in which officers frequently were incapable of communicating with one another. The academy was one of the most-progressive features of Maria Theresa's reign. Not only did it provide a sound military education, it fostered ideals of patriotism, sacrifice, and true honor. Although admission to the academy was not restricted to the nobility (indeed it was shunned by the higher nobility), it represented an attempt by the state to foster a sense of d'Arc's economy of function. Under Maria Theresa, deserving officers might gain nobility through distinguished service. Their sons might become part of a military class dedicated to the service of the monarch.

All of the major military monarchies strove to achieve this ideal through education. Thus the French École militaire of 1751 was limited to 500 young men of noble parentage. These institutions provided young officers with a sense of professional and corporate identity that distinguished the officer corps of the time from that of preceding generations. They provide evidence of the greater ability of the eighteenth-century state to shape the nature of its military forces. The educational program also reveals the limits of state influence. The numbers involved were too small in many cases to have an impact. In the case of Prussia, where one-third of the officers were graduates of the cadet corps, the influence was profound and no doubt contributed to the high quality of Prussian officers. Austria was late in the day with its educational program. Fewer than 6 percent of its officers during the Seven Years' War were products of the academy at Wiener-Neustadt. No state had the resources to provide a military education for all of its officers, and this in turn limited the effect of the Military Enlightenment.

Great Britain provided an education only for the officers of its technical services. Cavalry and infantry officers were for the most part self-taught or learned on the job. Some privileged officers were educated at military academies abroad, as in the case of Earl Cornwallis at Turin. Others, such as John Burgoyne, profited from service in continental armies. Not everyone regarded study at a foreign military academy as a privilege. At least this was the attitude of one of Burgoyne's characters in his play *The Heiress*. Commenting on the generosity of a relative, a young man observes: "He offer'd to send me from Cambridge to an academy in Germany, to fit me for foreign service: Well judging that a cannon ball was a fair and quick provision for a poor relation."[63] Some British officers expressed regret at the lack of an academy such as Wiener-Neustadt, and enterprising teachers sought to meet the need for a military education through private academies. Most successful was Lewis Lochée, an immigrant from the Austrian Netherlands, who presided over the Royal Military Academy at Little Chelsea between 1770 and 1789.[64] Lochée advocated a curriculum of bodily exercise and academic subjects. His approach was distinctly "modern," advocating the study of modern languages rather than Latin and Greek. He admitted that the latter was part of a gentleman's education but concluded that classical study did not make for a better or more useful person. Education was useless if it did not lead one in later life to enlarge his understanding and devote himself to public service. Academic subjects also included mathematics, fortification, and civil law (Montesquieu, Grotius, and Puffendorf being the recommended reading). Lochée also stressed the study of history "to obtain a true knowledge of human life and manners." He sought to produce prospective officers with an enlightened understanding of military affairs who would rise above the tedious detail of regimental routine.[65]

Lochée's educational philosophy reflected that of other military reformers who sought to establish an ethic of service. The most important object in cultivating a student's mind, he wrote, "is to establish those principles of moral truth and duty, and form those habits of several virtues, that will support the dignity of his character in all situations, and render his actions not less honourable and useful in the stillness of peace, than in the activity and bustle of war."[66] He believed that the spirit of self-sacrifice was the common source of all the virtues. Thus Christianity should form the core of a soldier's moral life. It embodied self-denial; engraved upon the heart it was more powerful than the "false honor" of monarchies, the human virtue of republics, or the servile fear of despotic states. While Lochée recommended teaching fencing as an important exercise, he cautioned that it frequently led to dueling out of false honor. He condemned the "perverted notions of honour, gallantry, and courage, inculcated in some schools."[67] Therefore he urged strict enforcement of the laws against dueling. Lochée's views on this subject should remind us that the abolition of dueling was not exclusively the product of a bourgeois spirit of Christian commercialism. Military reformers who sought higher professional standards and an ethic of true honor also sought to eliminate this evil.

Lochée's academy was successful, fashionable, and recommended by high-ranking officers. It attracted a steady stream of privileged young men already commissioned but underage, or those hoping to qualify for commissions. However, relatively few aspiring officers could afford his fees, which added up to 125 pounds a year by the 1770s. Few cavalry officers graduated from the academy, and Lochée graduates represented fewer than 10 percent of new ensigns commissioned in the 1770s. The academy came to an end in 1789, and in 1790 Lochée participated without any particular distinction in the Netherlands uprising as commander of the Belgic Legion. There was no successor to the academy, and the majority of British officers continued to enter the service without a formal military education.

In most armies, therefore, the majority of officers arrived at their first post without military education or training. They were expected to learn on the job and follow the example of their seniors, many of them regimental officers of long service. An ambitious young officer might read a book or actually set himself to becoming familiar with the expanding body of military literature. George Evelyn Boscawen, son of a distinguished admiral, arrived in Boston in 1774 as an ensign in the 4th regiment at the age of 17. He was fortunate to be taken under the wing of his kinsman Captain W. Glanville Evelyn, also of that regiment. Young Boscawen had boned up on Humphrey Bland's *Treatise* on the voyage and arrived full of self-confidence and opinions. Evelyn kept the family up to date on the youth's progress: "I will venture to stake my credit that, when you next see *the young General,* you shall approve him; this is a name the boys have given him from the gravity of his deportment, and some alterations he has proposed to have made in the management of our affairs; you must know that upon his first coming among us, he discovered that the system we had followed for many years was all wrong, and proceeded to lay down some regulations for us, and to set us to right; but to his great amazement the boys only laughed at his schemes, and called him *Humphrey Bland* and *the young General,* and I am afraid have laughed him out of his plans for reforming the army, for he now seems inclined to go on as other people do."[68] The regiment was a school in itself and taught young men to conform with established practice. Evelyn found that Boscawen also demonstrated a "love of indolence and luxury," traits unsurprising in a young man of privilege but ones that would have hardly met the real Humphrey Bland's approval. Evelyn had an eye out for his kinsman's future. He recommended that Boscawen remain in America for some time for the experience and then purchase a lieutenancy in a regiment returned to England, "but by no means ever think of putting him into the Guards or suffering him to be about London."[69] Boscawen was fortunate that he had someone to provide moral direction. He served with his kinsman in the reserve brigade during the Lexington and Concord action. Although Evelyn was a veteran of the Seven Years' War, he was shocked by the savagery of the combat that he witnessed on that day and subsequently at Bunker Hill. Concerned that Boscawen might suffer harm while under his care, he urged the youth's immediate transfer home. Boscawen was from a prominent family and this was quickly accomplished, but Evelyn himself rejected an offer to transfer and remained out of a sense of duty. Mortally wounded in action, he died in New York in 1776. Boscawen had lost a worthy mentor who embodied the ideals of true honor. Boscawen's experience offers a snapshot of how young officers learned their trade. Both British and American officers relied on Bland as their basic text. Beyond this they depended on regimental mentors. We do not know Evelyn's reading habits, but he had adopted the language and values of the military reformers of the time. Books were an important medium by which professional values might be transmitted to the officer corps. The lively business of publishing military treatises suggests a large market among the officers. Senior commanders, Frederick the Great above all, urged their officers to pursue professional reading. This could range from masters such as Folard to subjects such as "field fortification for dummies." The author of one such work assured his readers that "in the first place, it is not requisite that an officer who would wish to become a field engineer, should employ any of his time in the study of mathematics—too dry for everyone to relish."[70] From this essay an officer could learn some simple geometry that would assist him in an ordinary task of an infantry regiment. Ira Gruber's survey of British officer libraries indicates that a number of officers were serious readers on the art of war. Popular titles included Saxe's *Reveries*, Feuquières's *Memoirs*, and Turpin de Crissé's *Art of War*, as well as translations of the works of Polybius (made popular in the eighteenth century by Folard), Caesar, and Vegetius.[71] Officers had eclectic reading tastes. The catalog of one officer's library includes the following: Plutarch's *Lives*, Samuel Johnson's *Shakespeare* and *Dictionary*, the *Spectator* (eight volumes), Rabelais, Rousseau on education, Alexander Pope's *Works*, Pleydell on fortification, *Instructions for Officers*, *The Racing Calendar*, Thompson's *Seasons*, Milton's *Paradise Lost*, and Muller's *Attack and Defense*, as well as *Tristam Shandy, Amelia, Tom Jones*, and *Woman of Pleasure*.[72] Only three entries in this list dealt with military subjects, and none of the great military authors of the century were included. The list reflects the wide range of tastes one might expect in a not particularly intellectual young man of action. The author of *Advice to the Officers of the British Army* probably reflected the actual reading habits of many younger officers when he recommended "such books as warm the imagination and inspire to military achievements," in short, a list of pornographic works led by *Woman of Pleasure*.[73] Some officers dedicated themselves to the study of contemporary literature. Thomas Hughes served as a junior officer in Burgoyne's ill-fated army and remained a prisoner for some time after the British defeat at Saratoga. He was a lively, humorous, and observant young man with the conventional values of an eighteenth-century gentleman. In June 1783, while Britain and France remained at war, he took himself to Boulogne to study French. No one seems to have thought this unusual, as he found a lively English social set there. He established a reading program of "a few good books" by standard French authors, including Molière, Raynal, and Voltaire, but it is unclear how much progress he made. Boulogne was full of temptation.[74]

Another officer was enthralled with Rousseau. Captain James Murray wrote to his sister in 1773, "Must not forget to tell you that I am in raptures with *La Nouvelle Heloise.* Since I read Rousseau I can suffer nothing else. I insist upon your perusing the original. It is impossible to translate the force and fire of that admirable writer."[75] In 1771, George Harris tackled Adam Ferguson's *Lectures on Philosophy:* "You will say I ought to commend 'em, when I tell you they cost me a guinea—one so poor, should be a better economist."[76]

Not every officer could afford a library, and books were often extremely scarce. Captain John Knox, stranded in a garrison in Nova Scotia in 1758, lamented the lack of books and the "neglect paid by the Officers of each corps to the purchase of a good regimental library for their entertainment as well as improvement."[77] Many officers preferred to spend their time at the gaming table, and some were open in their contempt for intellectual pursuits. Nonreaders were likely to be nonwriters, but Sir Thomas Wilson, Bart., who served in the British expedition to the coast of France in 1761, was one who dismissed the theoretical side of war. He expressed contempt for engineer officers and others who had acquired their knowledge from books: "I have always been of the opinion that one ounce of Experience is better than a Tun of Theory." In directing mortar fire against the citadel at Palais, Belle Isle, he found that a poor bombardier "at 16 pence per diem had practice, but no Instrument, Traverses the Cohorns [mortars], Claps his Eye to the Thing of the Apron the Lead of which made the Perpendicular, fired many shells by this awkward method and never missed the place once; comes an officer—who was resolved to do better than well, claps a nice Brass Quadrant into the Mortar, Lays them all by it, fires away and by G-d never touched it once, so much for theory but give me practice." He denounced the civilians at the Board of Ordinance who had supplied inferior artillery. "They will imagine we don't think ourselves very much obliged to them and will for the future know what a vast difference there is between a plan upon paper of Vauban's, and the thing executed on Terra Firma."[78]

The intellectual life of the British army was probably no higher than that of the Prussian army as described by Duffy. Pockets of intellectual curiosity flourished amidst a sea of Philistines. The Prussians differed from the British in having a dynamic intellectual center in the person of the king, who encouraged his officers to read professionally and challenged them by setting forth tactical problems for them to solve. Prussian officers were at least in tune with intellectual fashions for, in the second half of the century, officers began to adopt a demeanor of wistful melancholy as a result of reading Goethe and Rousseau.[79] This fashion began to work its way into all Western armies. Charles Royster has observed that officers of the American Continental army "cultivated sensitivity—which the eighteenth century called 'sensibility.' He looked for things to feel: friendship with other gentlemen, love for a woman, compassion for the unfortunate, ardor for his country, nobility in self sacrifice."[80] Rousseau's influence was everywhere, even among the many who never read him. Officers might also be influenced by eighteenth-century discussions of aesthetics and thus see the world in new ways. Thomas Hughes waxed with romantic imagery in describing Montmorency Falls near Quebec in 1785: "[W]ith a lively imagination you might fancy a rock of crystal with a river gushing from a cavern at the top of it, the spray that rises higher than the fall freezing in the air looks like sparks of fire and forms in the falling a pyramid at the bottom sixty or seventy feet high."[81]

British officers in America during the 1770s often staged amateur theatricals as diversions from the routine of garrison life. An officer wrote from Boston in 1776, "Some Ladies and Officers for diversion, and for the Benefit of the sick and maimed Soldiers in this Army; and Faneuil Hall (a famous place where the sons of sedition used to meet) is fitted up very Elegantly for a Theatre. And on Monday the Eighth Instant was perform'd the *Busy Body* [a farce written in 1709 by Susanna Centlivre]. A new farce call'd *The Blockade of Boston* (written by Genl. Burgoyne) was to have been introduc'd."[82] Unfortunately Burgoyne's opening night was cancelled by an alert. Peebles attended many productions in Philadelphia during the winter of 1777–1778. He recorded his enjoyment of a series of farces in which officers played all of the parts.[83]

Peebles had a serious side. He read Gibbon on the Platonists, the Stoics, and the Epicureans and copied the following passage from Hume in his notebook: "[N]o course of life has such safety (for happiness is not to be dreamed of) as the temperate or moderate, which maintains as far as possible, a mediocrity, and a kind of insensibility in every thing."[84] Peebles could on occasion lapse into a pose of reflective melancholy:

> Let death attack us in the bed or field
> All Ranks and ages to his force must yield
> Happy the man who meets his foe unspar'd
> For death or his Enemy never unprepar'd.

After a mirthful dinner he added:

> Happy the man who sleeps at
> ease, nor stung by conscience nor
> yet bit by fleas[85]

JOHN ANDRÉ: THE TRUE KNIGHT

Peebles had the opportunity to witness the most elaborate production of all, the *Mischianza*, the elaborate pageant staged in Philadelphia on May

18, 1778, in honor of Sir William Howe on the eve of his departure from the
command of the British army in America. The impresario of this celebrated event was Howe's aide, John André. It was the most festive day of
the war, one marked by spirited extravagance. It cost the staff officers the
princely sum of 3,132 guineas to produce the *Mischianza;* one shop took in
12,000 pounds for silk goods and other fineries ordered by the participants. The day began with a colorful regatta on the Delaware followed by
the famous tournament between the knights of the Blended Rose and
those of the Burning Mountain. Appareled in the style of Henry IV of
France, the young staff officers tilted with lance and sword. Their audience included Philadelphia's most fashionable ladies (including the
famous Peggy Shippen) bedecked in Turkish costumes. A sumptuous and
elaborate banquet, fireworks designed by the chief engineer, John Montresor, and dancing until dawn completed the festivities. All of the events
were staged in public view of the army and the population of the city.[86]
   André summoned up the image of the 1356 battle of Poitiers in tribute
to his departing chief:

> Oft, while grim War suspended his alarms,
> The gallant bands with mimic deed of arms
> Thus to some favourite chief the feast decreed,
> And deck'd the tilting Knight, th' encountering steed.
> In many sport that serv'd but to inspire
> Contempt of death, and feed the martial fire,
> The lists beheld them celebrate his name
> Who led their steps to victory and fame.
> Thro ev'ry rank the grateful ardor ran,
> All feared the chieftain, but all loved the man;
> And fired with the soul of this bright day,
> Pay'd to a Salisbury what to Howe we pay.[87]

Mark Girouard, who has described the revival of interest in chivalry in
nineteenth-century England, observes that England's medieval chivalry
experienced an Indian summer during the reign of Elizabeth I. This Eliza-
bethan chivalry had an exotic and unreal quality for, while the rituals and
forms were retained and elaborated, they ceased to have any relationship
to contemporary war. According to Girouard, chivalry was eclipsed in an
eighteenth century that advocated that the standards of society be shaped
according to the dictates of reason, although there was a revival of interest
in the late eighteenth century as part of the romantic movement.[88] The
Mischianza represents the survival of chivalric forms in the eighteenth-
century military culture. The *Mischianza* itself remains a puzzling event. It
was a display of affection on the part of the staff officers who formed
Howe's military "family." It was also an elaboration of the theatricals and
entertainments often devised by officers in garrison and of the grimmer

ritual of the duel. But the pageant disguised a sober reality. Howe had neither defeated nor conciliated the Americans; he did not depart Philadelphia as a victorious chieftain. Ambrose Serle, secretary to Howe's brother, Admiral Lord Howe, was scandalized by the affair, writing, "Every man of Sense, among ourselves, tho' not unwilling to pay a due respect, was ashamed of the mode of doing it."[89] Serle's worldview was that of the early Enlightenment. To Serle the rational order of the universe proved the existence of God; liberty consisted of living under a system of civil laws.[90] The American subversion of this system filled him with dismay, but he believed that the *Mischianza* was simply silly. However, the escape into a world of myth and legend may provide insight into the persistence of certain arcane values among the officers that formed the culture of honor. The *Mischianza*'s mock tournament provided a ritual that may have helped to confirm the participants' aristocratic status and to integrate an officer of nonaristocratic status into the military elite. John André, like Delacherois, was the son of Huguenot immigrants, seeking acceptance within the British social elite. The *Mischianza* was perhaps not entirely a game for him.

André was the *chevalier sans peur et sans reproche.* He was a perfect aide-de-camp: bright, industrious, one who made life easy and pleasing for his seniors. Clearly he was enormously likeable, with a wide range of friendships in the army and in British society. Howe's successor, Sir Henry Clinton, made André adjutant general and treated him as a son. As adjutant, André was deeply involved in Clinton's most-secret plans. This led to his participation in the clandestine negotiations with Benedict Arnold and the plan to betray West Point to the British. The story of André's capture behind American lines while in civilian dress and General George Washington's insistence that he be hanged as a spy is well known. Washington's point of view is perfectly understandable. André had suborned Arnold to commit an infamous act of treason, and civilian dress deprived him of prisoner-of-war status. Although Washington's severity might have been motivated by anger that Arnold had escaped, he acted within the laws of war. Clinton's appeals for clemency failed to move the stern republican. This incident, however, secured enduring fame for André. His unflagging charm worked its magic even on American officers, and his calm bravery won their respect. He met his end in the spirit of self-sacrifice that was emblematic of true honor.

André's death was a tragedy that stood out from the many deaths from battle and disease suffered by eighteenth-century soldiers. He was eulogized by his friend the poet Anna Seward, in "Monody on Major André." She dedicated this work to Clinton: "With the zeal of a religious Enthusiast to his murdered Saint, the Author of this mournful Eulogium consecrates it to the Memory of Major André, who fell a Martyr in the Cause of his King and Country, with the firm Intrepidity of a Roman, and the amiable resignation of a Christian Hero."[91] For Seward, André's death was part of a double tragedy. His engagement to another friend, Honora Sneyd, had been dissolved by parental authority; the young woman had married another but died of consumption only a few months before André's execution. The "Monody" is a lament for lost love. Seward's initial sympathy with the American cause had cooled with the news of the French alliance. She now condemned what she considered to be Washington's brutality:

> Oh Washington! I thought thee
> great and good,
> Nor knew thy Nero-thirst of
> guiltless blood!
> Severe to use the pow'r that Fortune
> Gave
> Thou cool determin'd Murderer
> Of the Brave[92]

Many officers commented on the tragic nature of war. Seasoned warriors lamented the loss of friends. Thus General Jeffrey Amherst, commander in chief in North America in 1759, responded to the death in action of his friend Captain Townshend: "[T]he loss of a friend is not made up by all the success that a Campaign can give to one's self personally— *villain métier, celle du soldat.*"[93]

Lieutenant Richard Browne's letters in the wake of the ferocious battle of Minden in 1759 provide a full spectrum of responses to the calamity of war. On August 14, he expressed shock and dismay: "I thought formerly I could easily form an idea of a battle from the Account I heard from others, but I find everything short of the horrid Scene, and it seems almost incredible that any can escape the incessant fire and terrible Hissing of Bullets, of all sizes. The Field of Battle after is Melancholy, four or five miles of plain covered with human bodies dead and dying miserably butchered, dead horses, broken wheels and carriages and arms of all kinds. This was the ground we pitched our tents on after the battle and tho we removed many dead bodies out of the way, in the morning on the ground in our tents was pools of Blood and pieces of Brains. I am much of the opinion of the Hereditary prince [the nephew of Browne's commander Ferdinand of Brunswick] who thinks the profession of a soldier shocking to human nature and declares he'll never pursue it again longer than the continuance of the war."[94]

By August 28, Browne had gained perspective on the event and now adopted a stylized manner in writing what he thought *should* be said on such an occasion: "[M]y only secret prayer was, not for my safety, but that I should acquit myself properly of the trust reposed in me by my King and the publick, as well as what I knew due to my own Character, and thank

God I have hitherto escaped blame. Long life is what I would not waste a wish about, the utmost of my desire is that while I live it may be in Repute, and if I fall, that it may be in Character."[95] Shock had been replaced by a concern for honor and the good opinion of his peers. By November, Browne was anxious for action once again. Above all he was eager for advancement. He was the senior lieutenant of his company, and war brought vacancies and promotion. Peace was now the barrier to his professional advancement, and soon he was asking his father for a loan to purchase a company before the army was reduced to peacetime strength. It appears that, unfortunately, peace came too soon for a soldier who had put the horrors of Minden behind him.[96] Browne's letters remind us that it is dangerous to generalize about the attitudes of eighteenth-century officers. Officers often wrote what was expected depending on the circumstances. In 1741, then-Lieutenant Philip Browne responded to orders posting him abroad by observing, "it is most Agreeable to me to Court Dangers and Hardships abroad, rather than continue in Safety and Ease at Home. And my only wish and desire is that I may behave Gallantly and die like a Soldier, or return with Honour and in Higher Rank."[97] Philip Browne saw action at the bloody battles of Dettingen and Fontenoy and seems to have acquitted himself well. The bulk of his letters reflect the primary interest of most officers: how best to achieve advancement. Great battles opened the way, and senior commanders were likely to find themselves flooded by letters from officers seeking to fill new vacancies.[98] Young soldiers did not seem to linger long over war's tragedies.

HONOR AND THE PRIVATE SOLDIER

There is little evidence that the rank and file embraced the culture of honor. Literary evidence for the lower ranks is scarce, nor do officers provide us with much insight into the attitudes of the lower ranks. In the British army it was considered conduct unbecoming for an officer to consort with common soldiers, and thus a distance between the two groups was maintained. Peebles seldom mentioned the men under his command except to condemn them for thievery and drunkenness. Indeed, he spent more time in his journals discussing his own alcoholic consumption. The only reference to some emotional bond came with his description of his farewell to his company on February 8, 1782: "I could hardly make an end of the little speech, my voice faltered, and my knees shook under me. I was glad to get into my room where my heart swelled at my thought of it. I saw the poor fellows were affected too. I ordered them five gallons of rum to make a drink of grog in the Evening."[99] Ewald wrote of the exhausted British troops at Yorktown that they preferred captivity to continued starvation and hardship. "One must consider mankind as it is; every man is not a hero, and the rank and file does not think like an officer, who is spurred on to his utmost to win honor."[100] There were literate soldiers, and some left accounts that expressed their military values. Sergeant Roger Lamb of the Royal Welsh Fusiliers served in America under Burgoyne and became part of the "convention army" interned after the British defeat at Saratoga. He escaped, was recaptured at Yorktown, and escaped again. He set out to write an impartial history of the war and was generally successful in doing so. His journal, which is included in the history, is the best account of the experience of an NCO from the period. Lamb wrote from patriotic motives. He concluded that "it would be superfluous in him to press on the Reader's attention, that the flowers of literature are not to be expected from an old soldier, whose only object in the publication was the unfolding of truth in the defence of his country's honor, and the humanity of her officers."[101]

In his study of the Austrian army, Duffy has identified two private soldiers who became literary men after their period of service. Most notable was Joseph von Sonnenfels, who became a professor of administration and economics and an ally of Maria Theresa's reform programs. Unlike Lamb's, Sonnenfels's service was limited to about four years, but it may have contributed to his idea of patriotism, which consisted of loyalty to a state that protected an individual through good laws and good government. Sonnenfels remained proud of his military service and expressed fondness for the officers who had encouraged him to develop his potential. He believed that the common soldier shared in military glory, writing: "That which forms the honour of the entity is the honour of its individual parts."[102]

HUMANITY

"I chuse to carry on the war with strict Faith between the Nations and the greatest Humanity to the Particulars," wrote the earl of Loudon, British commander in North America, to Quebec governor Marquis de Vaudreuil in 1757.[103] His successor, General James Abercromby, returned British prisoners on parole to the French commander, Marquis de Montcalm, "to convince your Excellency how Desirous I am to carry on the War in this country with the same humanity and generosity it is in Europe and ought to be everywhere."[104] Courteous exchanges between European commanders were common in the eighteenth century. They upheld military conventions that assured the honorable conduct of war: prisoner paroles and exchanges, flags of truce, care for enemy wounded, honorable capitulations for defeated forces, and restraints on firing at pickets or at general headquarters. Such conventions gave substance to the confidence of Emmerich von Vattel and others that eighteenth-century warfare was conducted more humanely than in previous periods. Some officers took seriously their responsibility to the enemy's wounded. After the French

army's victory over the duke of Cumberland's German "army of observation" at Hastenbeck in 1757, the marquis de Valfons recalled that he had
spent three days searching the wooded ravines where the battle had been
fought in order to bury the dead and find the wounded who had gone
without assistance. "I was sufficiently fortunate to find my cares rewarded
by saving the lives of many Hanoverians, Hessians, and French who survived as a result of my zeal, not having wished it said of me that I had
neglected so precious a work."[105] Reginald Savory, in his discussion of the
treatment of prisoners of war, the sick, and the wounded by the Anglo-
German and French armies during the Seven Years' War, concludes that
"one may agree...that the middle of the eighteenth century was the
period during which the conduct of war was in this respect, the most
enlightened. It has never been the same since."[106]

The code of honor played a role in negotiations with the enemy. Folard
addressed the question of whether one should always abide by one's commitment to a defeated enemy. Was it sometimes necessary to massacre
prisoners in spite of the capitulations? He found historical precedents for
such actions in Hamilcar Barca's slaughter of the insurgent foreign mercenaries and in the fate of the vanquished Hussites in 1434. In contrast, he
praised the modern example of Marshal Villars, who adhered to his com-
mitments after defeating the Protestant Camisards of the Cévennes in
1704. Villars's honorable conduct had been an important factor in bringing
the rebellion to an end. It also suggested that, in comparison with previous centuries, eighteenth-century soldiers abided more strictly by a code
of honorable and humane conduct.[107]

It is difficult to imagine modern commanders conducting negotiations
over prisoners in the manner of French and British officers during the
British siege of the citadel at Belle Isle in 1761. In May of that year,
the British general Studholme Hodgson wrote to the citadel's commander,
the chevalier de St. Croix, to protest as contrary to custom the reduction of
British prisoners to bread and water. St. Croix replied that, although he
was following the orders of his superior the duke d'Aiguillon, he felt
deeply for the plight of the prisoners. Siege conditions made the 400
British prisoners a heavy burden on his resources. Hodgson thereupon
requested that the prisoners be transferred to British ships under parole
and promised that they would not be asked anything about the citadel. St.
Croix again pled the restrictions of his orders but assured Hodgson that he
would do his best to protect the prisoners from bombardment. Hodgson
then turned to Aiguillon, who insisted that the prisoners be sent to
England until the fate of the citadel was decided. If it fell, they would be at
liberty to serve without ransom or exchange. Hodgson sent Colonel Burgoyne to conclude a treaty on these terms, but the latter exceeded his
authority by agreeing to the return of French prisoners. The French did
not hesitate to pounce on Burgoyne's gaffe. Aiguillon expressed dismay at

the refusal to execute the agreement signed by Burgoyne, saying, "Military conventions have always been regarded, even among the least civilized nations, as sacred and inviolable laws and have always been executed with the most scrupulous exactitude." All this was settled by the capitulation of the citadel on June 7, with the French accorded all of the honors of war. The British prisoners gained their freedom, and Aiguillon agreed to ransom the French prisoners according to the standing cartel that established ransom rates.[108]

Both sides conducted the negotiations with profound courtesy. They were eager to establish that they conducted the war in an honorable and humane fashion. One has the sense that the officers involved wrote their letters with a wider public in mind. Hodgson was particularly exasperated that Burgoyne had placed him in the position of rejecting the agreement. Certain conventions and ideals of honor were observed in the exchange of letters, but the reality remained that the prisoners remained firmly where they were until the citadel fell. Aiguillon wrote to Hodgson that "my only motives have been the particular consideration that I have for you and the sincere esteem with which I have always been filled for the English troops and nation"—but perhaps his motives were more complex.[109] Anglo-French negotiations at the heart were poisoned by distrust. The French probably suspected that, despite the terms of the negotiations, paroled British prisoners would reveal important information about the defenses. Behind the courteous words there lurked a deep distrust of the enemy. Lord Loudon wrote of his experience in North America that the French "have kept no faith, and have committed every Cruelty in their power."[110] No French action escaped suspicion—the use of flags of truce as an opportunity for spying was a particular complaint.[111] This hostility toward the French contrasts with the high regard expressed for Spanish officers who accompanied to New York British prisoners exchanged after the fall of Pensacola in 1781. The Spaniards had observed the capitulation terms scrupulously and had acted with great courtesy. They were at liberty to do almost as they pleased in New York and were treated in the most-friendly manner.[112]

Vattel assumed that honorable officers would protect the weak and refrain from marauding and pillaging. Senior military commanders usually did their best to enforce the rules against this sort of thing. Pillaging led to indiscipline and the erosion of an army's preparedness. As is discussed in chapter 5, it might provoke a massive popular uprising. At times, commanders resorted to the devastation of the enemy's countryside as a matter of policy. The duke of Richelieu won the nickname Father Marauder for the devastation his troops caused in Germany during the Seven Years' War. In 1757 his troops sacked Celle, during which the children of a local orphanage perished. The allied commander Prince Ferdinand wrote to Richelieu to expostulate in the strongest terms: "Judging by the way that you have treated Celle, one would think one was dealing with an army of Russians."[113] This comment was very unfair to the Russians who, with the exception of the Cossacks, were at least as well behaved as any other army.

At the regimental or company level, enforcement of the rules was often at the discretion of the officers and thus depended on their sense of right and wrong. A good officer had to assure that his men were fed and warm. Poor finances and bad logistics could lead them to give a very wide definition to the term *forage*. The Hessian jaeger Ewald recalled that on the first night after his command disembarked in Westchester County and camp was pitched, "We heard cries of chickens, geese, and pigs which our resourceful soldiers had discovered. Within the hour, several roasts hung from long sticks before the fire. The whole camp was busy as an anthill. From this one can see how easily a good soldier knows his way about."[114] Ewald believed that although plunder might create enemies among the inhabitants, it was part of a soldier's rightful compensation. It was therefore a legitimate motive for military service. He recorded tensions produced by commanders who favored some troops over others with opportunities for plunder. Nevertheless, this issue presented him with a moral dilemma. He resolved it by drawing a distinction between plunder or booty shared by all and individual looting. He considered the latter to be robbery. He turned a blind eye to robberies committed by his soldiers, but he declined to turn robber himself, for this was unbefitting an officer's sense of honor.[115] Naval officers were usually spared these moral dilemmas, as their share of booty usually came from the seizure of enemy commercial vessels. In the British navy the entire value of enemy prizes condemned by an admiralty court was shared by the captors, with the lion's share going to the officers. N. A. M. Rodger wrote, "It was considered entirely proper in the eighteenth century that patriotism should have its reward, and no class persons were so highly rewarded for serving the Crown as sea officers."[116]

Officers might also find the law against rape to be against human nature. "A girl cannot step into the bushes to pluck a rose without being ravished, and they are so little accustomed to these vigorous methods, that they don't bear them with the proper resignation, and of a consequence we have the most entertaining courts-martial every day," wrote the British officer Lord Rawdon from Staten Island in August 1776.[117] Peebles recorded the incident of a man condemned to death for rape but pardoned because of the intercession of the injured party, the second such instance.[118] Officers seem to have had an ambivalent attitude toward rape; an analysis of rape courts-martial is needed. Most officers did not share Mercoyral Beaulieu's belief in chastity. Peebles expressed sympathy for the rape victim above, but he was a man of the world and was complimentary about a respectable prostitute who kept a highly regarded brothel in Newport, Rhode Island, with "a tolerable degree of modern luxury."[119] But Duffy concludes that "bad women" with whom the Austrian army associated "reduced many a good officer to an impoverished disease ridden wreck."[120] While many officers were happy to record successes with fashionable and unfashionable women, there was an understandable reluctance to discuss rape on their own part. An exception was Lancelot Turpin de Crissé, hussar officer and author of a major treatise on war. Crissé believed that many rapes were accomplished with voluntary compliance, and his fond recollection of a youthful exploit in a convent so shocked his editor that the latter deleted part of the account.[121] One has the sense that, as long as brutality was not involved, a reputation for amorous conquests did not detract from an officer's honorable reputation.

Honor established ideal standards of conduct for officers. These standards were not always clear, as the debate over true and false honor suggests. As with any standard of conduct, many officers might fall short. Nevertheless, they were aware that they were under constant scrutiny by their fellow officers. Loss of reputation for honorable conduct usually meant the end of one's career. True honor, with its emphasis on patriotism and self-sacrifice, served the cause of those who wished to increase professionalism in the officer corps. In this sense, honor appeared in a modern form and laid the ground for a twenty-first-century officers' code. The debate over the nature of honor reflects the eighteenth-century tension between the values of a traditional society and those of the emerging modern world. Honor contributed to the sense of the military spirit that Folard and other authors of the Military Enlightenment sought to revive. Indeed, the subject of honor was central to their thinking. The evolving definition of honor also contributed to the hope of Vattel and other Enlightenment writers that the conduct of war was becoming more humane. Officers do appear to have acquired a higher standard of conduct. Professor Jean Chagniot, comparing the attitudes of seventeenth- and eighteenth-century French officers toward pillage, found that the latter were far more critical of excesses than were their predecessors.[122] Armies did establish high standards of conduct. "The troops are desired to remember," pronounced one British order, "that clemency should go hand in hand with bravery, that an enemy in our power is an enemy no more, and the glorious characteristic of a British soldier is to conquer and spare."[123]

A commander who appeared to flout the rules of war risked ostracism by his professional colleagues. After the surrender of Lord Charles Cornwallis's army at Yorktown, French and American officers treated their British colleagues with courtesy and assisted them in what ways they could. The exception was Lt. Colonel Banastre Tarleton, whose troops had killed Americans attempting to surrender and whose very name evoked the horrors of the campaigns in the American South. Tarleton was snubbed by the allied officers. The French commander Count Rochambeau said of him: "Colonel Tarleton has no merit as an officer—only that bravery every Grenadier has—but is a butcher and a barbarian."[124] Tarleton and John André had ridden together as knights on the day of the *Mischianza*. How their careers had diverged —André to be remembered as the true knight of the code of self-sacrifice, Tarleton to be caricatured in the recent film *The Patriot* as the embodiment of the evils of war. In their cases, the judgment of the court of public opinion, was decisive.

NOTES

1. Johann Ewald, *Diary of the American War, A Hessian Journal,* trans. and ed. Joseph P. Tustin (New Haven: Yale University Press, 1979), 298.

2. Robert Donkin, *Military Collections and Remarks* (New York, 1777), 202.

3. Campbell Dalrymple, *A Military Essay Containing Reflections on the Raising, Arming, Cloathing, and Discipline of the British Infantry and Cavalry* (London, 1761), 378.

4. J.C. Pleydell, trans., *An Essay on Field Fortifications, Intended Principally for the Use of Officers of Infantry, Translated from the Original Manuscript of an Officer in the Prussian Service by J.C. Pleydell, Lieutenant in the Twelfth Regiment of Foot* (London, 1768), 122.

5. *The Military Mentor: Being a Series of letters recently written by a General Officer to his Son, on his entering the Army,* 2d ed., 2 vols. (Salem: Cushington and Appleton, 1808), I:248–49.

6. M. de Laissac, *De l'esprit militaire,* new ed. (The Hague, 1788), 231.

7. George Eid, "Diary of Lieutenant Eid," *Proceedings of the Massachusetts Historical Society* 18 (Boston, 1880): 78.

8. Jean François, Marquis de Saint-Lambert, "Honneur,"in *L'Encyclopédie, ou Dictionnaire raisonné des sciences, des arts et des métiers,* ed. Denis Diderot and Jean Le Rond d'Alembert, 28 vols. (1751-72; facsimile of the first edition, Stuttgart-Bad Cannstatt: Frommann, 1969), 8:289-91.

9. James Anderson, *Essay on the Art of War* (London: A. Millar, 1761), 2–3.

10. *The Military Mentor,* I:12.

11. Ibid., 33.

12. John Peebles, The Journals of Lieutenant (latterly Captain) John Peebles of the 42nd Royal Highland Regiment, during the War of American Independence, Cunningham of Thorntoun Muniments, 21/492/5/24, Scottish Record Office, Edinburgh, Scotland. For an example of an amicable settlement in lieu of a duel, see Samuel Graham, *Memoirs of General [Samuel] Graham with Notices of the Campaigns on which He was Engaged from 1779 to 1801* (Edinburgh: privately printed by R. & R. Clark, 1862), 17. Duels in the British army are discussed in some detail in Mark Odintz, "The British Officer Corps, 1754–1783" (Ph.D. diss., University of Michigan, 1988), 508–36. Also see V.G. Kiernan, *The Duel in European History: Honour and the Reign of the Aristocracy* (Oxford: Oxford University Press, 1988).

13. *The Military Mentor,* I:288–304.

14. Donkin, *Military Collections and Remarks,* 200.

15. Edward Barrington Fonblanque, *Political and Military Episodes in the Latter Half of the Eighteenth Century Derived from the life and Correspondence of the Right Hon. John Burgoyne, General, Statesman, Dramatist* (London: Macmillan, 1876), 33, n. 1.

16. H.W. Richmond, *The Navy in the War of 1739–48,* 3 vols. (Cambridge: Cambridge University Press, 1920), 2:183.

17. *The Lost War: Letters from British Officers during the American Revolution,* ed. and annotated by Marion Balderston and David Syrett (New York: Horizon Press, 1975), 60.

18. Eid, "Diary," 76.

19. J. Krafft, *Journal of Lieutenant Joseph Charles Philip Joseph von Krafft,* vol. 12, *Collections of the New York Historical Society for the Year 1882* (New York, 1883; reprint, New York: Arno Press, 1968). For duels, see 31, 33-34, 161–62, 170 (citations are to the reprint edition).

20. George Elers, *Memoirs of George Elers, Captain in the 12th Regiment of Foot,* ed. Lord Monson and George Leveson Gower (New York: D. Appleton, 1903), 82–89, 168–69. See also Odintz, "British Officer Corps," 517.

21. S. R. Lushington, *The Life and Services of General Lord Harris during His Campaigns in America, the West Indies, and India,* 2d ed., rev. (London, 1845), 11–17.

22. Elers, *Memoirs,* 217.

23. Gilbert Bodinier, *Les officiers de l'Armée Royale combattants de la guerre d'indépendence des États-Unis de Yorktown à l'an II* (Château de Vincennes: Service Historique de l'Armée de Terre, 1983), 193–200.

24. John Barker, *The British in Boston: Being the Diary of Lieutenant John Barker of the King's Own Regiment from November 15, 1774 to May 31, 1776* (Cambridge: Harvard University Press, 1924), 27–31.

25. Arthur Gilbert, "Law and Honour among Eighteenth-Century British Officers," *The Historical Journal* 19, no. 1 (1976): 75–87.

26. For a broader discussion of this issue, see V. G. Kiernan, *The Duel in European History,* particularly 165–85.

27. Donna T. Andrew, "The Code of Honour and Its Critics: The Opposition to Dueling in England, 1700–1850," *Social History* 5 (1980): 434.

28. Granville Sharp, *Remarks . . . on Manslaughter and Murder* (1773), in Andrew, Ibid., 426, n. 94.

29. Nicholas Delacherois, "The Letters of Captain Nicholas Delacherois, 9th Regiment," ed. S. P. G. Ward, *Journal of the Society for Army Historical Research* 51 (1973): 10.

30. J. A. Houlding, *Fit for Service: The Training of the British Army, 1715–1795* (Oxford: Clarendon Press, 1981), 104–5.

31. Christopher Duffy, *Instrument of War,* vol. 1 of *The Austrian Army in the Seven Years' War* (Rosemont, Ill.: The Emperor's Press, 2000), 140.

32. André Corvisier, *Armies and Societies in Europe, 1494–1789,* trans. Abigail T. Siddall (Bloomington: Indiana University Press, 1979), 102.

33. Christopher Storrs and H. M. Scott, "The Military Revolution and the European Nobility, c. 1600–1800," *War in History* 3, no. 1 (1996): 1–41.

34. Christopher Duffy, *Russia's Military Way to the West: Origins and Nature of Russian Military Power, 1700–1800* (London: Routledge & Kegan Paul, 1981), 154.

35. Frances St. Clair Vivian, "John André as a Young Officer: The Army in the Eighteenth Century and a Young Man's Impression on First Joining His Regiment in the 1770s," *Journal of the Society for Army Historical Research* 40 (1962): 28.

36. These relationships are well discussed in Odintz, "British Officer Corps," 536–66.

37. Alan J. Guy, *Oeconomy and Discipline: Officership and Administration in the British Army, 1714–1763* (Manchester: Manchester University Press, 1985), 37.

38. Humphrey Bland, *A Treatise of Military Discipline,* 9th ed. (London: R. Baldwin, 1762), 173–74.

39. Ibid., 134.

40. Guy, *Oeconomy and Discipline,* 165–67.

41. Bland, *Military Discipline,* 133.

42. Émile Léonard, *L'Armée et ses problèmes au XVIIIe siècle* (Paris: Libraire Plon, 1958), 150–57.

43. Ibid., 165–90.

44. Jean Chagniot, *Guerre et société à l'époque moderne* (Paris: Presses Universitaires de France, 2001), 220–21, 272.

45. *Campagnes de Mercoyral de Beaulieu, 1743–1763* vol. 370 (Paris: Société de l'histoire de France), 323.

46. Many writers seem to have counseled that a successful military career was jeopardized by a fondness for women. Folard abided by this principle. See Jean Chagniot, *Le chevalier de Folard: La stratégie de l'incertitude* (Paris: Editions du Rocher, 1997) 65.

47. David Bien, "The Army in the French Enlightenment: Reform, Reaction, and Revolution," *Past and Present* 85 (November 1979): 65–78.

48. Andrew Crichton, *Life and Diary of Lieut. Colonel John Blackadder, Deputy-Governor of Stirling Castle, Abridged from the Larger Work* (Edinburgh: H. S. Baynes, 1875), 76.

49. Ibid., 85–86.

50. Ibid., 139.

51. Charles de Mathéi, marquis de Valfons, *Souvenirs du Marquis de Valfons…1710–1786,* Mémoires sur le XVIIIe siècle (Paris: E. Paul, 1906), 277–78.

52. Roger Stevenson, *Military Instructions for Officers Detached in the Field Containing a Scheme for Forming a Corps of a Partisan….* (Philadelphia, 1775), 53.

53. M. de Zimmerman, *Essais de principes d'une morale militaire et autres objets* (Amsterdam, 1769), 37.

54. Ambrose Serle, *The American Journal of Ambrose Serle, Secretary to Lord Howe, 1776–1778,* ed. Edward H. Tatum, Jr. (San Marino, Calif.: Huntington Library, 1940; New York: Arno Press, 1969), 57.

55. Evan Charteris, *William Augustus, Duke of Cumberland, and the Seven Years' War* (London: Hutchinson, n.d.), 59–60.

56. "Patriotic Reflections," in Duffy, *Instrument of War,* 187. Duffy remains the best authority on the culture of the Prussian and Austrian officer corps.

57. Chagniot, *Guerre et société,* 231.

58. [Francis Grose] *Advice to the Officers of the British Army* (1782; reprint, London: Jonathan Cape, 1946), 50 (page citation is to the reprint edition).

59. Corvisier, *Armies and Societies,* 105–8.

60. Gunnar Lind, "Military Absolutism: The Army Officers of Denmark-Norway as a Social Group and Political Factor, 1660–1848," *Scandinavian Journal of History* 12 (1988): 221–43.

61. Christopher Duffy, *The Army of Frederick the Great* (New York: Hippocrene Books, 1974), 28-29.

62. Duffy, *Instrument of War,* 146.

63. John Burgoyne, *The Heiress: A Comedy in Five Acts as Performed at the Theatre-Royal in Drury Lane,* 2d ed. (London, 1786), 31–32.

64. See J. E. O. Screen, "The 'Royal Academy' of Lewis Lochée," *Journal of the Academy for Army Historical Research* 80, no. 283 (1992): 143–56. Lochée was a prolific writer of military textbooks. His ideas on education are contained in his *An Essay on Military Education* (London, 1776).

65. Lochée, *Military Education*, 42.

66. Ibid., 31.

67. Ibid.

68. W. Glanville Evelyn, *Memoirs and Letters of Captain W. Glanville Evelyn* (Oxford, 1879; reprint, New York: Arno Press, 1971), 30–31 (page citations are to the reprint edition).

69. Ibid., 33.

70. Pleydell, *Field Fortifications*, xii.

71. See John Morgan Dederer, *War in America to 1775: Before Yankee Doodle* (New York: New York University Press, 1990), 142.

72. Catalogue of Captain Moyle's Library, Peebles's Journals, 21/492/3.

73. [Grose] *Advice to the Officers*, 59–60.

74. Thomas Hughes, *A Journal by Thos: Hughes (1778–1789)*, with an introduction by E. A. Benians (Cambridge: Cambridge University Press, 1947), xi.

75. James Murray, *Letters from America 1773 to 1780, Being the letters of a Scots Officer, Sir James Murray to his home during the War of American Independence*, ed. Eric Robson (Manchester: Manchester University Press, 1951), 7–8.

76. Lushington, *Life of General Lord Harris*, 26.

77. John Knox, *An Historical Journal of the Campaigns in North America for the Years 1757, 1758, 1759 and 1760 by Captain John Knox*, ed. Arthur G. Doughty, 3 vols. (Freeport, New York: Books for Librarians Press, 1970), 1:272.

78. Sir Thomas Spencer Wilson, Bart., to Lord Fitzmaurice, 18 May 1761; Sir Thomas Spencer Wilson, Bart., to Lord Shelburne, 7 June 1761, Shelburne Papers 37:47, 183, William Clements Library, University of Michigan, Ann Arbor.

79. Duffy, *Army of Frederick the Great*, 47–50.

80. Charles Royster, *A Revolutionary People at War: The Continental Army and the American Character, 1775–1773* (Chapel Hill: University of North Carolina Press, 1979), 88–89.

81. Hughes, *Journal*, 139.

82. Balderston and Syrett, eds., *The Lost War*, 58.

83. Peebles, Peebles's Journals, 2/492/5.

84. Ibid., 21/492/11/1 and 21/492/10/42.

85. Ibid., 21/492/5/4.

86. For Peebles's description, see Journals, 21/492/5/26–29. John André provided an account for *The Gentleman's Magazine* (July 1778). Another version, "Major André's Story of the *Mischianza*," was published in *The Century Illustrated Magazine* 47 (1894), 684–91. The Hessian adjutant general Carl Leopold von Baurmeister described the event in his journal, published as *Revolution in America: Confidential Letters and Journals, 1776–1784, of Adjutant Major Baurmeister of the Hessian Forces*, trans. Bernard Uhlendorf (Westport, Conn.: Greenwood, 1973), 177–78.

87. André, *The Gentleman's Magazine*, 357.

88. Mark Girouard, *The Return to Camelot: Chivalry and the English Gentleman* (New Haven: Yale University Press, 1981), 17–23.

89. Serle, *American Journal*, 293–94.

90. Ibid., 59–60.

91. Anna Seward, "Monody on Major André" (1781), in Bernard J. Lossing, *The Two Spies* (New York: D. Appleton, 1886), 133.

92. Ibid., 149.

93. Jeffrey Amherst, *The Journal of Jeffrey Amherst, Recording the Military Career of General Amherst in America from 1758 to 1763,* ed. J. Clarence Webster (Toronto: Riverson Press; Chicago: University of Chicago Press, 1931), 145.

94. Richard Browne to Jeremy Browne, 14 August 1759, Browne Papers, Clements Library, University of Michigan, Ann Arbor.

95. R. Browne to J. Browne, 28 August 1759.

96. R. Browne to J. Browne, 2 November 1760 and 4 April 1761. According to Col. H. C. Wylly, *History of the King's Own Yorkshire Light Infantry, 1755–1914* (London: Percy Lund, n.d.), 95, Browne appeared in the army list for 1763 as a lieutenant in the 51st regiment. Peace had evidently overtaken him.

97. "Letter of Captain Philip Browne—1737 to 1746," *Journal of the Society for Army Historical Research* 5 (1926): 56–57.

98. For example, see M. de Pesteil au comte de Clermont, 11 May 1745 (after the battle of Fontenoy), in J. Colin, *Les Campagnes du Maréchal de Saxe* (Paris: Libraire Militaire, R. Chapelot et Cie, 1901), 226.

99. Peebles, Peebles's Journals, 21/492/13/38.

100. Ewald, *Diary*, 338.

101. Roger Lamb, *An Original and Authentic Journal of Occurrences During the Late American War from its Commencement to the Year 1783* (Dublin: Wilkerson & Courtney, 1809; reprint, New York: Arno Press, 1968), 438 (page citation is to the reprint edition).

102. Duffy, *Instrument of War*, 224.

103. Lord Loudon to the Marquis de Vaudreuil, 8 November 1757, Loudon Papers, LO 4788, Huntington Library, San Marino, Calif.

104. General Abercromby to the Marquis of Montcalm, 21 July 1758, Abercromby Papers, AB 463, Huntington Library, San Marino, Calif.

105. Valfons, *Souvenirs*, 279.

106. Reginald Savory, *His Britannic Majesty's Army in Germany* (Oxford: Clarendon Press, 1966), 464.

107. Jean-Charles de Folard, *Histoire de Polybe...avec un commentaire ou un corps de science militaire....*, 7 vols. (Amsterdam : Arkstée et Merkus, 1753), 2:90–99. I am grateful to Professor Chagniot for calling my attention to this passage. For Villars's skill in suppressing the Camisard rebellion, see Claude C. Sturgill, *Marshal Villars and the War of the Spanish Succession* (Lexington: University of Kentucky Press, 1965), 53–62.

108. Shelburne Papers, Belle Isle, vol. 37, pt. 1, 49–53, 75–76, 79, 90.

109. Ibid., 76.

110. Loudon to the earl of Holdernesse and William Pitt, 16 August–17 October 1757, Loudon Papers, LO 4230 A and B.

111. See the case of the Sieur l'Archer who was confined after escorting 74 British prisoners from Louisbourg to Boston, Loudon Papers, LO 4282, 4326, 4455, 4755.

112. Frederick Mackenzie, *Diary of Frederick Mackenzie, Giving a Daily Narrative of His Service as an Officer of the Regiment of Royal Welch Fusiliers during the Years 1775–1781 in Massachusetts, Rhode Island, and New York,* 2 vols. (Cambridge: Harvard University Press, 1930), 2:19.

113. Savory, *His Britannic Majesty's Army in Germany,* 54.

114. Ewald, *Diary,* 8.

115. Ibid., 19–20, 22, 31, 76, 159–60, 273.

116. N. A. M. Rodger, *The Wooden World: An Anatomy of the Georgian Navy* (Annapolis: Naval Institute Press, 1986), 256.

117. Great Britain, Historical Manuscripts Commission, *Report on the Manuscripts of the Late Reginald Rawdon-Hastings,* 4 vols. (London, 1934), 3:179.

118. Peebles, Peebles Journals, 21/492/3.

119. Ibid.

120. Duffy, *Instrument of War,* 187.

121. "Mélanges et documents: La campagne de 1761 en Westphale d'après les lettres du Maréchal de Crissé au Prince de Saxe," *Revue historique* (May-August, 1910): 323.

122. Jean Chagniot, "The Ethics and Practice of War amongst French Officers during the Seventeenth Century," *War and Society* 10 (May 1992): 19–36.

123. "St. Lucie, Reserve Orders, December 14, 1778" recorded by William Medows, in *Some British Soldiers in America,* by W. H. Wilkin (London, 1914), 197.

124. See Robert D. Bass, *The Green Dragoon: The Lives of Banastre Tarleton and Mary Robinson* (New York: Holt, 1957), 4.

CHAPTER 4

Field of Honor: Fontenoy, 1745

If this day was a great day for the nation, it was a thousand times greater for the eternal and personal glory of His Majesty.[1]

Oui, un beau jour, mais le dernier de l'ancienne France!
      –The Duke de Broglie, *La Journée de Fontenoy* (1897)

THE SPORT OF KINGS

Montesquieu's observation that war was the spirit of monarchies was supported by the close involvement of eighteenth-century monarchs in the practice of warfare. Some kings were accomplished generals in their own right. Charles XII and Frederick the Great were true soldier-kings and possessed military genius. Britain's first two Hanoverian monarchs were deeply interested in military affairs and sought to raise standards of military professionalism. As elector of Hanover, George I saw action during the War of the Spanish Succession, and George II commanded at the battle of Dettingen, June 23, 1743. This was the last occasion that a British monarch led troops in battle. Victor Amadeus II of Piedmont-Savoy exercised personal command over his army in battle, as did his successor Charles Emmanuel. Sovereigns such as Charles XII, Frederick the Great, and Peter the Great began their careers under the watchful eye of experienced commanders but emerged as great military leaders in their own right. Others, such as Louis XIV, Louis XV, and Joseph II of Austria, were involved in the planning of campaigns and were present at battles and sieges. For the most part, they deferred to their generals on operational matters.

There were good reasons for royal involvement at this level. Armed forces were the most important institutions of eighteenth-century states. Machiavelli's advice to princes continued to hold true. Kings who ignored their armies might lose their thrones to those who actually commanded them. Louis XIV's greatest commanders, Turenne and Condé, had participated in rebellions against royal authority. Thus Versailles came to hold its marshals on a short leash. A king might not possess the ability of Charles or Frederick, but his presence on the field of battle or at the siege lines was important all the same. The king was the fount of honor, and officers and men serving under his eye were inspired to feats of courage that might win them recognition and advancement. On the battlefield a king rekindled the chivalric bond with his nobility. This required that he assume some level of risk. His close circle of advisers might be horrified that he might be wounded, killed, or taken prisoner. This was a real prospect. Charles XII was killed in action and Frederick was slightly wounded at Torgau, Germany, in 1760. George II won praise for his coolness under fire at Dettingen in 1743. Things might have been worse. The "Pragmatic army" (so named because it had come into existence to uphold the Pragmatic Sanction insuring the integrity of the Habsburg inheritance) that George II led found itself in a trap skillfully planned by the French marshal Noailles. Penned between the river Main and a range of hills, the Pragmatic army found its path swept by French artillery and blocked at both ends by French troops. Only an error by the commander of the blocking force saved the day for the Pragmatic army. Ordered to remain behind a bog, the French commander led his men across and into the ferocious fire of the British infantry.[2] George was able to celebrate his victory, but he might have easily ended the day a prisoner.

Not all monarchs could participate in battle. Britain's Queen Anne, Austria's Maria Theresa, and Russia's Catherine the Great relied on the services of their male subjects. Maria Theresa, however, was a great war leader, even if she sometimes chose her generals unwisely. Even her enemy Frederick II admired her indomitable spirit, and she appealed to the chivalric sentiments of her subjects, particularly the Hungarians, in her time of need. All understood that, if they could not participate themselves, they remained the source of the honors and rewards that motivated eighteenth-century soldiers.[3] We should remember that eighteenth-century states had yet to develop a modern form. Monarchs depended on the nobility to sacrifice blood and treasure in their defense. However "absolute" these states might be, such sacrifice could not always be compelled. The nobility would not act against their interests or their honor. Monarchs had to recognize the tangible interests of the governing elites and also share the values associated with the less-tangible standards of honor.

FONTENOY

Such things were on the mind of the king of France, Louis XV, on the eve of the battle of Fontenoy, Belgium, which was fought on May 11, 1745, during the War of the Austrian Succession. The king had arrived in response to an invitation from the commander of his army in Flanders, Maurice de Saxe (Maurice of Saxony). Saxe had performed a brilliant maneuver. Massing his army near the town of Maubeuge, in northern France, he had left his opponents, an allied army commanded by William Augustus, duke of Cumberland, uncertain of his true objective—Mons or Tournai. The allies did not learn the truth until Tournai was invested and Saxe's covering army was strongly posted to prevent its relief. Tournai was the key fortress defending the Scheldt estuary. It was considered the strongest fortress in the Dutch barrier, a chain of fortresses in the Austrian Netherlands that the Dutch had won the right to garrison by the terms of the Treaty of Utrecht. Constructed under the direction of the great French military engineer Sébastien de Vauban, partially protected by the waters of the Scheldt, and garrisoned by 8,000 Dutch troops, Tournai presented a formidable obstacle to an invader. The weakness of fortresses, however, lay in the spirit of the defenders. Residents of towns in the Austrian Netherlands had little love for the Dutch, and morale among the mercenaries of the Dutch garrisons was low. Officers were susceptible to bribery, and the senior Dutch engineer at Tournai had actually sabotaged the preparation of the defenses.[4] Several barrier fortresses had already surrendered with no more than token resistance. The Dutch had been tight fisted in their maintenance of their hard-won barrier, and now it was proving distinctly permeable. In 1745, at least, the defense of the barrier relied more on armies in the field than on the passive defenses of the fortress system. Saxe was confident that he could take Tournai. If the allies hoped to prevent its fall, they would have to fight him in the field. He was determined that it be a field of his choosing.

Voltaire, the first of many historians of this battle, tells us that the arrival of the king accompanied by the dauphin was greeted with acclamations of joy in the French camp. Morale soared. Saxe wrote of this day, "His presence is worth an additional 50,000 men to us as much by the impression it makes upon our own troops as on the enemy who do not think that we have assembled in force."[5] Louis was in a festive mood. "The King was never more gay than on the eve of combat," Voltaire wrote. On the evening before the battle, conversation turned to the battles that kings had attended in person. Louis said that since the battle of Poitiers (1356) no

French king had fought in the company of his son. Indeed, no French king since Saint Louis had gained a significant victory over the English. Now he hoped to be the first.[6] It is a leader's duty to inspire confidence, and Louis played his part well. Nevertheless, the conversation must have inspired some sober reflection. All were aware that Poitiers had not only been a military disaster but that the French king John had been taken prisoner by the Black Prince, son of King Edward III. Now a French king would lead his army into battle against the younger son of George II, the 24-year-old William Augustus, duke of Cumberland. Concern for the king's safety weighed heavily upon his staff. They had no illusions about the troops they would face. In the place of the Black Prince's knights and archers, the British would deploy the famous infantry trained in the tradition of Marlborough. At Dettingen they had demonstrated a clear superiority over their French opponents. Noailles, who was now with the king as a senior aide-de-camp, had reported that the British infantry at Dettingen "were in close order and held together as a wall of bronze from which there burst a fire so lively and sustained that the most experienced officers had never seen its like, and so superior to ours that there could be no comparison."[7] The French troops, he concluded, lacked the discipline and the military spirit of old. Medieval and modern history lent the king's discussions added drama, but in a tragic vein. The scene of the king and his followers reminds one of the dauphin and the French nobles on the night before Agincourt in Shakespeare's *Henry V*.

BACKGROUND TO FONTENOY

Louis XV is remembered as neither a general nor a statesman. Compared to his gifted and dynamic peers among the "enlightened absolutists," he appears to posterity as a mediocre meddler and voluptuary. Even when he aroused himself to be a king, it was usually at someone else's bidding. When Cardinal Fleury died in 1743, the king, in the tradition of Louis XIV following the death of Mazarin, proclaimed himself his own prime minister. The result was government by committee with unclear war aims and plans. Still, French policy had undergone a shift in direction. Marshal Charles de Belle-Isle's ambitious coalition to dismember the Habsburg possessions had collapsed, and that soldier-statesman had achieved only a skillful and heroic retreat from Prague in December 1742. British subsidies and diplomacy under the guidance of Lord John Carteret offered the prospect of a great coalition against the Bourbon powers, France and Spain, but that great scheme also collapsed because of the conflicting interests and suspicions of its members. By November 1744, Carteret had also been removed from the scene. Nevertheless, Britain's financial and naval power focused French attention on her as the true national enemy. In September 1743, France declared war on Britain, thus ending the fiction of Britain's participation in the conflict as an auxiliary. Two forms of attack were contemplated. First was an invasion of England itself with a force commanded by Maurice de Saxe, an endeavor that was shelved when storms wrecked both the French and the British fleets. The second approach was to invade the Austrian Netherlands. In 1744 the king accompanied Saxe on a campaign that secured the surrender of demoralized Dutch garrisons in the barrier fortresses of Furnes, Menin, and Ypres, while the Pragmatic army stood by ineffectively. Only an Austrian invasion of Alsace and a serious illness suffered by the king delayed the French advance.

Louis recovered, but his inclination for hands-on statesmanship did not. In November 1744 he appointed the marquis d'Argenson minister of foreign affairs and returned to his life of ease and pleasure. Argenson has puzzled most historians. Many see him as even less qualified for the post than the king himself. Reed Browning describes him as a visionary utopian, a Wilsonian idealist lost in a maze of eighteenth-century realism.[8] Perhaps it is better to see him as Abbé de Saint-Pierre's statesman in action, one who sought to use France's military power to secure a lasting peace. He took the position that France was a disinterested power and an honest broker. However, he proved unable to define military priorities and to supply the energy and direction required of a war leader. France was fortunate only in the commander of its army in Flanders.

Saxe's advance to Fontenoy brought a prompt response from the allied army. The ineffective commander of the previous year, Field Marshal Wade, a notable road builder, had been replaced by the more-energetic Cumberland.[9] Cumberland had accompanied his father at Dettingen and had been wounded in action but possessed no experience in high command. He remains a controversial figure. To his credit, he took his responsibilities seriously and was devoted to increasing professionalism within the army. There is no doubt that he was personally brave and capable of generous gestures. That he was chosen for command is another reminder of the close connection between the monarchy and military affairs. He was the king's surrogate and brought to the army the inspiration that only a monarch could provide. He was no Marlborough, but the army had no Marlborough waiting in the wings. His rank assured him first place among allied generals, and he brought to his command the energy and decisiveness lacking under the dilatory Wade. As Saxe would prove, Cumberland's aggressiveness could be used against him, yet he had reason for confidence as he marched to the relief of Tournai. He knew history as well as did Louis XV, and he commanded the best troops. Cumberland's subsequent career has cast a cloud over his reputation. He was consistently outmaneuvered in the Flanders campaigns by Saxe, who thereby proved to be one of the great generals of the century. Cumberland's only battlefield victory was gained against the Jacobite army at Culloden Moor,

Scotland, in 1746. His performance on that occasion was coolly professional, but the subsequent brutal aftermath blackened his name. The savage repression of the Scottish Highlands was a government policy, but Cumberland has forever carried the burden of responsibility. He earned thereby the sobriquet "Butcher." In an age in which honor and reputation were all, this was a heavy price to pay. All of this was ahead of him on the eve of Fontenoy, but on that day at least would be no blot on his honor.

The presence of the king, princes of the blood, and rival generals complicated the command of the French army, but at least it was a unified national army. Cumberland's army was a coalition force fraught with all the dangers of conflicting procedures and goals. The British-Hanoverian element was the largest contingent, and the British could expect to appoint the commander. A general of royal lineage was an advantage among coalition partners jealous of their own privileges and claims to precedence. The Dutch Republic furnished the next largest contingent, about 20,000 men, led by the young, inexperienced, and enthusiastic prince of Waldeck. He was advised by an uninspiring group of senior officers. The cavalry officer Brigadier Schlippenbach left a scathing criticism of the four major generals of the Dutch cavalry. One, 78 years old, could scarcely mount his horse; another was forced to lead his men from a carriage especially made for his great paunch; a third was melancholy and often imbecilic; and the fourth was often sick.[10] On paper the Dutch army was large, reaching 65,000 men at its highest point. But it was a shadow of the great forces deployed in previous centuries. It was a garrison rather than a field army, without the military spirit so valued by military commentators. The Republic had little enthusiasm for this war. Indeed, it had refused to declare war on France and participated as a reluctant auxiliary in order to uphold the Pragmatic Sanction. The Austrians furnished a small mounted force, recruited from the Austrian Netherlands. Some of Austria's best soldiers came from that region, but the Austrian government saw the defense of the Netherlands as more important to British and Dutch interests than to their own. They were content to let the allies bear the primary burden while they concentrated on the defense of Austrian core lands. The Austrians were led by the elderly and experienced Count Konigsegg, but their commitment was too small to allow him to serve as a break to the youthful Cumberland's impetuosity.

The two armies were evenly balanced in numbers, between 50,000 and 60,000 each. David Chandler credits the French with 60,000 men in 69 battalions and 119 squadrons (the basic battle organizations for infantry and cavalry) and 70 field guns; the allies with 50,000 in 51 battalions, 90 squadrons, and 101 guns.[11] Saxe had to maintain additional forces for the investment of Tournai and its 8,000 Dutch troops. Everything depended on how these forces were used. The allies, for example, failed to take advantage of their numerical superiority in artillery. The ultimate French victory would owe much to the skillful deployment of the French field artillery in fighting a defensive action. In quality both armies were uneven. Saxe had some of the best regulars in the French army but also battalions of militia. Many of his general officers were unreliable. It was one thing to devise a good plan as Noailles had done at Dettingen. It was another thing to see that it was carried out. Indeed, on the day of Fontenoy, some noble officers were forbidden to give orders. Saxe did attract some officers of high ability and experience, most notably his chief lieutenant, the Danish professional Count Lowendahl. Senior officers attached to the king as aides-de-camp, particularly Noailles and the duke of Richelieu (grandnephew of the great Cardinal Richelieu), might have made for a divided command, but on the whole they played a constructive role.

In 1743 the king had expressed reluctance to give Saxe independent command in Alsace, even though he was the best available commander, because of his vaulting ambition and uncertain loyalties.[12] Louis's greatest contribution to his victory at Fontenoy was to place full confidence in his military commander. On the evening before the battle, recalled one officer, three-quarters of the army were persuaded that Saxe had chosen the wrong position and that the enemy would attack their left, seize the bridges on the lower Scheldt, and capture the siege works at Tournai. The king put an end to this clamor, saying to Saxe: "Monsieur Marshal, in confiding to you the command of my army, I have intended that everyone should obey you; I shall be the first to give an example of such obedience."[13] Perhaps the worst threat to Saxe's exercise of command was his health. He suffered from dropsy and had twice undergone surgical procedures to relieve the fluid. He was forced to resort to a litter in the days preceding the battle and endured intense pain. Saxe was not one to yield to physical infirmities, however. He remained a high liver and brought with him to the front a carriage filled with women described as actresses, or *putains*. His physician Senac prescribed chastity as a remedy and stood guard over the marshal's tent at night to enforce it. But in every other way it was clear who commanded the army.

As was the custom with young commanders who owed their position to high rank, Cumberland was provided with experienced veteran advisers, most prominent of whom was Lord Ligonier. It seems clear, however, that the key decisions on the allied side were made by Cumberland, sometimes against the strong advice of his subordinates. For all of his faults, the duke did not run his army by committee. He was Saxe's equal in energy, bravery, and decisiveness. But he was no match for his opponent's intellect, which had been shaped by long years of experience and reflection. As Voltaire observed, Saxe "joined profound theory with practice. Vigilance, secrecy, prudence, and foresight were his talents."[14] Cumberland's instincts were those of a good battalion commander, "to march towards the sound of the guns." Saxe was a true commander in chief, able to grasp the entire situation and to plan ahead. He possessed that rare quality known in the eighteenth century as coup d'oeil. In short, Cumberland was about to be taught lessons of command by one of the era's truly great generals.

Once Cumberland decided to march to the relief of Tournai, Saxe was forced to prepare for battle. The allies had the option of attempting to raise the siege by maneuvering against the French communications. A prudent commander might have chosen this course, but as Saxe's aide, the baron de Espagnac, recalled, "The ardent courage of the Duke of Cumberland and the great confidence of the English resisted such council."[15] However, as long as he was committed to protecting the besiegers of Tournai, Saxe knew, Cumberland could force a battle on him. He chose a defensive battle, one in which he could gain the maximum advantages from his position. The deliberate pace at which the allied army approached allowed the French time to thoroughly survey the countryside, to predict Cumberland's line of advance, and to sight their positions accordingly. Cumberland does not seem to have been in a hurry, for he thought that the French would withdraw on his approach.[16] Crossing to the eastern bank of the Scheldt by pontoon bridges, Saxe deployed across Cumberland's line of advance about two miles from Tournai. On the left of his position was the wood of Barri, and on his right the small farm village of Fontenoy, from which the ensuing battle drew its name. From Fontenoy the French right-angled back to the village of Antoing on the Scheldt. Between the wood of Barri and Fontenoy, astride the road to Tournai, was a gap of about one-half mile, and perhaps a mile separated Fontenoy from Antoing. The center of this position was unobstructed by woods or buildings and allowed free movement for French troops, particularly the cavalry, of which they possessed superior numbers. As Jean Colin observed, this represented both a strength and a weakness, for, if the position were penetrated, the French army might be thrown back into the river at its rear.[17]

Saxe's dispositions appear as if he had been planning them for years. He shared Noailles's concern that the French were not the equals of the British infantry and planned a battle that would compensate for that weakness. Two battles of 1709, Malplaquet and Poltava, appear to have influenced his plans on this occasion. Saxe had been present at Malplaquet, where the French marshal Villars had posted his army in trenches between two woods. In his usual style, Marlborough had attacked the two flanks in order to weaken the center that was to be in turn the target of his main thrust. The Dutch Guards assaulting the French right were massacred by French artillery, something the Dutch still remembered at Fontenoy, but British troops forced the wood on the left and Villars was driven from his trenches. Saxe believed that a trench once penetrated was a death trap for its defenders, and his dispositions were aimed at avoiding a repetition of

Figure 4.1
Battle of Fontenoy, May 11, 1745

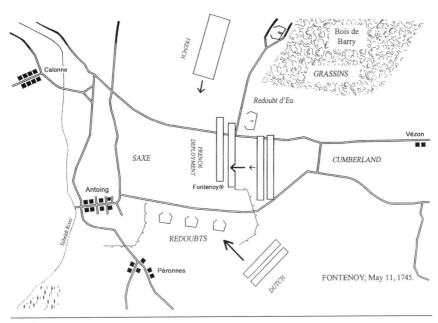

Adapted from R. Weigley, *The Age of Battles* (Bloomington: Indiana University Press, 1991).

Malplaquet. His defense featured three key elements. First, he occupied the wood of Barri with a specialized partisan regiment, the Grassins, trained in loose order and marksmanship, the kind of soldiers he had envisaged in his *Reveries*. Second, eschewing trenches, he employed a series of redoubts, small self-contained field fortifications of earth and timber containing artillery and infantry. This was the kind of field fortifications that had absorbed the fury of the Swedish charge at Poltava. Two redoubts were on the left, one of which—the redoubt d'Eu, occupied by two battalions and eight guns—was at the edge of the wood at the Barri-Fontenoy gap. Behind the wood of Barri was a strong force of infantry protected by an abatis. Fontenoy itself was demolished and fortified with batteries containing six guns. The one-mile gap between Fontenoy and Antoing was protected by three redoubts and infantry posted in a sunken road. Antoing was heavily fortified and covered by heavy siege guns planted on the far side of the river. Independent redoubts offered the opportunity of drawing the enemy into a cross fire. Saxe took full advantage by disposing his artillery to sweep the gaps between the fortifications. The majority of the heavy guns were allotted to the field fortifications with only the light "Swedish guns," probably four-pounders, available to maneuver with the troops. However, twelve guns were held in reserve. The author David Chandler commented, "This creation of an artillery reserve was practically unique at the period and really foreshadows Napoleonic practice—and equally notable was the degree of care Saxe took in selecting his battery positions. Not since the days of Marlborough had a commander-in-chief taken such pains based on careful thought and study of the ground."[18]

Among the allies, only Konigsegg seems to have counseled against an attack on this position. Cumberland did not rely on finesse. He intended to follow Marlborough's favored tactical plan by breaking through the enemy center. Informed that enemy troops were in the wood to the right, he ordered a brigade to clear it in preparation for the general advance. The Dutch corps was given the assignment of capturing Fontenoy itself. Once the flanks were secured the main thrust would take place. Colin observes that the plan was deeply flawed because insufficient forces were allocated to attack the two strongest positions in the French lines. This was partly due to a faulty reconnaissance conducted by the allied commanders on the previous day and to their failure to understand the strength of the French position on their right.

The allies assembled at 2:00 A.M., an hour before sunrise. Heavy fog obscured their movements, but by 5:00 A.M. they found themselves under artillery fire. The allied plan quickly began to unravel. Brigadier Ingolsby and the troops responsible for clearing the wood were pinned down by musketry from the Grassins and cannon fire from the redoubt d'Eu. Despite repeated orders from Cumberland to attack the redoubt, Ingolsby accomplished nothing. Uncertain of the number of the Grassins hovering in the woods and under heavy cannon fire, his men cowered in a sunken road. The commander of the British cavalry in the center responsible for covering the assembly of the infantry was killed by a cannon shot, and his men were left under fire without orders. It took some time for the allies to bring up guns to reply to the bombardment. The British artillery succeeded in killing the duke of Grammont, the officer responsible for the French debacle at Dettingen. It is unclear which side was most favored by this lucky shot. The allied failure to properly use their artillery was most evident in the assault on Fontenoy. Here there was no artillery preparation at all, and the Dutch twice failed in attacks on the village. Had they been able to penetrate the gap between Fontenoy and Antoing, the Dutch would have won the day. But they were stopped by crossfire from the redoubts. One cavalry regiment broke in panic and the attack failed ingloriously.[19]

By 10:00 A.M. the situation no longer resembled a battle directed by Marlborough. The duke had used attacks on the flanks to weaken the center for a final blow. In this case, the French flank positions were intact and the bulk of their army had yet to be engaged. A prudent commander might have paused to consider alternatives. But Cumberland now ordered the British and Hanoverian infantry to advance through the Barri-Fontenoy gap. Compounding this fateful decision, and against the urgings of his senior commanders, he joined his lieutenant general Ligonier at their head. In doing so, he not only placed at risk a royal life but abdicated his role as commander in chief. No one on the allied side remained in overall control, and thus it is not surprising that the Anglo-Hanoverians were left to themselves. Cumberland was determined to share his soldiers' risk and inspire them by his presence. His bravery was praised throughout the army. Cornet Philip Brown wrote shortly after the battle that "his Highness the Duke was never excelled by any Hero whatever. He exposed his person every where the same time as the most private soldier, this is no Compliment to his High Birth but a fact to my own eyes and certain knowledge which ought to endear him to the whole Nation—But Success is not always to the Valiant and Brave."[20]

Cumberland was known as a severe disciplinarian of the German school, but his bravery won him the respect and loyalty of his troops. He could be said to have fulfilled the code of honor discussed in chapter 3. Cumberland was not the only commander at Fontenoy whose judgment was clouded by a desire for glory. The sixteen-year-old dauphin is said to have twice demanded to charge the enemy at the head of his household troops.[21] At the climax of the battle, a number of French lieutenant generals deserted their commands to charge with the cavalry. Saxe, who knew that these young men had more breeding than sense, kept them on a short leash and gave them little opportunity to give orders on their own. When at one point in the battle it was suggested to the comte d'Eu, a prince of the blood, that it would be a good idea to charge the enemy, he replied that he agreed but could not give orders to the cavalry.[22] However, Cumberland was not a lieutenant general, but commander in chief, a fatal difference.

Following the repulse of the Dutch attack, an officer complimented Saxe on his success. "All is not said," replied the marshal. "Now we come to the English and they will be harder on the digestion."[23] Saxe who, ill and listless, had been carried to and fro in a wicker chariot, now roused himself to an extraordinary effort. At the height of the battle his officers were surprised to find him on horseback exercising a firm grip over developments. Indeed, at Fontenoy he appears to have exercised a mastery of command and control that was unusual in an eighteenth-century army. According to the fine distinctions drawn by military writers of the time, Cumberland displayed bravery, but Saxe courage.

Now began one of the extraordinary episodes in the history of the British army. Drawn up in two lines, the infantry advanced at a slow parade-ground pace through the Barri-Fontenoy gap. They were enfiladed by artillery fire from the French strongholds on the flanks and suffered from sniping by the Grassins. The narrowness of the front and the enfilading fire caused some battalions to bend back to face the flanks. The Anglo-Hanoverians thus began to form a hollow square or oblong, an act that appears to have been forced on them by necessity rather than as the result of a preconceived plan. There is no evidence that Cumberland was a student of Folard (as Saxe certainly was), and any resemblance between the British formation and the latter's famous column was coincidental.[24] The British infantry advanced up a gently rising slope until they came to a sunken road. There the French Guards, deployed in four ranks, waited to receive them.

THE CHALLENGE

According to Voltaire: "They were at a distance of fifty paces.... The English officers saluted the French by raising their hats. The Count de Chabones [sic], the Duke de Biron who were in the front and all the officers of the French Guards returned the salute. Lord Charles Hay, Captain of the English Guards, cried 'Gentlemen of the French Guards, fire.'

"Count d'Auteroche, then lieutenant and later captain of the Grenadiers, replied 'Gentlemen, we never fire first, open fire yourselves.' The English commenced a rolling fire, that is, they fired by divisions, so that one battalion in four ranks having fired, another battalion made its discharge, and then a third, while the first recharged their weapons. The line of French infantry had not fired; it was alone in four ranks, the line rather elongated and not sustained by any other force of infantry. Nineteen officers of the guards fell stricken at that single discharge....The first rank having been thrown into confusion, the three others looking to their rear and seeing only cavalry at three hundred toises [about 150 yards], they fled."[25]

But did it really happen this way? Voltaire had many friends in the French army, the most important of whom was the duke of Richelieu, who Voltaire credited with having rallied the French at a critical moment. Count d'Argenson, the secretary of war, provided Voltaire with all of the officers' letters; he also received material from Saxe and Noailles. Another close friend, the marquis d'Argenson, the foreign minister and older brother of the war secretary, was present at the battle and wrote him a detailed account four days after the battle. Argenson did not mention the famous challenge.[26] Even so, Voltaire's published account became the standard source for the events described above. Francis Henry Skrine, author of a standard twentieth-century history of the battle, dismissed Voltaire's narrative as a legend aimed at furthering his interests at court. Relying on a letter written three weeks after the battle by Lord Charles Hay to his brother, the marquis of Tweedale, Skrine expanded on the British officer's role. Hay stepped to the front of his battalion and saluted with his hat. Then he took out a pocket flask and drank their health, shouting, "We are the English Guards, and we hope that you will stand till we come up to you, and not swim the Scheldt as you did the Main at Dettingen!" He then turned and called for three cheers that were given with a will. The French officers, claimed Hay, were dumbfounded by his gesture. Biron, Auteroche, and others returned the salute and called for cheers, which were given with little enthusiasm. Then the French fired.[27]

Hay was not as polite as the British officers in Voltaire's account. Perhaps that gives him more credibility. He was an eccentric and unstable personality. In 1757, while serving on Loudon's staff in North America, he continually engaged in disruptive outbursts that made it difficult to carry on business. Eventually he was arrested, placed in confinement, and sent home.[28] It would appear that he was mentally disturbed. There is no reason to prefer the account of this bizarre individual to that provided by Voltaire. Perhaps there was no exchange of salutes at all. *The Gentleman's Magazine,* a periodical with good army sources, published an account of the battle in its May 1745 issue: "We advanced nevertheless to the Enemy, and receiv'd their Discharge at the Distance of thirty Paces before we fired."[29] The French historian Eric de Saint Denis notes that the dialogue is perhaps the only aspect of the battle retained in the national memory. He believes that it is unlikely that Voltaire made it up but finds it difficult to authenticate. He cites two other accounts that do not appear to provide definitive confirmation and concludes that the context of eighteenth-century military courtesy provides the best argument for the veracity of Voltaire's account.[30]

The marquis de Valfons recalled that as the British closed to within 300 paces from the French Guards, he turned to their captain, La Peyre, and said, "These men that I bring to you will pass their time badly for they will find the man of Rechswag," a memorable military exploit on the part of that officer. "He thanked me for my recollection and my politeness. These compliments—they are useful to everyone. They give an air of sang-froid to the one who makes them and augment the confidence of the one who receives them. Then the English gave their war cry: House! House!" Valfons confirms the spirit if not the fact of the dialogue: "An air of ease and of gaiety is useful in all of these adventures."[31] It is best to see in these dialogues, real or imagined, a manifestation of the military spirit prized by writers of the period.

Cheers and gasconades were a way of fortifying the spirit in the face of death. But there remains disagreement over who fired first. This is interesting in itself, for no eighteenth-century exchange has been so intensely scrutinized. Voltaire's account was stylized. "The [British] corps advances, always compact, always solid."[32] It appears to be a machine moving forward impervious to sound of cannon and musketry, the shriek of missiles, and the screams of men whose limbs were severed or who were disemboweled. The allied army had endured a hard march to the rescue of Tournai. The men had been under fire for five hours before they began their advance through billows of black-powder smoke. That they persevered under these conditions is remarkable and says much for their training and the leadership of long-service company officers and noncommissioned officers (NCOs). One wonders if the infantry was able to maintain the famous platoon fire (inaccurately referred to as rolling fire by Voltaire). If musket fire was as ineffective as is often suggested, how did they rout the French Guards so easily? It has been suggested that the French Guards were not the elite troops one would expect from their name; they were recruited from urban workers and journeymen who lacked soldierly qualities and were addicted to wine and every other vice.[33] It was reported that Saxe had ordered the Guards not to fire first because they would be left defenseless and demoralized before an enemy whose muskets were loaded. Noailles had ordered them to hold their fire at Dettingen but to no avail. French discipline was recognized as inferior to that of the British, and some may have fired without orders. At Fontenoy the same failure seems to have occurred. The French practice of four ranks may have reduced the effectiveness if they did fire first, because the rear rank could not see the target. Perhaps we are misled by the image of ranks of men standing and firing at one another at almost point-blank range.

After Dettingen, Lt. Colonel Charles Russell wrote to his wife that the British had made an irregular running fire, not "Hide Park firing," a reference to the precision drills displayed to the public in peacetime. The enemy dropped to the ground while waiting to receive fire, and the British waited for them to stand up again before firing. He recalled that the French had conducted a similar irregular running fire. Russell's commander, the earl of Stair, a veteran of Marlborough's wars, commented that he had seen many a battle and had never seen infantry engage in any other manner."[34] The nature of the action at Fontenoy makes it unlikely that the British infantry maintained parade-ground precision for long and suggests that they engaged in irregular firing. Skrine tells us that whole ranks were swept away by cannon fire. The soldiers were trained to close up, but surely this would have been difficult to carry out over the bodies of their dead and wounded comrades, who eventually numbered 6,000. The stricken men would have made it difficult for the troops to maneuver but were a source of ammunition, as the ensuing firefights would have exhausted an infantryman's standard supply of cartridges. The fallen British soldiers were a grim source of supply for those still fighting. The French also experienced ammunition shortages, particularly when the guns at the village of Fontenoy were reduced to firing blank charges. Voltaire's portrait of the battle resembles the battlefield paintings of the era that sought to provide viewers with an accurate, if romanticized, picture of events. Missing are the chaos, confusion, and the uncertainty that contributed to Carl von Clausewitz's concept of the friction of war.

But this was Voltaire's battle as well as Saxe's. The latter laid the plans and led his army to victory. Voltaire created a version of it for the historical memory. He had many agendas. Despite his hatred of war, he glorified the French in their victory. The French military historian Émile Léonard acidly observed that Voltaire's antimilitarism varied according to circumstances and always followed public opinion. He scorned the private soldiers, but eagerly sought the friendship of the generals.[35] Shortly after the battle, Voltaire whipped out his *Poème de Fontenoy*. Published on May 17, 1745, it sold a remarkable 20,000 copies. Skrine describes it as a rhymed bulletin, eagerly snapped up by those hungry for news. The poem celebrates the sacrifices of the French nobility and the heroism of his friends. Above all it credits Louis XV with the victory. Voltaire dedicated the poem to the king "as an authentic monument of all the glorious deeds performed in your presence in imitation of your own." Argenson recalled that at one moment in the battle the dauphin had drawn his sword but was prevailed upon to desist. Voltaire caught the drama of the event, for his readers at least:

> His son, his only hope...Ah! Dear prince, stop;
> Why do you draw your sword so hastily?
> Conserve that life so precious to the world.
> Louis fears for his son, the son fears for his father.
> Our bloodstained warriors fear for both,
> Dismay stirs the generous hearts of you who guard my king,
> You who avenge France,
> You, people of heroes, on whom the enemy advance,
> March! You will determine destiny,
> Louis, his son, the State, Europe
> Are in your hands.[36]

All this because the dauphin drew his sword! Overblown as Voltaire's language appears, it reminds us of the significance of the king's presence. Furthermore, Voltaire demonstrated a journalist's shrewd instinct in tapping the public's reverence for the monarchy. He basked in the reflected glow of the victory and sought to please those in high circles. The king was the embodiment of honor. The English might speak of courage,

> But they speak in vain; when Louis advances
> Their spirit is tamed, the English are overthrown,
> And ferocity gives way to virtue.[37]

There were reports that some British soldiers had shouted "no quarter!" as they had advanced. Against them Louis had marshaled true courage. Voltaire's readers would have understood the distinction between British bravery and French courage. His preliminary discourse to the poem struck another familiar theme: the civilized manner in which war was conducted among European people. "The peoples of Europe have principles of humanity not found in the rest of the world.... The European Christians are like the Greeks: they wage war among themselves, but retain in their disputes much of the decorum and common politeness that a Frenchman, an Englishmen, or a German, on meeting one another might think themselves to have been born in the same city."[38] Thus Voltaire's Fontenoy became celebrated as an ideal battle of the Old Regime, fought by men of honor, inspired by the presence of royalty, and bound even in the heat of action by civility and humanity. It was, in short, a battle of enlightened knights. But this was not the real battle. Argenson, whose letter contributed to Voltaire's version of the battle, was closer to reality when he wrote: "Certainly the artillery had the honour of this terrible slaughter."[39]

THE HONOR OF THE SLAUGHTER

When the French Guards gave way before the British advance, a crisis gripped the French army. The British plan now appeared to have succeeded. One would have expected a second line of French infantry to have been drawn up in support of the French Guards, but they fled into a vacuum. Chabannes, who commanded in the center, had dispatched the troops of the second line to support those defending Fontenoy. Cumberland had thus partially succeeded in replicating the Marlborough tactic of weakening the center by attacks on the flanks of the French position.[40] Now it appeared that the front had been ruptured and that the French might be driven into the Scheldt. Ligonier believed that the day was won for the British.[41] Panic gripped the king's headquarters. Earlier in the day, the king had laughed when splashed by mud from a cannonball, but now the mood had changed. Noailles and others feared for the king's safety and urged that he retire across the Scheldt. A cruel jest later circulated in Paris that during the battle the brave duc de Biron required three changes of horses, the feverish Maurice de Saxe three changes of shirts, and Noailles three changes of breeches.[42] Saxe recognized that the king's departure would spread panic throughout the army and initiate a rout. Fortunately, at this moment the duke of Richelieu arrived from a reconnaissance of the British force. Argenson referred to him as the Bayard of the army. He presented himself sword in hand, out of breath, and covered in gunpowder. According to Voltaire, Noailles asked him for his news and for his advice. Richelieu replied that the battle was won if they had the will. His advice was to concentrate four guns against the head of the British column and, while the artillery bombarded the enemy, to throw the *maison du roi* (household troops) and all the other available troops against them and attack like marauders.[43] Richelieu seems to have stiffened the king's resolve, and he remained at his post.

Although the king does not deserve credit for the ensuing victory, he could have lost the battle if he had fled.

Richelieu was not the only one who recognized that the British were in serious difficulty. Despite exhaustion and pain, Saxe roused himself to action and was encouraged when Lowendahl, in command of the reserve, arrived to congratulate him on the situation. Cumberland had staked all on one throw and had almost succeeded. Now the British infantry were deep in the French position but under cannon fire from the front, flanks, and rear. According to Ligonier's biographer, they withdrew under this fire to the line of the Fontenoy-Barri gap, reformed and again penetrated the French camp. There they are said to have formed a square, though this may have been true of only a portion of the corps.[44] The British might have intended to attack Fontenoy from the rear with a portion of the troops. It is unclear whether this was the result of an order on the part of Cumberland or Ligonier or a reaction among the troops to an attack from all sides. The conscious formation of square, a defensive formation, would indicate that the assault had come to an end. Were this deployment conceived of as a column, it would mean that the British intended to remain on the offensive. There may have been no decision at all, and the British troops may have huddled together to seek safety from the storm that broke upon them.

The British deployment later aroused much interest among military thinkers. Saxe gave the following account to his mentor Folard:

Let us speak a little of the column to which you always return. Chance produced that which the English made at the battle of Fontenoy; they attacked us by lines, but as their center encountered great resistance at the village of Fontenoy, their right attacked the brigade of guards whom they scattered, and then sought to effect a 90 degree turn to the left to take the village of Fontenoy from the flank and the rear. I attacked these two lines of infantry by several charges of cavalry that I reiterated for three hours to prevent them from achieving their objective; since they had occupied the field where the brigade of guards had been posted, these two lines presented us their flank, which everyone has called a column; and in order to protect this flank, they stationed a battalion or two across it, which formed a long square. I held them in that position until it was possible to reassemble the brigades of infantry that were upon my left, to attack that infantry and to make an effort on all sides of the square at the same time, and that decided the outcome of the battle. You well understand that, if I had allowed them to take the village of Fontenoy by the flank, the outcome of our affair would have become equivocal; there is the fact of the matter, and we leave there the column of Epaminondas and those of everyone else; you know my affection for you.[45]

Folard took a keen interest in the British deployment and as a result modified his tactical scheme to allow for a hedgehog of three columns with sufficient space between them for the movement of cavalry and artillery.[46] A later advocate of the column, Baron Mesnil-Durand, dismissed the idea that the British deployment was a true test. The so-called column lacked the mobility and energy offered by his "plesions," which would not have suffered, he maintained, the same fate. He believed that Fontenoy had provided a false lesson for military specialists. "That action contributed greatly to that rapture for artillery that began then and has only grown since."[47]

Their formation, however it may be termed, protected the British from the vigorous but poorly coordinated French cavalry attacks, but it offered a rich target to the French artillery. The British had no artillery support of their own. Skrine indicates that the British infantry were accompanied in their advance by 12 six-pound cannons, but they appear to have played no role. Such heavy field guns were difficult to move, and their horse teams were vulnerable to enemy fire. The gun crews were compelled to manhandle them forward. Perhaps this explains the deliberate nature of the British advance. However, when the British were forced into their defensive formation, which Skrine described as a hollow square, the guns remained in the center and were useless.[48] They were left behind when the infantry began its retreat. The cavalry, the arm on which Marlborough had relied to deliver the coup de grâce in his victories, were nowhere to be seen. They were unable to maneuver through the narrow Fontenoy-Barri gap, their way blocked by French fire and by their own infantry. Nor was there anyone to give them orders, for the commander in chief, as we have seen, had conceded his ability to exercise command and control when he went forward with the infantry. Thus the cavalry, the artillery, and the allies stood by while the French concentrated on the Anglo-Hanoverian infantry. Saxe struggled to bring the full combination of French arms to bear upon the British.

Saxe had prepared the way for victory by the excellence of his dispositions and now, to use Richelieu's expression, he summoned the will to win the day. The French Guards had uncovered the vital center, but they provided only a portion of the army. Other troops were at hand. First, there was the cavalry, including the *maison du roi*, which was thrown against the allied infantry. These attacks were poorly coordinated and made no impression on the British-Hanoverians, who remained in close order and whose fighting spirit was unchecked. Nevertheless, this sacrifice bought time and by forcing the British into close order exposed them to artillery fire.[49] Second, Saxe had posted a strong infantry force of Corsicans, Irish, and Swiss (a reminder of the role that foreign mercenaries continued to play in the French army) behind the wood of Barri as insurance against an enemy breakthrough on the left flank. Lowendahl, assuming command of these troops to which he added the Brigade of Normandy, brought them against the British right.

The French artillery at this time conformed to the Valliére system of heavy guns; these appear to have been positioned in the fortified areas and on the far side of the river. However, half of Saxe's artillery consisted of light four-pound Swedish guns, so called after the mobile field guns introduced in the seventeenth century by Gustavus Adolphus as infantry support weapons. Saxe had called for light artillery (*amusettes*) in his *Reveries*, and the Swedish guns seem to have been a realization of that vision. Heavy artillery, firing solid shot from fixed positions, was ideally situated to enfilade the British infantry. Solid shot was most effective if fired obliquely and allowed to bounce along the enemy line. The Swedish guns enabled Saxe to rush cannon to a critical point and engage the enemy at close quarters. These guns would have employed grapeshot, bags of musket balls, or scrap iron, having the effect of a large shotgun. Against massed troops, grapeshot wreaked deadly slaughter. A Dutch officer seeking to explain the failure of the attack on the left wing reported that as they reached the enemy trench they "were taken in the flank and attacked by a battery of twenty-five large battering pieces, which were planted in a wood and which discharged chain shot [cannonballs linked by chains] and partridge [grapeshot] so violently, that we were forced to cause our troops to fall back upon those advancing to sustain us."[50] (No such battery seems to have existed.) The Dutch lieutenant general Aylva also reported the use of grapeshot by the enemy.[51] Grapeshot was a controversial ammunition, and some legal authorities declared its use to be a violation of the laws of war. After the battle of Fontenoy, Cumberland ordered the collection of all of the grapeshot and irregular metal found in wounds as evidence that the French had violated the laws of war.[52] (On the other hand, Cumberland did not hesitate to employ grapeshot against Scottish rebels at Culloden in 1746.)[53] In eighteenth-century warfare, the attempt to regulate the destructiveness of weapons often broke down, even in battles between regulars. The restrictions were seldom observed when irregulars were the target.

The volume of French artillery fire now became irresistible, and Saxe ordered every available infantry regiment forward. The British now experienced their own moment of crisis. Once again we are told that their withdrawal was as calm and orderly as their advance. Indeed, the retreat became as celebrated as the attack. It is true that Cumberland and many of his troops reached their own lines, but they left 6,000 out of 15,000 killed and wounded. Although Voltaire claimed that French care for the allied wounded was exceptionally humane, even the best intentions would have failed to compensate for the deficiencies of the medical services. We can assume that many wounded were left to suffer where they fell. Although there was no rout, we must presume that discipline began to give way as the soldiers sought safety. Nevertheless, their retreat salvaged British honor. There seems to have been agreement that British courage had been overcome by the power of the French guns. Konigsegg praised the bravery of the allied infantry, which had been overwhelmed by enemy fire.[54] Contributors to *The Gentleman's Magazine* sought to find a moral victory in the midst of defeat. The true heroes of Fontenoy, claimed one writer, were the British common soldiers: "Where has the English history a nobler account of the strength and bravery of the common soldier?"[55] An excerpt from the *Westminster Journal* titled "The true British military spirit encourag'd" found that "the courage of our men was indeed sufficiently exhibited now, as at Dettingen, by standing the charge of a large train of artillery, without anything to oppose it."[56] The Dutch officer quoted above concluded that "if we had only fought against men, I can assure you that the siege of Tournay would have been quickly rais'd and that there would not have escap'd a third part of the French army, which, as we were eye witnesses, is composed of very contemptible people; but we fought against 266 pieces of cannon [an exaggeration] as well battering as field."[57] Aylva reported that "the Anglish and part of the Hanoverians attacked so furiously that they merit universal esteem, and the French could not have gained the battle or claimed any bravery, but solely by the infinite number of their artillery which massacred so many of us."[58] In *The True Patriot*, Henry Fielding scorned the conduct of the French who, he wrote, "have always fled before us, and who at Fontenoy run from our Forces (tho' they were but a third of their Number) till their Cannon gave them a dishonourable Victory; if they could be said to obtain any, over an Army which retreated in Order from the Attack, and which they did not pursue."[59] These comments were a rationalization of the defeat, but they are consistent in their contention that there was something dishonorable in a French victory that relied on technology in the form of artillery. There had been courage in abundance, but it was not enough.

Fontenoy was a turning point in many ways. On the British side, it is interesting that the common soldiers conducted themselves with honor. Cumberland, whose decisions contributed directly to the defeat, was shielded from blame because he had shared the danger with his men. Curiously, Saxe credited the attacks of his infantry from the left for his victory. He did not mention the role of the artillery. Perhaps it was indeed Richelieu or Captain Isnard who thought of the four guns that might be deployed at the critical moment, or perhaps Saxe did not believe that their deployment was significant. Perhaps he too believed that there was something dishonorable about winning a battle with artillery and preferred to give the credit to French bravery rather than to round and grapeshot. If that was the case, it was ironic that he had inaugurated a new era in warfare in which artillery would rule the battlefield. The way was open to the slaughterhouse that was the Seven Years' War.

The retreat was secured by the exhaustion of the French army, which had itself been on the verge of defeat. The king found Saxe writhing in agony on the ground. He had summoned every ounce of energy to save the day and could do no more. The French cavalry was in no condition to pursue the enemy, whose own cavalry now moved forward to cover the retreat. Allied reserve infantry and the hitherto-useless artillery provided insurance against a French pursuit. But Tournai remained securely in the French grip.

RESULTS

Estimates of casualties vary. David Chandler, who provides statistics for all major eighteenth-century battles, cites 12,000 allied casualties (including 3,000 prisoners) and 6,000 French casualties. Browning indicates that both sides suffered losses of 7,000-7,500.[60] Saxe said to the king after the battle: "Sire, now you see what war really means."[61] Séchelles, the dauphin's tutor, observed that the latter was fortunate to see for himself, at his age, to what he owed his kingdom." A senior officer seems to have been in shock: "This terrible spectacle scarcely had any effect in its first moments. I walked about and informed myself about my friends, and I saw a great number dying, with a calm that has astonished me."[62] The allies acknowledged the French victory by abandoning their attempt to succor Tournai. That city fell on June 19, followed by the collapse of the Dutch barrier in western Flanders, including the fortified cities of Ghent, Oudenaarde, Bruges, Dendermonde, Ostend, and Nieuport. This phenomenon places the role of fortresses in their proper context. Along with the battle fleet, fortresses were the greatest technological, capital-intensive, military projects of the era. But their usefulness depended on many factors. The barrier fortresses were in an alien country. The Habsburg state considered the Netherlands as marginal to its interests and contributed little to its defense. There was little enthusiasm for the Dutch garrisons in the Catholic barrier cities, and commanders could not depend on support from the inhabitants. Poor morale and underfinancing undermined the foundation of the Dutch defense system. The barrier depended on the existence of a powerful field army; the Dutch, perhaps, would have done better to invest in one rather than in isolated, ineffective garrisons. But the politics and the defensive inclinations of a republic in decline obviated such a policy. The Dutch defense system really was one of hope: hope that the French would not come and that Britain would protect them if they did. Fontenoy and its aftermath were the result.

Saxe was far from finished. His victory not only delivered western Flanders into French hands but cleared the way for the Jacobite rising in Scotland that required the recall of Cumberland and British troops for home defense. By the end of 1746, Brussels, Antwerp, Mons, Charleroi, and Namur were in French hands, a conquest assured by Saxe's victory over an allied army at Raucoux in October. Saxe defeated the unfortunate Cumberland again at Lauffeld in 1747 despite a hard-fought defense by the British infantry. On this occasion Cumberland displayed the same failures as a commander as those revealed at Fontenoy. Much of the allied army stood by, while the British infantry made their stand. Cumberland was nearly captured while attempting to rally the fleeing Dutch cavalry. Saxe also was nearly captured, but he retained overall control of the battle.[63] Jeremy Black concluded, "Saxe's generalship was instructive not only because of his battlefield ability to control large numbers in both attack and defense, but also because of his determined espousal of a war of manoeuvre.... His preference for bold manoeuvres, emphasis on holding and gaining the initiative, and stress on morale contrast markedly with the stereotyped views on non-Frederician mid-eighteenth-century warfare."[64] In the same year a French corps under Lowendahl overran Dutch Flanders and laid siege to one of the Netherlands's most powerful fortresses, Bergen op Zoom, at the mouth of the Scheldt River, the western gateway to an invasion of the homeland of the republic. Lowendahl had 30,000 men to accomplish this task while, by threatening Maastricht, the eastern gate, Saxe prevented Cumberland from marching to the relief of Bergen op Zoom.

That city appeared to be a far more difficult conquest than barrier fortresses of the Austrian Netherlands. Menno van Coehoorn, Vauban's great rival, had designed the defenses to take advantage of its situation. The river and sea gave the city access to reinforcements and supplies throughout the siege. Surrounding wetlands hindered the normal approach techniques, and Lowendahl was compelled to rely on series of redoubts rather than usual trenches. His sappers were threatened by countermines that might explode without warning. There were numerous eruptions of such mines during the siege. Coehoorn's outer-works were famed for their strength, and the Dutch commander, the 86-year-old General Cronstrom, was confident that the city could withstand any attack. But all was not well within the city. The unbroken string of French successes did not help the morale of the citizens—or the members of the allied garrison. Lowendahl submitted the city to a severe bombardment, aiming red-hot shot at the steeple of the great church, which was set alight. Houses were set ablaze by mortar bombs. In the midst of this chaos, soldiers of the garrison began to pillage the inhabitants they were assigned to protect. Three of the culprits drew lots to determine which should be shot, and the execution followed immediately. Indiscipline seems to have been rife in the garrison. On one occasion the British gunners and the Dutch engineers proclaimed their intention to serve no longer if they did not receive additional money and drink.[65] Despite the material strength of the fortifications, the defense was vulnerable because of the low morale and lack of discipline among its defenders.

On September 16, 1747, Lowendahl launched a surprise attack at 4:30 A.M. The outer-works were carried without a fight, and the French poured in through the gates while many of the defenders and their commander fled for their lives. Some 2,000 were taken prisoner. Some continued to resist by firing on the French from houses within the city. At this point, an event occurred that made a mockery of Voltaire's notion of polite war. It was always a tricky business when soldiers carried a town by storm. There remained the time-honored tradition that plunder was a soldier's right. A town defended too long risked provoking the wrath of soldiers who had endured long periods of danger and hardship. The wine shops helped fuel the frenzy of the French soldiers, who now began to rob and murder defenseless civilians. By 10:00 A.M., 2,000 civilians had perished in this indiscriminate slaughter and another 1,000 were injured. Lowendahl was unable to restore order until the soldiers were sated with drink and murder.[66]

This sort of thing had happened before, but enlightened opinion held that it could not happen again. That it did reveals the dark side of the wars of the Enlightenment and provides a grim footnote to the legend of Fontenoy. In his account of the incident, Count Pajol blamed Cronstrom for failing to recognize that the French had secured a breach that would allow them access to the city. A retreat or an honorable capitulation would have spared the city. Pajol concluded that Cronstrom's failure to act exposed Bergen op Zoom to a sack as provided by the laws of war.[67] Lowendahl was made a marshal of France as a result of the capture of the city for, as Saxe told the king, the only alternative was to hang him. As for Saxe, his final achievement was the capture of the great fortress of Maastricht in 1748. Fittingly, peace negotiators at Aix-la-Chapelle met within the distant sound of his guns.

This concluded one of the most extraordinary military campaigns of the century or perhaps of any century. It is not as well remembered as others because French diplomats gave back all of Saxe's gains at the peace table. The intricacies of this diplomacy may be followed in Reed Browning's *War of the Austrian Succession.* In retrospect, we know that the peace was but a truce foreshadowing the far more destructive Seven Years' War. Louis XV would have no Saxe and no glorious victories in that conflict.

Fontenoy illustrates some of the themes of this work. It reveals Voltaire as one who responded to military glory and patriotism. His stylized and romantic description of the battle at Fontenoy and his belief in the common humanity of the combatants suggests the optimism of the early Enlightenment. Both his narrative and his poem convey a sense of quaint anachronism in their focus on the role of the king and the courtier officers. At this point in his life, Voltaire saw the king as the living embodiment of France and drew a connection between monarchy and military glory. Napoleon is said to have observed that Fontenoy prolonged the monarchy by 30 years.[68] Perhaps Voltaire's antimilitarism would not have become so pronounced had France's experience in the Seven Years' War proved less disastrous. He seems to have been genuinely embarrassed by France's military decline. It is significant that his account of Fontenoy focused on the king. Louis had acted bravely and sensibly. Perhaps he did so for the last time. His turn to other pursuits deprived the Old Regime in France of a vital moral quality. The king ceased to be the standard of honorable conduct. For all the deficiencies of his narrative, Voltaire was a good military historian, one who scrupulously, if selectively, relied on the primary sources. As Jean Chagniot observes, when the impulse to engage in flattery did not blunt his critical spirit, Voltaire excelled in the description of battles and the puncturing of myths.[69] It would be unfair to expect him to have written about war in the manner of John Keegan. His influence on subsequent military history was profound. When one reads standard accounts of the "rational" and "polite" wars of the eighteenth century, we must remember that Voltaire was the creator of that image.

It is Saxe who emerges from the slaughterhouse of Fontenoy as a modern figure. As we have seen, he possessed the most creative military mind of the time. He possessed all of the qualities of a great general. A brilliant maneuver allowed him to gain the initiative from Cumberland and to choose the ground on which to fight. His dispositions demonstrated that quality that eighteenth-century writers called coup d'oeil. His field artillery achieved an unprecedented mobility that allowed it to concentrate against the most-vital targets. Fontenoy was an artillery battle that pointed the way to the destructive actions of the Seven Years' War. The Grassins were a new feature in western-European warfare, regular troops trained to operate in loose formation. This required a new kind of training and discipline; ultimately many military thinkers believed that it would require a new kind of soldier. Finally, few generals could equal Saxe's ability to retain command and control over a large army amidst the fog and chaos of battle. Saxe seems to have viewed the field with an eye as clear as that possessed in retrospect by historians and painters of battlefield scenes. His great intellectual gifts and iron will allowed him to translate dreams into action. In the wake of Fontenoy, the 76-year-old Folard acknowledged that his pupil had surpassed his master. It was in many ways a turning point. The world of the early Enlightenment played out its last days on the field of Fontenoy and the other scenes of the War of the Austrian Succession. A new and more turbulent world was at hand.

NOTES

1. "Projet de relation de la bataille de Fontenoy.... " In J. Colin, *Les Campagnes du Maréchal de Saxe* (Paris: Libraire Militaire, R. Chapelot et cie, 1901). In addition

to providing a detailed account of the battle of Fontenoy, Colin provided a large appendix of primary documents titled "Pieces Justificatives" (hereinafter cited as PJ); see PJ, 307. Other detailed accounts of the battle of Fontenoy include Francis Henry Skrine, *Fontenoy and Great Britain's Share in the War of the Austrian Succession, 1741–1748* (Edinburgh, 1906) and Charles Pierre Victor, comte de Pajol, *Les Guerres sous Louis XV*, 7 vols. (Paris: Librairie de Firmin-Didot, 1881-91), 3:chapter 10. Saxe's aide and admirer, Jean Baptiste Joseph Damazit de Sahuguet, the baron de Espagnac, published an account 30 years after the battle. See his *Histoire de Maurice, comte de Saxe, duc de Courland et de Sémigalle*, 2 vols. (Paris: Saillant and Nyon, 1775), 2:48–61. For a recent appraisal, see Jean-Pierre Bois, *Fontenoy, 1745: Louis XV, arbitre de l'Europe* (Paris: Economica, 1996). Saxe's other biographers and those of Cumberland and of Lord Ligonier also give detailed attention to this battle.

2. For Noailles's description of the battle, see *Correspondance de Louis XV et du Maréchal de Noailles*, ed. Camille Rousset, 2 vols. (Paris: Didier et Cie, 1869), 1:109–20.

3. The role of monarchs in wartime is described by Jeremy Black, *European Warfare, 1660–1815* (London: UCL Press, 1994), 213–17.

4. Skrine, *Fontenoy*, 139–40.

5. Marshal Saxe to the comte d'Argenson, 3 May 1745, PJ, 141.

6. Voltaire, *Précis du siècle de Louis XV* in *Oeuvres completes de Voltaire*, 52 vols. (Paris, 1878; reprint, Lichtenstein: Kraus Reprint, 1967), 15:237 (page citation is to the reprint edition).

7. *Correspondance de Louis XV et du Maréchal de Noailles*, 1:123.

8. Reed Browning, *The War of the Austrian Succession* (New York: St. Martin's Press, 1993), 190–91. For a different view of Louis XV and Argenson, see Bois, *Fontenoy*, 124–32. Bois argues that Louis restored his conquests through the peace of Aix-la-Chapelle because, as leader of Europe's most powerful state, he wished to be a disinterested arbiter, more concerned with justice than with territorial gain. Bois believes that Louis needed a military victory to enable him to assume that role and that Fontenoy provided him with one.

9. Cumberland's character and ability as a leader has received a staunch defense from Evan Charteris, *William Augustus, Duke of Cumberland, His Early Life and Times (1721–1748)* (London: Edward Arnold, 1913). For Fontenoy, see 177–93. This positive view of Cumberland is reinforced by Rex Whitworth, *William Augustus, Duke of Cumberland: A Life* (Hamden, Conn.: Leo Cooper, 1992). One may conclude that although Cumberland was not an especially gifted commander, he was not the cruel bumbler pictured by his detractors.

10. PJ, 287.

11. David Chandler, *The Art of Warfare in the Age of Marlborough* (New York: Sarpedon, 1995), 306.

12. *Correspondance de Louis XV et du Maréchal de Noailles*, 1:178.

13. Colin, *Campagnes de Saxe*, 79–80.

14. Voltaire, *Siècle de Louis XV*, 239.

15. Espagnac, *Histoire de Saxe*, 2:48.

16. Colin, *Campagnes de Saxe*, 67.

17. Ibid., 85.

18. Chandler, *Art of Warfare,* 212. For Saxe's description of his dispositions, see PJ, 216–20. Also see Colin's discussion of the French artillery plan, *Campagnes de Saxe,* 86–88. Saxe's plans are also discussed in Bois, *Fontenoy,* 74–80.

19. For the Prince of Waldeck's journal, see PJ, 265–67. Also see Schlippenbach's account, PJ, 288.

20. Jeremy Black, "New Accounts of Dettingen and Fontenoy," Buckinghamshire Record Office, *Annual Report and List of Accessions* (1992), 18.

21. PJ, 314.

22. Colin, *Campagnes de Saxe,* 143–44.

23. Ibid., 107.

24. Jean Chagniot describes the British formation as a large column of attack with 15 guns on each flank; see *Guerre et société à l'époque moderne,* 193. However, it would appear that the British intended to advance in line and that they altered their formation in response to circumstances. The guns were in the center of the "column" and provided no support.

25. Voltaire, *Siècle de Louis XV,* 240.

26. Theodore Besterman, *Voltaire* (Chicago: University of Chicago Press, 1976), 284–85. See also pp. 641–43 for Voltaire's "Autobiography," in which he describes his sources and includes the full text of Argenson's letter.

27. Skrine, *Fontenoy ,* 171–73.

28. Lord Louden to the Earl of Holdernesse, August 5, 1757. Loudon Papers, LO 4072 A, B, and C. Huntington Library, San Marino, Calif. There are many other references to his strange behavior.

29. *The Gentleman's Magazine* (May 1745): 271.

30. Eric de Saint Denis, "Fontenoy: Une bataille, un homme, un dialogue," *Histoire économie et société,* 4e trimestre (1985): 479–95. I am indebted to Professor Jean Chagniot for calling my attention to this article. Francis Hulot follows the dialogue as reported by Skrine. See Hulot's *Le Maréchal de Saxe* (Paris: Pygmalion, 1989), 169. In PJ, Colin published an undated letter on the battle of Fontenoy that supports Voltaire's version, but the letter's source appears to have been Voltaire! See PJ, 274–76. Espagnac clearly based his account of the incident on Voltaire; see *Histoire de Saxe,* 2:55. Also see Bois, *Fontenoy,* v-vii.

31. Charles de Mathéi, marquis de Valfons, *Souvenirs du Marquis de Valfons...1710–1786,* Mémoires sur le XVIIIe siècle (Paris: E. Paul, 1906), 132–33.

32. Voltaire, *Siècle de Louis XV,* 241.

33. Chagniot, *Guerre et société,* 245.

34. Charles Russell, "Letters of Lieut. Col. Charles Russell," *Report on the Manuscripts of Mrs. Frankland Russell-Astley* (London: Historical Manuscripts Commission, 1906), 278.

35. Émile Léonard, *L'Armée et ses problèmes au XVIIIe siècle* (Paris: Libraire Plon, 1958), 217–33.

36. Voltaire, *Poème de Fontenoy,* in *Oeuvres,* 7:388.

37. Ibid., 391.

38. Ibid., 377.

39. Bestermann, *Voltaire,* 642.

40. Comte de Chabannes, "Projet de relation de la bataille de Fontenoy...par M. le Comte de Chabannes....," PJ, 311.

41. Rex Whitworth, *Field Marshal Lord Ligonier: A Story of the British Army, 1702–1770* (Oxford: Clarendon Press, 1958), 101.

42. Colin, *Campagnes de Saxe*, 119. The saying was recorded by Baron Friedrich Melchior Grimm.

43. Voltaire, *Siècle de Louis XV*, 243. Skrine, who had little patience for Voltaire's inclination to glorify his friends, credited Captain Isnard with the suggestion to bring the artillery to bear; see *Fontenoy*, 181. Colin and Pajol were equally critical of Voltaire and awarded the credit to Isnard; see Colin, *Campagnes de Saxe*, 138, and Pajol, *Guerres sous Louis XV*, 3:385. However, Chabannes, in his account, attributes the deployment of the guns to Richelieu; see PJ, 313.

44. Whitworth, *Ligonier*, 101–2.

45. PJ, 221–22.

46. Jean Chagniot, *Le Chevalier de Folard: La stratégie de l'incertitude* (Paris: Editions du Rocher, 1997), 256–57.

47. PJ, 364.

48. Skrine, *Fontenoy*, 181.

49. On this point, see Espagnac, *Histoire de Saxe*, 2:59–60.

50. *The Gentleman's Magazine* (May 1745): 251.

51. PJ, 281.

52. Ibid., 218. For the illegality of grapeshot, see G. F. von Martens, *The Law of Nations Being the Science of National Law, Covenants, Power, etc. Founded on the Treatise and Customs of Modern Nations in Europe*, trans. William Cobbett, 4th ed. (London, 1829), 287.

53. W. A. Speck, *The Butcher: The Duke of Cumberland and the Suppression of the 45* (Oxford: Basil Blackwell, 1981), 143.

54. PJ, 248–49.

55. *The Gentleman's Magazine* (June 1745): 293.

56. Ibid., (May 1745): 242.

57. Ibid., 252.

58. PJ, 281.

59. Henry Fielding, *The True Patriot*, no. 6 (December 10, 1745), ed. Miriam Austin Locke (University: University of Alabama Press, 1964).

60. Chandler, *Art of Warfare*, 306; Browning, *War of the Austrian Succession*, 212.

61. John Manchip White, *Marshal of France: The Life and Times of Maurice, Counte de Saxe* (Chicago, 1962), 164.

62. Colin, *Campagnes de Saxe*, 146.

63. Skrine, *Fontenoy*, 332.

64. Black, *European Warfare*, 128–29.

65. "A Journal of the Works in the Trenches during the Siege of Bergen-op-Zoom," in *Remarks on the Military Operations of the English and French Armies commanded by His Royal Highness the Duke of Cumberland and Marshal Saxe during the campaign of 1747*, by an officer (London: T. Becker, 1760), 111–86.

66. Browning, *War of the Austrian Succession*, 320.

67. Pajol, *Guerres sous Louis XV*, 3:557–63.

68. Evan Charteris, *William Augustus, Duke of Cumberland, and the Seven Years' War* (London: Hutchinson, n.d.), 5.

69. Chagniot, *Guerre et société*, 316.

CHAPTER 5

Popular War

MILITIAS

Fontenoy was a classic battle of the Old Regime, a conflict fought primarily by regular troops. It was a matter of a few hours full of horror and glory for those involved. However, battles such as Fontenoy represent but one facet of the eighteenth-century military experience. There was, for example, the military career of Edward Gibbon. The Seven Years' War rekindled British fears that France would seek to eliminate Britain from the war by a direct invasion. Now the call came for true-born Englishmen to prepare to defend their country. As Gibbon recalled, "in the outset of a glorious war the English people had been defended by German mercenaries. A national militia has been the call of every patriot since the Revolution, and this measure, both in Parliament and in the field, was supported by the country gentlemen, or Tories, who insensibly transferred their loyalties to the House of Hanover. In the language of Mr. Burke, they have changed the idol, but have preserved the idolatry."[1]

Gibbon received a commission as a captain in the Hampshire militia regiment and found himself "condemned more than two years and a half (May 10, 1760–December 23, 1762) to a wandering life of military servitude." He needed only a few pages in his autobiography to describe his "bloodless and inglorious campaigns." His only contact with the enemy "was in our duty at Portchester Castle and Sissinghurst, which was occupied by five thousand Frenchmen. These enemies, it is true were naked, unarmed prisoners: they were relieved by public and private bounty. But their distress exhibited the calamities of war, and their joyous noise, the vivacity of their nation." Like many soldiers, he found much that was tedious and dull in military life. "The loss of so many busy and idle hours was not compensated by any elegant pleasure, and my temper was soured by the society of our rustic officers, who were alike deficient in the knowledge of scholars and the manners of gentlemen." We may assume that the gambling, drinking, and affairs of honor that consumed the idle hours of so many officers offered no attraction for this bookish captain. Still, like many old soldiers in hindsight, he concluded that military life had been good for him: "My principal obligation to the militia was the making me an Englishman and a soldier." His foreign education and retiring disposition had set him apart from the life of his contemporaries, but in the army one learned to live with all sorts and to feel a part of the national culture. As one might expect, Gibbon took his duties seriously and began to read up on his new profession by consulting ancient authorities. He recognized that his practical training had its benefits as well: "The discipline and evolutions of a modern battalion gave me a clearer notion of the phalanx and the legions, and the captain of the Hampshire grenadiers (the reader may smile) has not been useless to the historian of the Roman empire."[2]

British naval victories forestalled a French invasion, and fortunately Gibbon was saved for greater things. Was the bookish historian up to being a real officer? Regulars have always tended to look down their noses at militiamen as amateurs. However, as we have seen, few British regular officers had any serious preparation before joining their regiments, and most learned on the job and by reading textbooks. Defenders of the militia system argued that no one expected these officers to become generals. All they had to do was learn the basics required of a company officer, which meant the proper drill and exercise of the men. Six months of experience was all such an officer needed to acquire this skill. Since Gibbon probably took his responsibilities more seriously than many young officers, he no doubt became proficient enough. Beyond this he was a gentleman and thus, by the hierarchical standards of eighteenth-century society, qualified to exercise command over a company of peasants. Perhaps no more was needed. Thus the authors of a treatise for the establishment of a militia denounced those military pedants who insisted that war was a mystery understood by a chosen few "as ignorant monks opposing the diffusion of knowledge."[3] The British militia was never put to the test of battle, but it did serve as a vehicle by which military knowledge and experience spread among the larger population. The role of militia service in the development of a national consciousness deserves further study.

Militia service was a permanent part of eighteenth-century French life. The Crown had long relied on militia forces for local defense and as a manpower reserve. Prior to the reign of Louis XIV, the militias were a two-edged sword, for they might resist as well as support royal authority. This was particularly true of bourgeois militias of fortified towns. Under Louis XIV, towns within the interior of the country lost their fortifications and their militias became less significant. At the same time, the royal militia drawn from the peasantry evolved in a manner that made it an agent of state power. The militia could be used to preserve internal order, as guards and garrisons, and as a reserve for the regular army. In 1726 the Provincial Militia was established by royal ordinance in the form that it was to retain until the revolution. It was distinguished from the regular army in that service was enforced rather than voluntary. This made it one of the most unpopular institutions of the Old Regime, particularly since its burden fell on the rural poor. Militiamen were chosen by lot under the supervision of the intendant or his delegate, but exemptions and paid substitutes made the proceeding appear unfair. The militia formed an important reserve army at a low cost for the government. Members of the militia were paid only while in active service; the king supplied weapons, which were returned to depots at the end of the service period. Local authorities, however, were responsible for the militiamen's equipment. When incorporated into the army, the militia might serve in battalions of their own or be drafted to fill gaps in the regular forces. The War of the Austrian Succession imposed a particularly heavy burden, with 145,520 men being mobilized. For the most part, the militia replaced regular troops, because guards and garrisons and militia battalions were most likely to serve on secondary fronts. However, 10 battalions were with Marshal Maurice de Saxe's army in 1745, and at the battle of Fontenoy they protected the crucial Pont de Calonne, across which the king would have escaped if the battle had been lost (see Fig. 4.1). Despite the philosophes' interest in the idea of a militia, the Provincial Militia suffered from a negative image throughout its history. It had bad officers, poor weapons, and low morale. It was a common scapegoat for the problems confronting the French army in the period. Marshal Noailles, for example, when seeking to excuse the conduct of his nephew the duke of Grammont at Dettingen, blamed the militia in the French ranks for the defeat.[4] Nevertheless, the Provincial Militia meant that there was a broader military experience under the Old Regime than is commonly supposed.

German states also relied on militias from which to recruit and supplement their armies. In Prussia, militia service gave way to the cantonal system. Each canton was required to provide a specified number of peasants for service in the regular army. Thus the army was a mix of mercenaries and conscripts honed to perfection by Prussian discipline and training. In peacetime, however, peasant soldiers spent part of the year in agricultural labor at home. In Prussia's highly militarized society, service as a soldier attracted respect not accorded to French militiamen. Furthermore, a peasant soldier's status protected him from some of the harsh consequences of serfdom. However, even the cantonal system failed to satisfy the army's appetite for men during the Seven Years' War. Militia service was revived, and the militia bore the principal burden in defending Pomerania from Swedish assault.[5]

During the period covered by this study, France and England escaped invasion by foreign armies and were relatively free from rebellion, the exceptions being the 1715 and 1745 Jacobite uprisings in Britain and the 1702–1704 Camisard rebellion in France. Whatever the demands placed on them, the peasantry lived in a peaceful environment. This was far from being the case in the war zones: Flanders, Germany, Piedmont-Savoy, Italy, and Spain, where peasants and town dwellers suffered from the depredations of marauding armies. They did not do so passively, however, and in many cases they determined the outcome of military campaigns. Beset by invasion during the Nine Years' War and the War of the Spanish Succession, Victor Amadeus II of Sardinia-Piedmont had to supplement his regular troops by calling out the militia to serve as garrisons and drafts for the regular army. Peasant guerillas attacked occupying armies on their own initiative. Armed peasants continued to play a role in the defense of the Savoyard state throughout the century. Their attacks on Franco-Spanish lines of communications made an important contribution to the relief of the key fortress of Cuneo in 1744. Such military service was unpopular, and the government recognized that it had negative economic consequences. On the other hand, lack of resources forced the government to rely on armed peasants, who could act in their own defense if necessary.[6] The French government also employed armed peasants in wartime, in addition to the established militia, to guard important boundaries. Allied forces arriving in Catalonia during the War of the Spanish Succession found a warm reception from the population. The countryside was dominated by armed peasants known as the Miquelets, who had a long tradition of fighting the government or one another. They seem to have possessed no loyalty other than to family or gang and strode around the countryside armed with knives and short-barreled pistols. They lived in a culture of violence from which they procured a livelihood. Although they had often allied with the French against the Spanish Crown, they now offered their support to the allies. They were tough irregulars, well suited for attacks on enemy outposts and communications, but they had no liking for the discipline that regular officers sought to impose. The Miquelets were in fact a law unto themselves; they underscore the fact that governments had not gained a monopoly over the forces of violence in the eighteenth century.[7] They offer an interesting contrast to the urbane Gibbon, the epitome of Enlightenment culture, and remind us of the complexity of the eighteenth-century military experience.

The most famous eighteenth-century militia was that of the American colonies, a force that has gained almost mythological status as a band of citizen-soldiers. Modern research has not been so kind to this institution. Virginia and New England militias had had a mixed record of success in the Indian wars of the seventeenth century, but by the eighteenth century these institutions were in decay. Eighteenth-century North American colonial wars were fought by hired soldiers recruited from the margins of society or by imperial forces dispatched from the metropolis. Many militia organizations had evolved into social clubs, with the exception of South Carolina's, which functioned as a slave patrol. Only the French Canadian militia, hardened by participation in the long-distance fur trade and assimilated into the Native American way of war, represented a formidable irregular force. A recent work has dismissed the popular notion that American colonists possessed a "gun culture." Rather, historian Michael Bellesiles argues that few Americans possessed firearms and fewer knew how to use them effectively. Although Bellesiles's evidence has been questioned, it appears that the reality of the frontier militia fell short of the standard established in American national mythology. For example, when as late as 1790, U.S. General Josiah Harmar summoned Kentucky and Pennsylvania militia for a campaign against midwestern Indians, few famed frontier warriors appeared. The militia were largely paid substitutes without experience and without firearms. The result was a military disaster. One must rethink the traditional view of popular and irregular military service in the eighteenth century. Although Britain lacked a standing militia until the Seven Years' War, Continental military experience was very different. A French peasant had much more chance of actual military experience as a militiaman than did an American colonist. The military experience was much more diffused among the European population than among the people of North America.[8]

Many eighteenth-century European soldiers were not regular or professional troops. The nature of irregulars varied widely. They included militia officers and soldiers, partisans such as the Grassins operating as adjuncts to regular forces, guerilla fighters such as the Miquelets; soldier-colonists such as the Croats of the Austrian military border with the Ottoman Empire; Cossacks; members of "free companies" raised by military entrepreneurs, such as the notorious Pandours of Francis, Baron von Trenck; peoples in arms, such as the Highlanders of Scotland and the Corsicans; and peasants who resisted the depredations of invading armies. There was no single eighteenth-century military experience and, as this brief list suggests, there was not one military culture.

Not every country had peasant warriors as colorful as the Miquelets, but the peasantry was a factor in most campaigns. Frederick the Great gave detailed attention to their role. "If my sole object were glory, I would never wage war anywhere except in my own country because of all the advantages I would find there. For every man is a spy and the enemy cannot stir a foot without being betrayed. You can send out detachments boldly and have them play all the tricks of which war is capable," he said. Things were different in the country of the enemy. In Bohemia and Moravia, Frederick had learned how difficult it was for an army to subsist when the countryside was against it: "You must keep your eyes open.

Most of the light troops will then be employed to escort convoys, for you must never expect to gain the affection of these people." The lack of good maps was exacerbated by the unwillingness of local people to act as guides from one village to another. The villages were deserted because the peasants fled with their cattle into the forests on the army's approach. Hostile inhabitants were thus a "force multiplier" for Frederick's Austrian opponents.[9]

Frederick observed that in neutral countries it was necessary to win the friendship and confidence of the inhabitants. "If the country is Protestant like Saxony, play the role of the protector of the Lutheran religion and seek to inspire fanaticism of the lower classes, whose simplicity makes them easy prey. If the country is Catholic, speak only of tolerance, preach moderation, and blame the priests for all the causes of animosity between the Christian sects which, despite their arguments, are in basic agreement on the principal articles of faith." It was essential, wrote the royal cynic, to do everything to blacken the reputation of the enemy and to accuse him of pernicious plans. Most important, however, was one's own conduct. One should observe the strictest discipline and prohibit marauding and pillage. Soldiers guilty of such crimes should receive severe public punishment. The iron discipline imposed on the Prussian troops was intended not only to make them invincible in battle but to secure them from the inhabitants around them.[10]

Marauding, pillage, rape, and murder were common crimes that accompanied the advance or retreat of the armies. Frederick would have been well aware of the difficulties these disorders caused military commanders. There is no complete record of peasant attacks on the military, nothing like David Chandler's tidy and useful tables of statistics for the major battles of the century.[11] However, there were enough major incidents to illustrate the scale of the problem. Count de Merode-Westerloo recalled that as the French army withdrew from Germany through the Black Forest in 1704, a soldier blew on a great brass alpenhorn that he had found. To the soldiers' delight, many cattle emerged from the woods in response to the call. The troops "regarded this as manna from heaven, and in no time the camp resembled a slaughterhouse. However, this droll incident had one unfortunate repercussion; it encouraged the troops to scatter in the woods and hills—we could do nothing to stop them—and a few regrettable incidents resulted. The outraged peasantry eventually killed several thousand of our men before the army was clear of the Black Forest."[12] Similarly, French pillaging of the German countryside in 1761 provoked an uprising by townspeople and some 4,000 peasants. Marshal Conflans, fearing that his army would be cut off and unable to retreat was forced to evacuate the town of Emden.[13] The actual nature of these large-scale peasant attacks has not been described. However, undisciplined soldiers with single-shot weapons were vulnerable when confronted by angry peasants. In the local population there were war veterans, deserters, and men with militia experience fully capable of confronting such troops. Nor can we assume that peasants in war zones were without arms, for, as we have seen, governments were often forced to rely on armed peasants. Unfortunately, there is little in the way of documentary evidence to give a clear picture of the anatomy of peasant uprisings. Nevertheless, behind the calm facade of the Old Regime there lurked the threat of a restless and violent peasantry.

The Grassins demonstrated at Fontenoy the value of specially trained light infantry and cavalry. As discussed in chapter 2, the War of the Austrian Succession revived interest in the employment of specialized forces. The Habsburgs made good use of their border people, the Croats, a name that in the eighteenth century embraced Orthodox Serbs and Albanians, as well as Catholics. These people received farms and other privileges to guard the Ottoman border. Essentially they were militiamen required to do part-time service, but during the midcentury wars the Austrians enrolled Croat regiments of infantry and hussars to serve in central and western Europe. They added an exotic air to the Austrian army with their distinctive red cloaks and martial swagger. Although there were attempts to make them more like the regular troops, it was understood that they were best at *petite guerre:* patrols, raids, and outposts, a form of war that was considered natural to them. They were so good that they played havoc with Frederick's logistics and forced him to reorganize his army. The Croats have often been confused unfairly with the murderous and thieving Pandours of Trenck. The nature of their operations required a form of discipline different from that of the regulars, and often they did not have the best officers. Indeed, the language problem that bedeviled the Habsburg army was particularly bad in their case, for they were not always able to communicate with their superiors. Homegrown officers were few, and it was even difficult to find enough literate men to serve as noncommissioned officers (NCOs). However, discipline seems to have been a serious problem only when the Croats as a group believed that their privileges had been denied. On these occasions they mutinied and headed for home. Army commanders sometimes were able to apply a remedy of negotiation and punishment but on other occasions simply had to let them go. The midcentury wars weighed heavily upon a people who were called on to provide increasing numbers of soldiers while continuing to guard the border and tend to their farms. By the end of the Seven Years' War, the number of Croats in arms against Frederick had declined, along with their effectiveness. Nevertheless, they had served the monarchy well and had contributed to the profound change in military thought described in chapter 2.[14]

One commander who had particular success with the Croats was General Johann Sigismund Maguire von Inniskillen, one of the famous Austrian Irishmen who formed a substantial part of the Austrian officer corps in the midcentury. Christopher Duffy has identified a network of 33 Irish families that contributed officers, including distinguished commanders such as Franz Moritz Lacy and Maximilian Browne. Young Irish gentry, forbidden by British authority to serve in France, found their way into the Habsburg service through this network. Maria Theresa looked to them to aid her in establishing a military caste in Austria, and many became prosperous in her service. They did not lose contact with friends at home. Duffy notes that many "existed in three worlds—their own ancient culture, that of the demeaning conditions of life in Ireland under the Protestant Ascendancy, and that of their Austrian environment."[15] Such officers were not irregulars, but they came from a poor country where a military career abroad was one of the few avenues for advancement. The same may be said for the Welshman Henry Lloyd. The poor countries of Europe—Ireland, Scotland, Switzerland, and Corsica—continued a long tradition of providing mercenaries for service abroad. However, there was always a two-way traffic in this trade, for foreign military experience might return home to fuel resistance to government authority. Rebels in arms against eighteenth-century governments were not necessarily amateurs in an era when military experience was widely diffused.

POPULAR RESISTANCE

In chapter 1, I provided a list of the major European wars of the eighteenth century prior to the French Revolution. Parallel to these wars are other conflicts that offer insight into the nature of eighteenth-century society:

Catalan resistance to the Bourbon monarchy, 1705–1714

The Protestant Camisard Rebellion in France, 1702–1704

The Jacobite Rebellions in Scotland, 1715, 1745

The Genoese Revolution, 1746–1747

Corsican resistance against Genoa and France, concluding in 1769

The Pugachov Rebellion in Russia, 1773–1774

The Dutch "Patriotic" uprising of 1787

This is but a partial list and excludes the most important revolution of all: the American. The Polish resistance of 1794 and the Irish rebellion of 1798 are outside our period, but they are perhaps more characteristic of the Old Regime than of the Revolutionary-Napoleonic era. Was there an "eighteenth-century crisis"? One must be cautious in offering a generalization to link these uprisings together, for they occurred under unique circumstances. However, two themes stand out. First many of these conflicts were related to the demands imposed on society by the great wars of the period. Reed Browning has observed that the strain imposed by the War of the Austrian Succession exposed cracks in the "cake of custom" and contributed to revolutionary ferment. These uprisings also tended to occur upon the margins of society and were the product of resistance to political centralization and what may be called cultural imperialism. Scottish Highlanders and Cossacks were borderlanders who resisted inclusion in modern states they regarded as an alien world. The Corsicans resisted foreign occupation, whether Genoan or French. Many uprisings were not modern in nature and sought to protect or restore ancient privileges. However, some groups, such as the Corsicans, were able to portray their struggle in terms that appealed to an enlightened European public. Religious issues played a prominent role in revolts by the Camisards and the Jacobites. This helps to explain the harsh and emotional response of the authorities on these occasions. Although eighteenth-century rationalists sought to identify a new age of order, tolerance, and humanity, governments responded to the revolts with a savagery that recalled the seventeenth-century religious wars.

The revolts demonstrate that eighteenth-century peoples were prepared when provoked to take arms into their own hands and to defend their rights. Few of the revolts succeeded in their objectives, but they managed to cause serious crises for eighteenth-century regimes before being contained. These events seldom elicited much sympathy from Enlightenment writers. Highland Scots and Cossacks were not portrayed as freedom fighters but as barbarians who threatened enlightened civilization. Voltaire, eulogist of the French monarchy and nobility in its role at Fontenoy, was no friend of the Cossacks or the Poles. Only Rousseau seems to have possessed empathy for popular causes, particularly with respect to Corsica and Poland. However, as we have seen, he too sensed the dark undercurrents that threatened more harm than good. With that exception, participants in popular revolts seldom had support from the shapers of enlightened opinion. This rendered them more vulnerable to repressive action when their armed resistance failed.

During the War of the Spanish Succession, the Catalans sided with the Austrian candidate for the throne, Charles III, against the Bourbon Philip V, grandson of the king of France. The war in Spain was in this sense a civil war pitting the defense of Catalan rights against Bourbon Castile. The Catalan cause was more promising than that of other popular movements, for they received direct aid from the allied powers and were able to rally around the person of their own king. Catalans played an important role in the allied capture of Barcelona in 1705. Miquelets assisted the allies in their initial campaigns in Catalonia and, although the latter's artillery was the key to overcoming Barcelona's defenses, the inhabitants took matters in their own hands when the capitulation was signed. There was an insurrection in the city, and allied troops had to intervene to save the lives of the viceroy and the military governor. Abandoned by the allies through the Treaty of Utrecht, the Catalan estates voted to continue to fight in defense of their privileges. The center of their resistance was Barcelona, which they were determined to hold against Philip V's army, even after the withdrawal of the imperial troops. Villaroel, the commander of the defense, had about 5,000 trained men and another 5,000 auxiliaries. The trade guilds and the lower clergy were prominent in organizing the resistance in an atmosphere of religious fervor. Deserted by their temporal allies, the defenders hoped for a miracle. In the last days of the siege, conducted on Philip's behalf by the duke of Berwick, Villaroel resigned and was officially replaced by the Virgin Mary, whose image presided at all meetings of the council of war. The Virgin's role seems to have symbolized the defiance of an abandoned people. Some Italian cities had professed their loyalty to the Virgin Mary as a statement of their independence from higher authority, and this seems to have been the case with Barcelona. However, there was no miracle. Following seven breaches in the walls, the city surrendered on September 13, 1714. The terms of the capitulations were not honored, and the leaders of the resistance were imprisoned or put to death. There was no prisoner-of-war status for rebels. Although Berwick prevented looting and the city soon went about its business, the Catalans had lost their privileges. Despite shedding crocodile tears, their friends could do nothing to help them.[16]

Religious issues, local rights, and international conflict also coalesced in the Cévennes mountain range of southern France in 1702–1704. This rebellion was in response to the religious persecution of Protestants in the wake of the Edict of Nantes, but it had deep roots in the resistance of remote religious communities to Catholic orthodoxy enforced from the center. The fact that France was engaged in a major war made the rebellion a serious drain on resources, for some 25,000 men were tied down by 2,000 peasant guerilla fighters. The Camisard leadership was divided between an experienced old soldier identified as Rolland and Jean Cavalier, a charismatic individual said to be inspired by the Holy Spirit. This helps to explain how the Camisards skillfully exploited their knowledge of the mountainous terrain while demonstrating a disregard for danger. The mountainous terrain was unfavorable for conventional operations by regulars, and the intendant in the Cévennes requested that Miquelets from the Pyrenees be recruited to provide the kind of specialized light infantry needed. With regulars needed elsewhere, much of the manpower deployed by the government came from local militia.[17] Initially, commanders attempted to end the revolt by employing cruel repression, a policy that only strengthened the ties between the Camisards and the peasantry of the region. The Camisards responded by defeating royal troops in a series of skirmishes. The government then turned to Marshal Villars, who had recently fallen from royal favor but was recognized as an officer of extraordinary ability. Villars conducted what might be considered to be a model counterinsurgency operation. While deploying mobile forces in ruthless pursuit of the Camisards in their mountainous hideaways, he met with peasant communities and assured them of the government's desire for peace. His offers of amnesty and freedom to leave the country led to a split in the Camisard leadership, with Cavalier choosing to accept the peace terms. Rolland proved to be a tougher case, and his band continued to resist until spies revealed his location and he was tracked down and shot. His companions were broken on the wheel. Villars had demonstrated that honesty and fair dealing in negotiations, combined with an implacable determination to destroy those who continued armed resistance, were the recipe to bring the revolt to a swift conclusion. It had taken him only five months.[18]

The Camisard Rebellion occurred on the margin of French society. Unlike previous religious civil wars it did not threaten the throne, although it was a serious distraction in wartime. The Camisards could be expected to draw sympathy and support from France's Protestant enemies, but the allies were unable to exploit the revolt.

Nevertheless, emerging states could still be threatened by communities on the margin whose religion and culture did not conform to that of the core society. Religious conflict could still stir passions in France. This was even more true in Great Britain, where a blend of Catholicism, Jacobitism, and Gaelic culture offered a competing vision of society.

THE '45

Eighteenth-century Englishmen might congratulate themselves that they had emerged from the civil wars of the preceding century as a stable and progressive society. This stability was guaranteed by the Revolution Settlement, the Hanoverian Succession, and the Protestant religion. The settlement allowed for the development of religious toleration and individual freedoms that were the foundations of enlightened society and a model for the European Enlightenment as a whole. However, this settlement did not occur without opposition. The "bloodless revolution" in England had required military conquest in Scotland and Ireland, where supporters of the Stuart dynasty had made their stand. As in the mid-seventeenth century, English politics were complicated by events in the Irish and Scottish kingdoms, which possessed different religious, political, and social institutions. English politicians sought to settle matters in these kingdoms, after militarily defeating the Jacobites, by a policy of repression in Ireland that guaranteed a Protestant ascendancy and by the Act of Union with Scotland in 1707, which bound that country more tightly in wartime. The act offered England greater political control over Scottish affairs while securing Scotland's own form of Protestantism. Furthermore, it was one of the first attempts to use free trade (in this case within the British Empire) as a means of fostering political unity. The Act of Union was a success but was not popular in Scotland, where it appeared to threaten traditional liberties and cultural identity. Rational arrangements such as the Act of Union can provoke emotional patriotic responses. It could not replace Scottish nationalism with British nationalism as devolution, the first alteration of the Act of Union has recently demonstrated. An early-twenty-first-century perspective suggests that for all the successes achieved by the Revolution settlement, a principal theme of post-1689 British history has been opposition to many of its aspects.

The principal voice of opposition to the Revolution settlement was Jacobitism. It bears attention in this chapter, for it exposed the insecurities behind the serene facade of Georgian England. It suggested that the Revolution settlement was not permanent and that the dark days of religious fanaticism and civil war might return. Robert Walpole both feared Jacobitism and recognized its political value by using it to taint his political opponents. There was substance to his fear. The eighteenth century witnessed two serious Jacobite uprisings, in 1715 and 1745, in addition to numerous plots. Jacobitism was a curious amalgam of loyalty to the exiled Stuarts, Catholicism, high-church Toryism, dislike of a German dynasty, resentment of Whig political ascendancy (usually defined as corruption), Irish and Scottish nationalism, and Gaelic culture. Historians have tended to disagree over the relative strengths of the ingredients in this political cocktail.

These loyalties produced adherents to the Stuart cause, but they also point to the fundamental weaknesses of Jacobitism. Its adherents did not necessarily agree on an alternative vision of society. Those who were prepared to sacrifice their lives for the cause came from the margins of the society. They produced a martial people, who could win local military successes over government forces. But their links with a so-called barbaric culture, as in the case of the Scottish Highlands, Catholicism, and France made them suspect in the eyes of members of the core culture.

France's battlefield victory at Fontenoy in 1745 was followed by the arrival of Prince Charles Edward Stuart (known as the Young Pretender and Bonnie Prince Charlie) and seven companions in the western Highlands of Scotland. It was the beginning of the rising known as The '45, which swelled into a movement that defeated the British regular forces in Scotland and penetrated England as far as Derby. Charles Edward had only modest support from France. A handful of troops detached from the Irish regiments in France eventually reached him, but the French government showed no interest in launching an invasion similar to the one attempted in the previous year. Charles Edward was therefore compelled to rely on what was at hand, and that was very good indeed. Sufficient numbers of Highland chiefs brought their clansmen to provide Charles

Edward with an irregular army that defeated the Hanoverian regulars in two battles, Prestonpans, near Edinburgh (October 2, 1745) and Falkirk, near Stirling (January 28, 1746), and in a number of smaller skirmishes as well. In experience Charles Edward was even less qualified for high command than was his cousin the duke of Cumberland, but he was an inspirational leader whose outstanding quality was certainty of success. He was fortunate that one of the Scottish nobles who joined him, Lord George Murray, was a man of military talent who understood how to lead Highland troops. Charles Edward lacked the sophisticated apparatus of an eighteenth-century field army. There was no artillery of any consequence and few mounted troops. He did possess, however, an infantry force capable of striking fear in the hearts of its opponents.

Charles Edward's Highland troops, volunteers or men forced into service, understood war in different terms than did their regular opponents. Many Highlanders had been trained to arms from youth and lived in a culture that esteemed martial feats over material rewards. Many possessed their own weapons or found them readily available. These were relatively simple, for the broadsword and shield (or target) remained the Highlanders' weapons of choice. They also carried muskets into battle but did not rely on them as their main weapon. The Highland charge was their preferred battle tactic. This meant that they approached the enemy in loose order and fired a volley to disrupt the enemy line. Then the Highlanders threw down their muskets, drew their swords, massed in groups and pounced on the enemy troops, who might manage only a single volley before the onset of the charge. The Highlanders rivaled Charles XII's Swedes in the effectiveness of their shock tactics.[19]

Charles Edward's victories in this brief war came at the expense of relatively small numbers of poorly trained regulars. At Prestonpans, Sir John Cope's force of about 2,500 consisted of garrison soldiers who ran away when Charles Edward's Highlanders surprised them with a charge after finding their way over a supposedly impassable bog. At Falkirk the British cavalry fled after receiving a volley, and the infantry collapsed when the Highlanders charged. Their commander, General Hawley, blamed his soldiers' cowardice for the defeat. These were small battles by Continental standards, and the Jacobite general Lord George Murray has often been regarded as one of the century's most-able small-wars commanders. The defeat of regular troops attracted much attention. The author of "An Essay on Regular and Irregular Troops," in a 1746 issue of *The Gentleman's Magazine,* argued that, "if war be a peculiar science, as all wise nations have understood it to be, that discipline which proves useless ought to be rejected, and a better substituted in its place." He continued to believe that the Highlanders could be defeated by continuous regular infantry fire supported by cavalry charges, but he called for the establishment of Highland regiments and hussar training for the cavalry. A private soldier of

Barrel's regiment, writing in the same issue of *The Gentleman's Magazine,* insisted that even though a quarter of the regulars' muskets misfired in the rain at Falkirk, the rebels had made no impression on his regiment, which stood its ground. The Highlanders waved their swords at a distance and ran off when they received another volley.[20]

At Culloden the advantage was with the government forces. The Highland army was exhausted by a failed night march against the royal camp and was short of food and ammunition. Murray advised against a battle on an open moor that was ideal for the employment of the enemy's cavalry and artillery. Cumberland now commanded the royal army. Whatever his limitations at Fontenoy, he was a more able commander than his charismatic cousin. Many of his troops were Flanders veterans of proven mettle, and he was bound to them through shared danger in the field. Although he never demonstrated the ability to command large armies in battle, the size of the engagement was perfectly within his capacities. In short, he was a very good brigadier. Cumberland's soldiers did not flinch before the Highland charge, delivered only by the Jacobite right. Much has been made of this action on the left of the royal line. The Highland charge broke upon a single regiment, Barrel's, and a portion of that stationed on its right. A bloody hand-to-hand fight followed, after which it was reported that there was not a single bayonet in Barrel's regiment unbloodied or unbent. Cumberland was credited with training the infantry to thrust their bayonets to the right to catch the Highlanders under their sword arms. It was a sensible tactic and one already advocated by the author of the "Essay on Regular and Irregular Troops," although in a rather impracticable manner. Michael Bellesiles, who dismisses the value of eighteenth-century firearms, has argued that Culloden was a military turning point for the eighteenth-century British army in that it introduced a tactic of firing a single volley and charging home with bayonets. This is a puzzling position, since Barrel's fought a desperate defensive battle and the Highlanders attempting to outflank them were driven off by volleys from regiments in the second line.[21] The remainder of the Jacobite army, battered by cannon fire, enfiladed by musketry, and flanked by cavalry, gave way in a rout. This was, for practical purposes, the end of the rebellion. Some followers urged Charles Edward to fight a guerrilla war in the Highlands, but he showed no interest. He was right, for such a war could not achieve the objective of overturning the dynasty.

In fact, Charles Edward's fate was apparent as early as December 15, 1745. His army of about 5,500 had penetrated England; captured Carlisle; been greeted with celebration at Manchester, where a number of English volunteers formed a regiment; and advanced to Derby. He had eluded two armies, and the way appeared open to London. Only the arrival of 6,000 Dutch troops in violation of their Ostend capitulation agreement (they were later replaced by Hessian mercenaries) prevented panic in the capital. Murray, however, advised withdrawal, because the government would soon be able to concentrate three armies against the Jacobite force. Furthermore, whatever the ideological or political components of Jacobitism, its fighting ingredient was limited to the Highlands. With the exception of the ill-fated Manchester regiment, few English Jacobites were willing to risk their lives. Derby was the high point of the Jacobite effort, and now the road pointed to Culloden rather than London.

The Jacobites' success had come so easily that their weaknesses were not immediately apparent. Britain was ill prepared for war at home and, unlike the Flanders cockpit, relatively unfortified. Not until experienced commanders and troops could be returned from Flanders could a respectable army be formed to confront the rebellion. Once this was effected, the tide shifted against the Jacobites. Marginal French support for the Jacobites undermined Jacobite hopes, particularly since their leaders promised a substantial intervention by the French. This may have been the main reason English Jacobites stayed home. Ultimately, the rebellion lacked sufficient popular support, even in Scotland.

No major Scottish nobleman supported the rebellion, and in the Lowlands the Highland army was regarded with outright hostility. The Highlanders were formidable irregular troops but possessed an evil reputation. Presbyterians recalled the Highland Host of 1678, dispatched by the Stuart regime, to disarm and overawe the Covenanters of the western Lowlands. A body of about 6,000 Highlanders were quartered in the western shires and left behind them a legacy of pillage and oppression. In fact, the Highlanders' conduct was probably no worse than that of regular soldiers in such circumstances, but the sober eighteenth-century Presbyterian historian Robert Wodrow portrayed them as barbaric villains. Wodrow provided shire-by-shire accounts of the financial losses incurred through free quarters, robberies, destruction of property, and slaughter of animals. More to the point were his descriptions of the menacing presence of these "savages." Wodrow was the most prominent Scottish historian of the early eighteenth century, one who emphasized facts over felicitous prose. Through him, the Highland Host was etched in Scottish historical memory. Charles Edward's reliance on another such host placed him at odds with those Scots who had settled into modern civil society.[22]

Bruce Lenman, who has played down the rising as a French-sponsored coup, has also dismissed the idea that it was as conflict of cultures. He points out that the Highland aristocracy, far from being primitive Gaelic chiefs, were part of cosmopolitan continental culture.[23] Perhaps this was so, but many contemporaries did define the Jacobite rising in those terms. Wodrow's account of the Highland Host recognized a strong cultural divide between the two sections of the country. The Highlanders occupied a place outside the pale of civilization. The irregular nature of Highland warfare lent credence to this view. Many Highlanders drew no real dis-

tinction between cattle theft and its attendant violence and war. The rules
of war, acclaimed by Enlightenment writers as part of the framework of
civilization, were unknown to illiterate Highland warriors, who did not
always observe the protocols regarding the wounded, prisoners, and noncombatants. This of course was grist for the mill of anti-Jacobite propa-
gandists. Charles Edward and the officers of the Jacobite army were aware
of the rules of war and knew that it was important for the success of their
cause that they be observed. After Prestonpans, Lord George Murray and
the duke of Perth intervened to protect officer prisoners from rough han-
dling by their followers. Highland discipline on the march to England was
exemplary and began to crumble only during the retreat. A "gentleman at
Derby" reported in *The Gentleman's Magazine* that six officers and 40 soldiers had been quartered upon him. His description of them as looking
like "so many fiends turn'd out of hell to ravage the kingdom, and cut
throats" recalls Wodrow's portrayal of the Highland Host. These Highlanders seem to have eaten their way through all his provisions and to
have been exceedingly casual in their sanitary arrangements. However,
they did no real damage and harmed no one.[24] Defeat undermined discipline in all armies, and in this case it would have been surprising if the
Highlanders had behaved differently. Still, every irregularity committed
by a Highland soldier was likely to be inflated into an atrocity. This attitude set the stage for the events in the wake of Culloden.

Lenman's view that the rebellion had little real significance was not
shared by all contemporaries. For example, Henry Fielding launched his
newspaper project *The True Patriot* in order to rouse Englishmen to meet
the danger represented by Charles Edward Stuart and his followers.
Although Fielding had been a critic of Robert Walpole's "corrupt" regime,
he was a staunch supporter of the Hanoverian monarchy as the guarantor
of the English Revolution settlements. The Jacobites represented the
restoration of absolute monarchy and religious persecution. Liberty and
property would no longer be safe. The connection between liberty and
Protestantism was obvious to Fielding. His Protestantism was rather
broader in outlook than that of the Presbyterian Wodrow, but it is worth
observing that Fielding, the enlightened humanitarian, did not neglect the
religious dimension of the crisis. He urged his readers not to condemn all
Catholics but urged Protestant Jacobites to consider the folly of supporting the Catholic Charles Edward. He employed his most beloved fictional
character, Parson Adams, to draw attention to the moral issues raised by
the rebellion. Displaying his usual naïveté when confronted by the vices of
the town, Adams considered the rebellion a judgment of God against an
offending people. It is a theme that Wodrow would certainly have
sounded in such a situation. Adams's concerns about morality coincided
with Fielding's conception of "true patriotism," defined as the "love of
one's Country carried into Action." True patriots were prepared to sacri-

fice private interest for the common good. It was on this quality that the security of the country depended. Thus the true enemy was luxury, sloth, and self-indulgence. Fielding's political and religious views coincided in his patriotic ideology.

This ideology was the basis of his call for a national militia incorporating all men between the ages of 18 and 50 (with some exceptions, such as Catholics and Quakers). He believed that all should participate in the defense of their freedoms. His plan for a militia reflected the hierarchical nature of his society, with a superior militia of property owners who would provide regiments of infantry and cavalry. He assumed that educated men of property possessing a sense of honor would more quickly acquire military skills than would the peasants and artisans, who should be formed into independent companies for local defense and into pioneer regiments. Especially interesting is Fielding's rejection of the need for harsh punishments to uphold military discipline. He recognized that one could not impose such a regime on a free people. Rather, he advocated the encouragement of example, emulation, and reward with punishments limited to fines. If the superior orders set the example, military service would become the fashion, and men would turn from frivolous pursuits to the service of their country. Fielding's militia proposal was thus more than a plan for national defense; it was to be an instrument for national regeneration.[25]

Fielding was discriminating in his approach to the rebellion. He recognized that it had little Lowland support and was careful not to brand all Scots or Jacobites as rebels. The focus of his paper was to arouse the nation to the consequences of a Jacobite victory. His hero was the man of the hour, the duke of Cumberland, who returned to restore order in a demoralized army. Fielding wrote, "This young Prince, who is an Englishman in his Nature, as well as in his Birth, will soon become the Darling of a People, who have always paid the highest Regard to Bravery and Generosity, Virtues for which, among many others, he is greatly eminent."[26] Whatever his reputation became in the aftermath of Culloden, it is worth remembering that during the crisis, Cumberland was the only military commander of stature to whom supporters of the Hanoverian regime could turn.

Charles Edward's Highland followers were unfortunate in that they were not considered regular soldiers protected by military custom, but rebels and "savages." They were thus beyond the protections of "civilized" warfare praised by contemporaries. Emmerich von Vattel never included "savage" peoples in his laws of war, and there is no reason to assume that Cumberland should have. The latter was in no mood for half measures, for the Hanoverian regime had good reason to view the Highlands as a center of disorder. Clansmen had taken up arms against the regime in 1715 and 1719, and now was a time to put an end to the matter. This view was shared by almost all of the governing class, and Cumberland was its willing agent. Rebel leaders could expect trial and execution; their followers were subjected to transportation. Rebel wounded were fortunate to survive to serve such a sentence—120 men, including four British peers, were ultimately put to death for complicity and 1,000 were transported. The English Manchester regiment suffered most severely, with 24 officers and men put to death for "High treason and levying War." Such figures do not seem excessive given the context, but there were incidents of indiscriminate violence committed by officers and men who made no distinction between loyalists and rebels. There were English writers who urged moderation in the treatment of the Highlanders. A contributor to *The Gentleman's Magazine* wrote, "I was as much against the rebellion as anybody; but I am neither for killing in cold blood, nor transporting them to the plantations." This author recommended addressing the "root causes" of the rebellion by introducing modern manufactures, and thus civilization, into the Highlands. Some contributors were much harsher in their attitudes and defended the actions of royal troops, but the periodical offered a balanced debate by publishing essays for and against mercy.[27] Bruce Lenman, no admirer of the Hanoverian regime, has concluded that "judiciously spread over England from London to York and Carlisle, the executions made their point and cannot be said to constitute a holocaust." Indeed, however bloody-minded most Hanoverian generals and many Westminster politicians may have been in early 1746, the legal processes which followed the '45 can be seen as the start of the rehabilitation and reintegration into the political nation of that not-at-all-representative minority of families who had fostered the rising. ... people who mattered were handled with some discrimination."[28]

GENOA AND CORSICA

In his history of the War of the Austrian Succession, Reed Browning has described the revolutionary forces unleashed by that conflict. As the Jacobite effort was coming to an end, new revolutionary strife erupted in Genoa, Italy, a city recently under Austrian occupation. This small-but-influential banking republic found itself caught between the forces contending for the control of Italy, on the one hand the Bourbon powers France and Spain and on the other Austria and Sardinia-Piedmont, supported by the British fleet. The time-tested formula for small commercial republics in such circumstances was neutrality, and the patrician-dominated senate pursued such a policy until 1744, when fears of Sardinian gains at Genoese expense drove the dominant faction into the hands of the Bourbons. Unfortunately, that was the losing side in the Italian wars, and their loss led to the Austrian occupation of 1746.

Genoa had a reputation as a wealthy city, and the Habsburg troops who arrived as occupiers were determined to enjoy themselves at the city's expense. The Austrian commander did nothing to restrain them while imposing a huge indemnity that Genoese authorities chose to meet by tapping the city's great charitable foundation, the Casa di San Giorgo. This attempt on the part of wealthy patricians to pass along to the poor the financial penalty incurred as a result of their policies naturally produced great social tension within the city. On December 5, 1746, Genoese resentment erupted in a spontaneous insurrection primarily by the lower orders, but (as at Barcelona) including members of the clergy. The insurrection forced the Austrians to evacuate the city. The success of this rebellion reminds us that regular troops had no advantage in street fighting against an aroused citizenry. Once in control, the Genoese set about the business of defending themselves and recovering territory still in Austrian hands. There remained widespread distrust of the patricians, whose bankrupt and cynical policies had produced such distress. A new government, the Assembly, including delegates from craft guilds, was formed to direct the war effort. It coexisted uneasily with the patrician Senate in a unity imposed by the external threat represented by the enraged Maria Theresa of Austria, who demanded that her troops recover their lost honor. Although the allies controlled land and sea access to the city, its defenses were much stronger than earlier in the year. The Assembly mustered popular resolve to man the fortifications, and the Senate was able to overcome Louis XV's distaste for rebels in order to obtain modest but essential French assistance. It was enough to allow resistance to continue to the war's conclusion. Genoa could not have maintained this defense without France, but her case demonstrates that in some circumstances popular uprisings could prevail against regular forces in the wars of the Old Regime.[29]

By the eighteenth century the island of Corsica had been under Genoese rule for some 300 years. A poor, mountainous land, it nevertheless occupied a strategic position in the western Mediterranean that engaged the attention of the great powers throughout the century. Genoese presence on the island was for the most part limited to the maritime towns; the interior was dominated by such local authorities as clan chiefs and the "fathers of the communes." These leaders feuded with one another but could be relied on to resist the extension of Genoese authority over the island. In 1729 a Genoese attempt to raise taxes, coupled with an attack on Corsican soldiers serving on the mainland, provoked a revolt that simmered through various stages for 40 years. The small numbers of mercenaries in Genoese pay were insufficient to impose its rule, and the republic was compelled to seek foreign help to subdue the rebels. First Austrian and later French troops arrived to restore order, but the rugged terrain and warlike nature of the inhabitants limited them to brief occupations of coastal towns. The Corsicans in turn asserted their independence by choosing an adventurer, Baron Theodor von Neuhof, as their king.

Although Theodore I, as he was called, spent little time on the island, by 1743 the Corsicans had organized a regency to govern in his name. The Corsicans sought Turkish assistance against Genoa, which in turn was now backed by the Bourbon powers. Until the 1760s the European equilibrium appeared to have prevented any of the great powers from exploiting the situation, and Genoese weakness preserved a considerable measure of Corsican independence. It was in this environment that a new kind of independence leader appeared in the form of Pasquale Paoli, one who in retrospect seems to have been a harbinger of the great democratic revolutions to come.

Few Europeans in the eighteenth century knew much about Corsica. It was far removed from the glittering cosmopolitan culture of Enlightenment salons and courts. The Corsicans themselves appeared to be similar to the rude and uncivilized Scottish Highlanders. Their poverty and their clan feuds caused them to be dismissed as brigands and savages. It was Paoli—who became an international celebrity—who changed all this. A charismatic leader and idealist, familiar with the works of Locke, Montesquieu, and Rousseau, Paoli was the first European independence leader to explain his movement in terms that struck a chord with the enlightened public. Through Paoli the Corsican image was transformed into that of a poor-but-virtuous nation of patriots. It was a country that provided ready materials for Rousseau's political thought.

Paoli's celebrity was to some extent the creation of James Boswell, who took the unusual step of including the island on his grand tour in 1765. "I wished for something more than just the common course of what is called the tour of Europe; and Corsica occurred to me as a place which no body else had seen, and where I should find what was to be seen no where else, a people actually fighting for liberty, and forming themselves from a poor oppressed nation, into a flourishing independent state," he wrote.[30] He arrived with a letter of introduction from Rousseau and was prepared to view Corsica through the lens of the man he called "the wild philosopher." He was not disappointed. The political leaders he met at Corte he found to be "solid and sagacious, men of penetration and ability, well calculated to assist the General in forming his political plans, and in turning to the best advantage, the violence and enterprises of the people."[31] At Bastelica, he wrote, "I happened at the time to have an unusual flow of spirits...I harangued the men of Bastelica with great fluency. I expatiated on the bravery of the Corsicans, by which they had purchased their liberty, the most valuable of all possessions, and rendered themselves glorious over all Europe. Their poverty, I told them, might be remedied by a proper cultivation of their island, and by engaging a little in commerce. But I bid them remember, that they were much happier in their present state than in a state of refinement and vice, and that therefore they should beware of luxury."[32] One wonders what the Corsicans made of this opinionated young man, but these words reflect the newly emerging image of the Corsicans that flourished in Rousseau's imagination.

Boswell portrayed Paoli as an ancient Roman patriot: wise, virtuous, and brave, seeking only the welfare of his country rather than fame or fortune. We see him at ease with the rough followers who share his table consisting of but a few plain dishes and no foreign wine. He is well versed in ancient and modern literature and can talk knowledgeably on many subjects. His followers are convinced that he has the gift of prophecy. Boswell cannot help but be skeptical. He recognizes that Paoli has exploited this "gift" as a means of gaining authority over a rude people but concludes, "I cannot allow myself to suppose that Paoli ever required the aid of pious frauds."[33] Whatever Boswell may really have thought, he has transformed Paoli into a romantic figure, one sure to capture the imagination of his time.

Thus Paoli compared himself to Maurice de Saxe: "If a man would preserve the generous glow of patriotism, he must not reason too much. Mareschal Saxe reasoned; and carried the arms of France into the heart of Germany, his own country. I act from sentiment, not from reasonings."[34] These sentiments were reflected in his thoughts about Corsican bravery. Boswell wrote, "The French objected to him that the Corsican nation had no regular troops. 'We would not have them,' said Paoli. 'We should then have the bravery of this and the other regiment. At present every single man is as a regiment himself. Should the Corsicans be formed into regular troops, we should lose that personal bravery which has produced such actions among us, as in another country would have rendered famous even a Mareschal.' "[35]

Perhaps few of Paoli's followers were aware that they had become exemplars of fashionable Enlightenment ideas, but the general could draw on a nationalism developed over a period of rebellion lasting almost 40 years. Corsica was not a modern state, but a form of national unity had evolved out of resistance to Genoese control. The Corsicans had the ability to sustain their independence against Genoa, but their fortunes changed in 1768 when Genoa acknowledged the end of its role as a colonial ruler by ceding the island to France. French troops were already in occupation of Bastia and St. Florent in the north of the island, and it was unclear initially what the cession implied for Corsican liberty. The French minister, the duke of Choiseul, carried out negotiations with Paoli that suggested that Corsican self-government might continue in the interior of the island. Thad Hall, the leading modern expert on the Corsican question, has said he believes that Paoli and his associates distrusted French intentions and that their long struggle for liberty made it impossible to agree that a treaty between Genoa and France could settle the matter of sovereignty over the island. Hall concludes that Choiseul, fearing British intervention in this strategic island, could settle for nothing less than total control if he was to gain the security that he sought in the western Mediterranean. Thus he was prepared to achieve his goals through military conquest, while Paoli determined on a resistance that he knew to be futile.[36]

Initially the French underestimated Corsican resolve and powers of resistance. Their initial expeditionary force was inadequate to the task at hand, and its commander, the marquis de Chauvelin, had not held military command since the War of the Austrian Succession. "He had lost the habit of war and understood nothing about it," was the judgment of Charles-François Dumouriez, the future victor of Valmy, who served in the Corsican campaigns of 1768 and 1769. Chauvelin was accompanied by young nobles from the court who thought that the campaign would be as easy as going to the opera. They expressed contempt for a rabble of peasants armed with fowling pieces without bayonets and did not expect that irregulars dressed in the brown clothes of the peasantry could offer any resistance. Although Chauvelin was chosen because he was supposedly familiar with the Corsican situation, he lacked an understanding of Corsican nationalism. Particularly fatuous was his dismissal of Paoli as an unpopular, opportunistic tyrant with money salted away abroad. Boswell's judgment was closer to the mark. French preparations for 1768 were hasty and inadequate, with only 3,000 effectives available after garrisons had been established. As a result, French operations in the autumn of 1768 were a disaster. In the battle of Borgo, October 5–9, 1768, the French suffered 200 casualties in a failed attempt to rescue a detachment isolated in that village. The Corsicans appear to have employed aimed fire from cover to defeat the French column. The French "were riddled by invisible enemies who fired with accuracy."[37] The besieged contingent of 530 men with 20 guns was forced to surrender. French humiliation seemed complete when they negotiated an armistice in order to secure the return of their prisoners. In contrast, the Corsicans, energized by success, responded with a mobilization of their society for total war. In March 1769 they voted a *levée en masse* for all men between the ages of 16 and 60 to prepare for war. Hall explains, "Under the pressure of foreign danger and the threat to their particular revolution, the Corsicans developed institutions and principles that appear decidedly modern in spirit.... In December 1768, Paoli's government established a special tribunal to hunt out and punish suspects. The *levée en masse* that was formulated three months later established the principle of the nation in arms and committed Paoli's Corsican followers to total war."[38] These new revolutionary institutions inevitably caused tensions in a society in which individualism had always prevailed. When French commanders claimed that the Corsicans were unhappy with Paoli's tyranny, they no doubt reflected the views of some of the inhabitants.

Choiseul had no intention of allowing the French to be expelled from the island and sent a substantial force to reduce it. It consisted of 24,000 regulars with a powerful artillery train, commanded by the comte de Vaux. He was an altogether different commander from the Chauvelin, who now had to defend himself at court against the criticisms of those same young nobles who had so seriously underestimated the Corsicans. Unlike the unfortunate Chauvelin, Vaux was a seasoned soldier who had served two previous tours on the island.[39] He was accompanied by a professional staff, including the respected mountain-warfare expert Bourcet, who attended as a volunteer, and Dumouriez's friend and rival, the brilliant young comte de Guibert. Paoli took his stand at the battle of Ponte-Nuovo on May 8. The exact nature of Corsican tactics is unclear, but they acted offensively. Two thousand Corsicans crossed the Golo River and attempted to seize the high ground on the French right. They were forced back after a fight of four hours. While retreating toward the bridge, they were inexplicably fired on by mercenaries previously in the Genoese service but now under Paoli. Vaux estimated their loss at more than 500. Voltaire wrote that they had made a rampart of their dead, observing, "One sees such actions only among free peoples."[40] This defeat ended organized Corsican resistance, and Paoli was forced to leave for exile on June 13. Vaux then proceeded to root out remaining resistance. Considering the mountainous terrain and the temper of the people, this was no easy matter. A detachment of about 250 men of the Burgundy regiment seeking to capture a rebellious village in the mountains on May 12 found itself in a hornet's nest. The first shots aroused the countryside, and the French found themselves beset on all sides by an estimated 2,000 inhabitants. Only the timely arrival of the colonel with a strong reserve saved the French from a complete defeat.

Paoli's departure was followed by the submission of the communes and the dispersal of the Corsican army. However, Vaux found that Corsican soldiers reappeared as brigands. Worst of all were the priests and monks who had been Paoli's strongest supporters. Choiseul approved of the destruction of rebel convents and went even further: "If we follow French or Roman procedures for the monks and priests, we will never have an end of them. My advice would be, Monsieur, that all of the bandits be executed without remission, and that all suspects of whatever order be transported to Italy and prohibited from returning."[41] Vaux believed that the Corsicans no longer wanted war but were engaging in their usual habits of robbery and vengeance. He regarded them as a half-savage people who required strong measures if government was to function. Ironically, he cited Paoli's own practices in dealing with his opponents as precedents for the harsh measures he employed. These included treating inhabitants in arms as criminals and burning the villages and farms of their relatives. With these measures he extended French authority across the island, but he continued to be plagued by guerrilla activity until his departure in 1770.

Boswell, who had won celebrity as "Corsica Boswell" with the publication of his journal in 1768, lobbied hard for British intervention and raised money for Paoli. There was considerable sympathy in Britain for the Corsican cause, but the government had no stomach for a war with France. Such intervention was the Corsicans' only real chance of resisting French power. In exile in England, Paoli became a symbol not only of Corsican patriotism, but of the new forces of nationalism and liberty that were stirring the world during the late Enlightenment. It appears that the French government never understood him. In 1776 it sounded him out on the possibility of returning to Corsica, in exchange for unspecified advantages, to assist the French in restoring tranquility to the island. He replied that he would very much like to return but only in an entirely different capacity. French authorities never comprehended Paoli's commitment to Corsican freedom. Returning to the island after the French Revolution, he was again forced into exile by the revolutionary regime, whose idea of freedom did not include Corsican independence.[42]

THE PUGACHEV REBELLION

Yemelyan Ivanovich Pugachev appears in sharp contrast to Paoli, the ideal popular leader of the Enlightenment. This illiterate Cossack and former soldier inspired a revolt against the Russian Empire that produced the most destructive jacquerie of the eighteenth century. During the period of 1773–1775, Russia's southeastern frontier was reduced to a shambles. The number of dead cannot be established with certainty, but the revolt ignited a social war in which 5 percent of the Russian nobility perished. This figure included women and children who were hanged, stabbed, bludgeoned, beheaded or drowned. The upheaval produced a frisson of horror throughout Europe as the so-called dark people shook the foundations of the Old Regime. Pugachev had no Boswell and struck no chords in Enlightenment thought. Rather, it was his enemy the Russian empress Catherine the Great (Catherine II) who remained the darling of the philosophes. Voltaire, who was urging her to kill Turks, had no sympathy for those who appeared to threaten her policy of enlightened reform. Ironically, it was Catherine who compared herself to Paoli in describing her war against the Ottoman Empire, saying, "He knows how to fight for his home and his independence."[43] Pugachev appealed to groups outside the circle of the Enlightenment: Cossacks; non-Russian-speaking Tatar peoples; religious dissidents in the form of the Old Believers, who resisted state control of the Orthodox Church; and Russian peasants. It was a revolt of the frontier against the heavy hand of a centralizing monarchy and of the poor against the privileged. The revolt had deep roots, echoing the rebellions of Bolotnikov (1606–1607), Razin (1670–1671), and Bulavin (1707–1708).[44] All of these people had reasons to oppose Catherine's "enlightened regime." Cossacks and Tatars resisted encroachments upon their autonomy and the demands for military service exacerbated by the empress's war with the Ottomans. Factory workers in Ural Mountains industries that supported Russian military expansion resented their condition of forced labor. Old Believers deplored westernizing cultural influences and the foreign advisers on whom Catherine relied. War imposed a huge burden on the entire state, and landlords passed that burden on to their peasantry, increasing existing social tensions. As everywhere, war strained the fabric of the Old Regime and, at the margins, the fabric ripped.[45]

Pugachev remains a remote figure. He was a charismatic adventurer who knew how to play on the hopes and fears of dissident peoples. He appealed to them in a manner they understood by adopting the pose of the czar Peter III, Catherine's late husband. In doing so he followed in the path of many other pretenders who claimed to have been the victims of noble plots and sought a "return" to power through popular support. Since Peter III's reign had been brief, it was possible to credit him with many good intentions in contrast to an oppressive and foreign-born empress. Peter had relieved the nobles from their service responsibility, and it was widely thought that he had been prepared to emancipate the serfs before his overthrow by the nobles. It appears that none of Pugachev's closest followers took his claim seriously but that they understood it was the means to gain legitimacy for their movement and inspire a millennial fervor among the peoples of the region. In some respects the movement was conservative, for by claiming to be czar Pugachev signaled an intention to retain the Russian state. He organized a military administration on the imperial model and was careful to issue decrees in the form consistent with that of other emperors. He was dependent in this respect on the literate members of his following, who formed a version of a traveling imperial court. At times Pugachev found it necessary to adopt the remote aspect expected of a true czar; at others he appeared as a simple man of the people. These conflicting roles created tensions among his followers and raised questions about his agenda. This included restoration of autonomy, freedom from military service and taxation, freedom for Old Believers, and an attack on the nobility. However, there was no suggestion that the institution of serfdom would be abolished. Indeed, many serfs who had recently been transferred to private ownership hoped to be restored to the status of state peasants under a benign czar. Although his movement gained wide popular support, Pugachev himself never articulated a revolutionary agenda that could appeal to an enlightened audience. Instead, he represented the dark forces that led even Rousseau to recoil from the prospect of an overthrow of the social order.

Militarily, Pugachev caught the government at the time when it was preoccupied by the Turkish war. Military garrisons in the area of the revolt consisted of poorly trained, second-class regulars and native troops who frequently deserted to Pugachev at the first opportunity. By the time St. Petersburg became aware of the serious nature of the revolt, Pugachev had assembled a large army and gained effective control over an extensive area of the southeast. In addition to the unreliable nature of the forces opposing him, Pugachev had considerable advantages. He himself was a soldier with experience as an artilleryman. The Cossacks who formed the core of his army were trained warriors and superb cavalrymen. As garrisons came over to them, the rebels acquired a large number of light field guns, which gave them an early superiority over forces sent to oppose them. Pugachev also gained support from metal workers in the Urals industrial region and with it a level of technical proficiency. However, these advantages proved fleeting. The majority of the rebel army was poorly armed and undisciplined. The successful conclusion of the Turkish war doomed the rebellion as the state turned its full military resources against Pugachev. Despite their bravery and skill, this irregular army was no match for the regular forces of a great power. From the beginning the rebels failed to capture fortified towns that were resolutely defended. This was a unique aspect of the Pugachev Rebellion, for earlier uprisings had attracted much support from the towns. It was one thing to have experience as a gunner and another to understand engineering. Thus the rebels were totally lacking in siegecraft. Furthermore, they could not withstand well-disciplined regular troops on the battlefield. Pitched battles invariably resulted in the massacre of rebel combatants. Thus the revolt moved from one place to another with regular forces on its heels. Pugachev's army wasted away in these conditions, and his end came when he was betrayed by his remaining followers, who sold him to the government.

The Pugachev Rebellion provides insight into the strengths and weaknesses of Catherine's regime. She was able to establish herself as an enlightened monarch and thus gained respect and legitimacy in the eyes of Europe. But Catherine's reforms aiming at the creation of a modern centralized state provoked a violent and formidable response from those on the margins of society. These included people with military skill and experience. However, the development of the Russian regular army was one of the greatest successes of the eighteenth-century Russian state. It was a peasant army whose officers were nobles. Unlike armies in the West, peasant soldiers endured 25 years of forced service, the equivalent of a life sentence in the context of life expectancies of the time. Russian policy ensured that these soldiers were removed from their native societies so their loyalty would be focused on the army. In this they were successful. Pugachev's appeals fell on deaf ears among the highly trained, long-service regulars who slaughtered his followers. Behind Catherine's enlightened rhetoric, the reality was that her regime depended not on the good opinion of Voltaire or d'Alembert but on this formidable instrument of force.

THE DUTCH REVOLT

Compared to such events as the Pugachev Rebellion, the Netherlands Patriot Revolution of 1787 was a pallid and rather middle-class affair. The Patriots, who were anti-Orange and anti-British, replayed old themes in Netherlands politics but recast them in the style of the late Enlightenment. In particular, they were inspired by the example of the American Revolution (American War of Independence) and sought to appeal to a broader political nation than did the wealthy Regents. They relied on a militia, the Free Corps, as their armed force. These citizen-soldiers had roots in earlier militia organizations, the *schutterig* (shooters), who appear in so many seventeenth-century paintings. The Free Corps opened its ranks to any denomination and gave commissions to burghers of modest means, but, as Simon Schama has indicated, it was not a revolutionary army. It served as a means of achieving the Patriots' political goals, but it was socially defensive. "On the whole the Patriot revolution was remarkable for its extreme reluctance to resort either to open violence or to punitive measures against its enemies."[46] The Free Corps was thus more significant as a political organization than as a military force. It quickly collapsed before the Prussian invasion of 1787. This underscores how far the Netherlands had fallen from the great days of the seventeenth century.

COMMON THREADS

The conflicts described above have few common threads. They occurred in response to particular circumstances and, except for Genoa, which retained its independence due to French assistance, all were ultimately defeated. Further east, Pugachev's Cossacks and Polish rebels were equally unsuccessful. In the end, peoples in arms could not prevail against regular troops unless they received outside support. Most eighteenth-century rebellions were in defense of old liberties threatened by a foreign power or by a new and alien regime. Scotland and Corsica offer similar cases of clannish and warlike peoples inhabiting poor mountainous countries on the margins of great-power politics. Charles Edward Stuart and Pasquale Paoli raised significant military forces from this material and scored surprising victories against unprepared regular troops. However, both required foreign assistance if they were to succeed, and both were disappointed by their friends among the great powers. Here, however, the similarity ends. The Jacobites could not count on a unified Scotland. Their political program, such as it was, was tainted by fears that they were the cat's-paws of an absolutist and Catholic France. Charles Edward presented the romantic image of an idealized past, one that frightened those with enlightened opinions in England and in Scotland. Paoli rode a movement of national unity and cast it in Enlightenment terms. The Corsican war of resistance against France looked forward to the ideas and policies of the Jacobins. The Jacobites and the Camisards lacked a broad base of support. It is interesting that other resistance movements sought to recruit from all classes within their society. This caused them to become revolutionary, as in the case of Genoa, while the Dutch remained socially conservative. In many cases religion and religious orders played important roles. All resistance movements were able to find sufficient arms to mount serious resistance against the forces arrayed against them. These movements did not lack military experience. Lord George Murray and Paoli were distinguished commanders. The Dutch produced no leader of this ability, but it is worth noting that Lewis Lochée, master of the military academy at Little Chelsea, closed his school and formed the Belgic Legion to aid the Dutch in their defense. These movements receive attention today only to the extent that they threatened the existence of an established state. This was beyond their means, however, and thus the memory of even so heroic figure as Paoli has faded. Nevertheless, they remind us that the foundations of the ancien régime were shaken by frequent tremors. In 1789 there was an earthquake that toppled the central pillar of that world.

   Whatever the ideological content of these popular conflicts and however they were perceived by enlightened public, the response of the military remained constant. French comments about the lack of regular troops among the Corsicans are significant. European officers regarded irregulars with contempt because they did not observe the forms and conventions that had contributed to the enlightened conduct of war. Therefore regulars were not prepared to extend to irregulars the protection of the laws of war. It was a small step to brand irregulars who wore exotic dress and who fought unconventionally as uncivilized or savage. Rousseau's noble savage, whom the Corsicans appeared to have epitomized, was simply a savage in the eyes of French regulars. As we have seen, Vattel did not believe that such savages were included in the protections of the laws of nations. Added to this was a general sense of revulsion against rebellion. Officers, as members or aspiring members of a social elite, were united in the defense of the social order. The code of honor discussed in chapter 3 guaranteed a social conservatism among even the most-enlightened elements of the corps. Rebellion, or a threat to established society from members at the margins of society, provoked a harsh response from most. Thus a rebel or an irregular who was wounded or captured could expect very different treatment than could a regular soldier. After Culloden the duke of Cumberland's troops bayoneted Highland wounded found on the battlefield. Other wounded Highlanders were simply left to bleed to death. This may be compared to the duke's concern for a wounded French officer after Dettingen or to Valfons's search for the wounded of both sides after Hastenbeck. Guerrilla war provoked an especially brutal response, as one had difficulty in distinguishing between combatants and noncombatants. Commanders did not hesitate to use scorched-earth tactics to destroy the roots of such resistance. Neither Charles Edward Stuart nor Pasquale Paoli engaged in guerrilla war. They sought to achieve their goals through large-scale battles fought by irregulars. When they were defeated, British and French commanders turned against the societies that had supported them and sought to crush the foundations of resistance. Guerrilla or partisan resistance flickered on in Corsica, but guerilla war was not the cause of the brutal policies associated with Cumberland and Vaux.

AMERICAN INDEPENDENCE

Of all the great eighteenth-century rebellions before 1789, only America's succeeded. Geographically at the margin of the European world, the thirteen colonies were of central importance to the British imperial system, and thus their rebellion had more-profound consequences than the conflicts discussed above. Discussions of the origins of the American War of Independence (American Revolution) include the particular tensions that arose in the wake of British imperial victory in 1763 and the debates over taxation and imperial authority. The intellectual origins have been viewed as part of the development of a culture of liberty in the Atlantic world (R.R. Palmer), as part of a tradition of British constitutional freedom (Bernard Bailyn), or as an extension of the religious revival of the Great Awakening (Jonathan Clark).[47] Particular grievances melded with broader intellectual, cultural, and social currents to form a combustible mix. American revolutionaries were skillful in explaining their goals in a way that could appeal to enlightened opinion. The Declaration of Independence was crafted with that in mind. Its general principles drew on the greatest Enlightenment political thinkers, from Locke to Rousseau, and thus claimed for the Americans the center of the Enlightenment mainstream. Its detailed indictment of Great Britain's King George III provided ammunition for parliamentary allies who sought to place the rebellion within the context of the British struggle for constitutional liberty. Before 1789, no other eighteenth-century popular leaders, not even Paoli, had come close to this achievement. It was the most-brilliant political manifesto crafted to that time, perhaps the most brilliant ever.

Still, wars are not won with pieces of paper. George III's parliamentary critics were a minority and remained so almost to the end of the American War of Independence. A shared Enlightenment culture provided American spokesmen an entrée to the world of French salons and to influential circles in Paris. However, it is unlikely that the ideas of the Declaration of Independence struck a responsive chord among the king and the government officials, such as Charles Gravier de Vergennes, who were more likely to calculate the opportunities and risks presented by the rebellion in terms of traditional great-power politics. Thus American independence was a near thing. As is often observed, Britain was the world's greatest naval, commercial, and financial power. Despite the rhetoric of some members of parliament, it possessed a stable and constitutional government capable of directing and sustaining a distant war. As was usually the case at the beginning of a war, the British government had to scramble to put together an army of sufficient size, but it possessed in its small standing force an experienced and highly trained core with a proud tradition. Its senior officers were veterans of the Seven Years' War, the most successful in British history. Many of those officers had North American experience. Against this formidable power, the Americans had to cobble together a government, an army and a navy, and a financial system. They did so with remarkable ingenuity but even they, as was the case with other eighteenth-century rebellions, could not have succeeded without foreign support. Unlike the Jacobites and the Corsicans (but like the Genoese in 1746), the Americans received substantial foreign assistance. France's intervention transformed the war. The battle of Saratoga was perhaps more instrumental in bringing this about than the Declaration of Independence.

The cultural components of the American Revolution were complex. After all, many Americans supported the Crown. At the end of the war, shiploads of American loyalists embarked for Canada from the harbor of Huntington, New York (where I wrote this portion of this book). The Crown found supporters among many different cultures: former Scottish Jacobites in North Carolina, German immigrants in Pennsylvania, Native Americans, and African slaves. British authorities sought to harness this support for their war effort, but they had indifferent success. Indeed, the recruitment of forces from the margins of colonial society exposed the British government to charges that it waged a cruel and savage war. The appearance of former slaves in British uniform was guaranteed to drive their masters to the cause of "liberty," no matter how ironic such a choice might be. From the beginning, there was a debate on both sides as to the nature of the war. If Americans were rebels, were they entitled to the protection of the laws of war or should they be treated in the manner meted out to the Jacobites and the Corsicans? To what extent might the Americans be conciliated, or should they be exposed to "hard war" to bring them to their senses? On the American side there was a similar debate. Should the Americans fight as a people in arms as at Lexington and Concord, an approach favored by General Charles Lee? Or should they, as Washington advocated, create a regular army that might meet the British on their own terms? These were crucial debates, and their resolution provides us with insight into the eighteenth-century culture of force.

The American resolution of the debate over how to wage war was perhaps the most significant in shaping the character of the conflict. The Continental army provided the Americans with a force of regulars that could be included within the military conventions of the century. Indeed, it was organized under articles of war similar to those that governed British forces. Although the British did not recognize the authority of the Continental Congress and refused to address George Washington as a general, they soon found it necessary to deal with him on matters of prisoners, treatment of the wounded, and soldier conduct. In doing so they offered de facto recognition of his authority. British prisoners in American hands were in a sense hostages, requiring the British to follow normal conventions between regular armies. However, the organization provided by Washington made it possible to engage in formal protocols. Washington's determination to create a regular army was probably the only realistic alternative open to the Americans. Recent scholarship has discounted the traditional picture of the Americans as a heavily armed people with great experience in the use of firearms. The colonial militias were often short of muskets and possessed only rudimentary training. They were far from being the martial people found in the Scottish Highlands and in Corsica. Throughout the war they played a greater role in internal security than as a fighting force. It is unclear how long the Americans would have sustained the kind of partisan war advocated by Lee. Such an approach would have played into the hands of British officers who urged a scorched-earth policy and would have undoubtedly made the war more violent. The partisan conflicts of the Southern campaigns would have been written on a larger scale. Southern partisans did cause difficulties for the British, but only the existence of a small force of Continental regulars prevented the British from dispersing to make an end of them. Furthermore, it seems unlikely that France would have taken seriously a rebellion fought entirely by irregulars. The existence of the Continental army under an established figure such as Washington was a prerequisite for critical foreign assistance. Without it the Americans could have found themselves reduced to the condition of Ireland, for whom French help was always too little and too late.

The strategic problems confronting the British were significant, but for the most part manageable. However, the British government's policy of negotiating while fighting led military planners to see the war through a strategic fog. Thus, there was the hope that by British seizure of strategic territory—whether it was New York, Philadelphia, the Hudson Valley, or South Carolina—the rebels would become demoralized and the loyalists empowered. The true strategic center of the American war effort was Washington's army. Had Howe destroyed it in New York in 1776, the military outcome most certainly would have favored Britain. On the whole, Britain fought the war with an eye to the hearts and minds of the colonists and exercised restraint over the conduct of their forces. It need not have happened that way. Notwithstanding the policy of the government, many

British officers—by 1779 probably a majority—advocated a scorched-earth policy in order to end the rebellion.

Charles Royster, the historian of the Continental army, has expressed his belief that America was gripped in a passion for arms in 1775, a *rage militaire.* This passion was partly a result of religion and the Great Awakening, which gave Americans confidence in the justice and the invincibility of their cause. Americans were also confident that they possessed special military skills and a natural superiority over foreign professionals. Thus, we may say that America's military enthusiasm was based on twin myths. British regulars quickly dispelled the nonsense of innate military superiority and raised troubling questions about the intentions of Providence. Royster finds that the *rage militaire* vanished by the end of 1775, never to return. In its place was the Continental army, a professional force that relied on discipline as much as patriotism to preserve its integrity. This army suffered from many of the problems confronting the British. Pillaging and desertion were common concerns in both armies. One historian concludes that a large percentage of the troops on both sides during the southern campaigns consisted of deserters from the other side. Royster finds that American officers were as prone to dueling as their British counterparts and shared their culture of honor and sensibility. By the end of the war, Continental soldiers began to regard themselves as a distinct class within American society, one forged by military professionalism and a common sense of patriotism and sacrifice.[48]

Some historians, such as Sylvia Frey, have observed that the social origins of the two armies were similar, the rank and file being drawn from poor-but-respectable men who chose the military for economic reasons.[49] Royster argues that Americans had better economic choices than the army, particularly when one considers the poor pay awarded American soldiers. The ease with which men deserted the Continental army suggests that those who remained did so for patriotic reasons. But one should not assume that British soldiers lacked patriotism.

There were approximately 3,500 British army officers at the beginning of the war. What was their attitude toward the rebellion? Studies by Ira Gruber and Stephen Conway find that although there was some pro-American feeling in the officer corps, it had little effect on its willingness to serve. A few high-ranking generals and a number of company and field-grade officers refused service in America, but this did not threaten the army's stability. The majority of those who opposed the government's coercive policies accepted service out of a sense of duty and loyalty to the Crown. For young officers war meant professional advancement, particularly since battlefield vacancies in higher ranks were not filled by purchase. Loyalty and career advancement were primary motives for officer participation in the American war.[50] One also finds a sense of patriotism among British officers. Most were proud of the sense of freedom provided by British institutions, even if they thought their government's policies were misguided. Many saw the American rebels as fanatical zealots who would impose mob rule. Few were attracted to American ideas of equality. Thomas Hughes, for example, was taken prisoner near Ticonderoga and was treated well enough. But he found that "people here have not the least idea of a gentleman. Our servants are treated just like ourselves, and they are surprised to find that our men won't eat at the same table with us, to which they are always invited."[51]

German officers expressed similar views. "You know the Huguenot wars in France: what Religion was there, Liberty is here, simply fanaticism, and the effects are the same."[52] Another officer observed that "The [American] regiments here are militia and nearly all of their officers are artisans. It cost a lot of pains to get the idea into the heads of the inhabitants here that our officers have no [civil] occupation; it was thought that they simply refused to ply their trade from caprice."[53] British, German, and French officers were united in a general contempt for American ideas of freedom and equality and for the amateur nature of their officers.

British officers were particularly outraged at the act of rebellion, a feeling that intensified when the Americans allied themselves with Britain's ancient enemy France. In September 1774 the British general Lord Hugh Earl Percy observed from Boston: "In short, this country is now in as open state of rebellion as Scotland in the year 1745." Two months later he wrote, "The People here are the most designing, Artful Villains in the World. They have not the least Idea of either religion or Morality."[54] The obvious parallel with the Jacobite revolt was ominous. W. Glanville Evelyn wrote to his father, "We have great confidence that we shall shortly receive such orders as will authorise us to scourge the rebellion with rods of iron."[55] When the war erupted, Lord Rawdon proposed that "we should (when we get further into the country) give free liberty to the soldiers to ravage at will, that these infatuated wretches may feel what a calamity war is."[56]

At the beginning it was unclear whether they were repressing a rebellion or fighting a conventional war. Frederick Mackenzie served as a staff officer in America during the period 1775–1781. He believed that American prisoners were treated too leniently, for rebels in arms customarily "forfeit their lives by the laws of all Countries."[57] Failure to impose capital punishment on the rebels, he thought, merely fed the rebellion. Once the Americans gained control of a number of British prisoners, however, the government had no choice but to recognize captured Americans as prisoners of war.

As the war progressed, Mackenzie continually weighed the question of humanity versus severity. In November 1776 he observed that it was right to treat one's enemies as if they might become one's friends. He shared the belief that humanity was the natural characteristic of British troops—an honor not lightly conceded. As a result, he rejected the idea of severe punitive actions, even though he believed that the government's conciliatory policy was not having the desired effect.[58] In 1778 the news that General Clinton intended to evacuate Philadelphia convinced him that that policy was bankrupt. He concluded that Philadelphia should be burned and New Jersey and New England laid waste. "Such a mode of Warfare might appear cruel, but it would be the most effectual towards the conclusion of the War, and in the end the most Economical," he wrote.[59] Thereafter he continued to advocate severe action against the Americans while denouncing the policy of leniency that appeared to prolong the war.[60] Mackenzie's outlook was similar to that of many soldiers who chafe at restrictions that seem to stand in the way of victory. A grim realist who was prepared to do whatever was necessary to win the war, he departed in no way from the standard of necessity established by Vattel, the most important expert on international law of the period.

Mackenzie's evolving attitude is representative of that of a majority of the officer corps in America. Stephen Conway has explored the issue of hard-liners versus conciliators in the corps and concludes that by late 1779 the advocates of severity had gained a numerical majority and were able at a local level to undermine the conciliatory policies of their superiors.[61]

PAOLI

On the night of September 20, 1777, British soldiers advancing stealthily through the darkness burst upon a detachment of Americans by their campfires near Paoli, Pennsylvania. The result was the Paoli Massacre.[62] Ignoring their victims' pleas for mercy, the British went about their sword-and-bayonet work with a savage gusto. According to one survivor, "They had with fixed bayonets formed a cordon around him, and...every one of them in sport had indulged their brutal ferocity by stabbing him in the different parts of his body and limbs."[63] A British officer confirmed the nightmarish nature of the event with its "shrieks, groans, shouting, imprecations, deprecations, the clashing of swords and bayonets, etc."[64] At least 150 Americans were stabbed to death and many others wounded by British soldiers, who concluded their task without firing a shot. Their commander, Sir Charles Grey, who had ordered them to remove the flints from their muskets, won a certain celebrity as No Flints Grey.

This was to be a recurring nightmare for the Americans. On September 23, 1778, a force commanded by Grey surrounded the village of Old Tappan, New Jersey. There he caught the men of Baylor's Light Horse asleep in the village's barns and houses. Although the Americans "Beg'd and Pray'd for Quarter," their enemies were "deaf to all their crys and Butcher'd a number of them in their Beads and swore they would give the Reables no Quarters."[65] Within a month, on the night of October 15, 1778, a force led by Captain Patrick Ferguson, nephew of the philosopher Adam

Ferguson, decimated the Casimir Pulaski Legion at Little Egg Harbor. About 50 Americans died from bayonet and sword thrusts for, as Ferguson observed, "It being a night attack Little Quarter could be given, so there were only five prisoners."[66] It is certainly true that night actions made it more difficult for officers to exercise control over their men, but it is worth noting that they had things well in hand until it became time for taking prisoners. It appears that they relished this bloody work. Captain Sir James Baird of the 17th Regiment, reported to have been a major perpetrator of the massacre of Baylor's dragoons, later swaggered through the streets with his bloodstained bayonet hanging from his back. He was one of the officers of the flank companies, the light infantry and grenadiers, who, it has been suggested, "cultivated a consciously ferocious image for themselves and their men."[67] There were British officers who were shocked by these events. Colonel Charles Stuart, younger son of the earl of Bute and a consistent critic of government policy, believed that the action at Paoli was murder rather than war.[68] Lieutenant Loftus Cliffe, who frequently expressed distress over the harsh nature of the war, rationalized the massacre at Paoli on grounds of military necessity. Others, probably representing majority opinion, expressed no scruples but only satisfaction over the outcome of these events.[69] Paoli, Old Tappan, and Little Egg Harbor were small actions with relatively few casualties compared to major European battles such as Fontenoy. However, they indicate that British officers had consciously departed from the rules of war and were prepared to engage in a higher level of brutality than usually seen in conventional operations in Europe. They reflect a deep tension in the British army over the conduct of the war, with many officers endorsing a hardline war and expressing frustration over the restraints imposed on them. This tension marked the relations of Major General Charles Cornwallis and his commander of light troops, Colonel Banastre Tarleton. The latter won notoriety in the South when his British Legion slaughtered Americans attempting to surrender at Waxhaws. Tarleton later offered an oblique defense of his own behavior by criticizing Cornwallis for the latter's "lenity and generosity," which "did not experience in America the merited returns of gratitude and affection."[70] Were Cornwallis and other senior commanders doddering McClellans who failed to wage a vigorous war to defeat the rebellion? Cornwallis's modern biographers have faulted him for failing to understand the need for ruthlessness in revolutionary war. But Cornwallis, who never hesitated to seek out the armed forces of the enemy, also, to his credit, played by the rules. He had no interest in following a Highland model of "pacification."[71]

Were the rules important? On July 15, 1779, an American brigade of light infantry under General Anthony Wayne carried out a night assault on the British position of Stony Point on the Hudson River. It was a position of great strength, defended by an abatis of sharpened trees and men

of the experienced 17th regiment. Ironically, Wayne had been the unfortunate American commander at Paoli and had barely escaped with his reputation intact. Now he achieved a signal revenge. While one portion of his
force opened fire on the center of the abatis, Wayne led the remainder
through chest-high water to outflank the defenders and seize the height.
There was a desperate melee as the Americans drove home their attack
with bayonets. British soldiers knew what to expect if defeated. Captain
Lawrence Robert Campbell of the 71st Grenadier Company, wounded
twice in the defense of the abatis, sought to retire to the rear for assistance
but was prevented by soldiers of the 17th regiment fleeing the upper
works. They told him that the Americans had put everyone to the sword.[72]
However, as British troops realized that continued resistance was hope-
less, they began to throw down their arms and beg for mercy. The Americans had killed 63 of the enemy and wounded 70 in the fighting. But 543
were spared and taken prisoner.

The Americans were conscious of having achieved a moral as well as a
military victory. "The American soldier," wrote general Wayne, "is not
so...divested of every tender feeling of humanity so as to strike a pros-
trate and unresisting foe—that is a business suited only to a base and
degenerate Briton, who has refined upon every species of Villainy."[73] Benjamin Rush wrote to Wayne, "You have established the national character
of our country. You have taught our enemies that bravery, humanity, and
magnanimity are the virtues of the Americans."[74] The significance of this
event was not lost on the British. "It was something not unworthy of
observation that the bayonet which had been so often fatally employed
against the Americans in similar cases, was the only weapon used in this
attack," wrote the *Annual Register* for 1779. "The laws of war," wrote the
British naval commander Sir George Collier, "give a right to the assailants
of putting all to death who are found in arms; justice is due to all men, and
commendation should be given where it is deserved. The rebels had made
the attack with a bravery they never before exhibited and they showed at
this moment a generosity and clemency which during the course of the
rebellion has no parallel."[75] The British general James Pattison reported
that "the attack was commanded by a Brig'r Gen'l Wayne, and it must in
justice be allow'd to his credit , as well as to all acting under his Orders,
that no instance of Inhumanity was shown to the unhappy captives."[76]

A significant percentage of British officers thought that the laws of war
should be suspended when dealing with rebels. This opinion was based
on the experience of regular officers dealing with irregular opponents in
places such as Scotland and Corsica. They were slow to comprehend the
significance of the revolution with which they were now confronted. They
were not alone for, as Gilbert Bodinier has found, the revolution made little impression on French officers sent to America during this time.[77] Captain Ewald recalled that, after the surrender at Yorktown, "one scarcely

knew whether he was among his friends or foes. Indeed I found on more than one occasion that the French officers preferred the company of the English, Anspach, and Hessian officers to that of their own allies."[78] The harsh attitude of the British officers conflicted with the strategy adopted by the government and senior commanders. It also was in conflict with the spirit of the Enlightenment that emphasized humane treatment for those unable to resist. Stony Point provided the Americans with a concrete action that supported the rhetoric of the Declaration of Independence. The Americans as a humane and enlightened people were entitled to govern themselves. Washington's regular army demonstrated discipline superior to that of the established British army. Stony Point was not an isolated incident. Don Higginbotham has called attention to the Continental army's respect for property, which stood in sharp contrast to the destruction caused by the British. Washington's army displayed a "visible virtue" that helped it win the battle for public opinion.[79] In doing so, it undercut the position of those British officers who sought to portray them as lawless rebels and proved the case for independence. Foreign officers might mock the Continental officers as amateurs and autodidacts, but there were times when they recognized the virtuous qualities of their opponents. A German officer prisoner wrote with surprise after the battle of Saratoga, "I must still say there was not a man among them (the American officers) who showed the slightest sign of mockery, malicious delight, hate, or other insult." The captive officers received the same courtesies that they would have encountered in Europe.[80] Ewald developed a respect for Continental officers, who seemed to work harder at their profession than their British counterparts. He also observed something in the American army that distinguished it from those of the Old Regime. He was one of the few commentators to recognize its revolutionary character: "With what soldiers in the world could one do what was done by these men, who go about nearly naked and in the greatest privation? Deny the best disciplined soldiers of Europe what is due them and they will run away in droves, and the general will soon be alone. But from this one can perceive what an enthusiasm—what these poor fellows call 'Liberty'—can do!"[81]

NOTES

1. Edward Gibbon, *The Autobiography of Edward Gibbon,* ed. Dero A. Saunders (New York: Meridian Books, 1961), 131.

2. Ibid., 132–34.

3. W. Windham and Geo. Townshend, *A Plan of Discipline for the Use of the Norfolk Militia in Three Parts…with an Introduction from Aelian, Vegetius, Folard, K. of Prussia, M. Saxe, Wolfe, and the most celebrated Ancient and Modern Authors* (London, 1763), xxviii–xxix.

4. I have based this paragraph on Jacques Gébelin, *Histoire des milices provinciales (1688–1791): Le triage au sort sous l'ancien régime* (Paris: Libraire Hachette et

Cie, 1881). For Noailles, see *Correspondance de Louis XV et du Maréchal de Noailles,* ed. Camille Rousset, 2 vols. (Paris: Didier et Cie, 1869), 1:112.

5. German militias are discussed in Peter H. Wilson, *German Armies: War and German Politics, 1648–1806* (London: UCL Press, 1998). For Prussia, see p. 244.

6. Christopher Storrs, *War, Diplomacy, and the Rise of Savoy, 1690–1720* (Cambridge: Cambridge University Press, 1999), 36–40; Reed Browning, *The War of the Austrian Succession* (New York: St. Martin's Press, 1993), 187–88.

7. David Francis, *The First Peninsular War, 1702–1713* (New York: St. Martin's Press, 1975), 181–83.

8. John Shy, "A New Look at the Colonial Militia," chap. 2 in *A People Numerous and Armed: Reflections on the Military Struggle for American Independence* (New York: Oxford University Press, 1976); W.J. Eccles, "The French Forces in North America during the Seven Years' War," in *Dictionary of Canadian Biography,* vol. 3, *1741 to 1770,* ed. F.G. Halpenny (Toronto: University of Toronto Press, 1974), xvii; Michael Bellesiles, *Arming America: The Origins of a National Gun Culture* (New York: Knopf, 2000), 5 (for the controversy surrounding Bellesiles's book, see the *New York Times,* 8 December 2001, sec. A, p. 13); Armstrong Starkey, *European and Native American Warfare, 1675–1815* (London: UCL Press; Norman: University of Oklahoma Press, 1998), 141-42.

9. *Frederick the Great on the Art of War,* ed. & trans. Jay Luvaas, (New York: Free Press, 1966), 126–29.

10. Ibid., 128.

11. David Chandler, *The Art of Warfare in the Age of Marlborough* (NY: Sarpedon, 1995).

12. R. Parker and Comte de Merode-Westerloo, *The Marlborough Wars,* ed. David Chandler (Hamden, Conn.: Archon Books, 1968), 160.

13. A.-R. Mopinot de la Chapotte, *Sous Louis le Bien-Aimé, correspondance amoureuse et militaire d'un officier pendant La Guerre de Sept-Ans (1757–1765),* ed. J. Lemoine (Paris, 1905), 370–71. See also *Correspondance inedited du Lieutenant General Lancelot Turpin du Crissé, litterateur et tacticien du XVIIIme siècle addresse au dauphin, fils de Louis XV et paraphé ou annoté par lui, 10 mai-10 decembre 1761 Édition de la "Revue des Independants"* (Paris, 1934), 47.

14. Christopher Duffy, *Instrument of War,* vol. 1 of *The Austrian Army in the Seven Years' War* (Rosemont, Ill.: The Emperor's Press, 2000), 301–15.

15. Ibid., 96–97.

16. Francis, *First Peninsular War,* 190–91, 371–80.

17. John A. Lynn, *Giant of the Grand Siècle: The French Army 1610–1715* (Cambridge: Cambridge University Press, 1997), 375, 455.

18. Claude C. Sturgill, *Marshal Villars and the War of the Spanish Succession* (Lexington: University of Kentucky Press, 1965), 53–62.

19. For Prince Charles Edward's tactics, see James Michael Hill, *Celtic Warfare, 1595–1763* (Edinburgh: John Donald, 1986), 127–56. See also, Jeremy Black, *Culloden and the '45* (New York: St. Martin's Press, 1990), and Katherine Tomasson and Francis Buist, *Battles of the '45* (London: B.T. Batsford, 1962; reprint, 1978).

20. *The Gentleman's Magazine* (January 1746): 31–32, 42.

21. Ibid., (April 1746). For Cumberland's account and other reports, see pp. 209–20. For an attempt to bend the facts to a theory, see Michael Bellesiles, *Arming America,* 145. British battlefield tactics during the century are best described in

David Chandler, *The Art of Warfare in the Age of Marlborough* (New York: Sarpedon, 1995).

22. Robert Wodrow, *The History of the Sufferings of the Church of Scotland from the Restoration to the Revolution*, 4 vols. (1721–22; reprint, Glasgow: Blackie, Fullarton, 1829), 2:389–432 (page citations are to the reprint edition). See also, John R. Elder, *The Highland Host of 1678* (Glasgow: James Maclehose, 1914).

23. Bruce Lenman, *The Jacobite Risings in Britain, 1689–1746* (London: Eyre Methuen, 1980), 146–147.

24. *The Gentleman's Magazine* (January 1746), 16.

25. Henry Fielding, *The True Patriot*, ed. Miriam Austin Locke (University: University of Alabama Press, 1964) nos. 7, 14, and 15. For Adams, see no. 12.

26. Ibid., no. 5.

27. *The Gentleman's Magazine* (May 1746): 261–62; (June 1746): 366–67; (July 1746): 412–18.

28. Bruce Lenman, *The Jacobite Risings in Britain 1689–1746*, 275–76. See also, W. A. Speck, *The Butcher: The Duke of Cumberland and the Suppression of the '45* (Oxford: Basil Blackwell, 1981).

29. Reed Browning, *The War of the Austrian Succession* (New York: St. Martin's Press, 1993), 291–94, 297-98.

30. James Boswell, *The Journal of a Tour of Corsica; and Memoirs of Pascal Paoli* (1768; reprint, London: Williams and Norgate, 1951), 49 (page citation is to the reprint edition).

31. Ibid., 63.

32. Ibid., 67.

33. Ibid., 102.

34. Ibid., 91.

35. Ibid., 72.

36. Thad Hall, *France and the Eighteenth Century Corsican Question* (New York: New York University Press, 1970), 176–79; for the French conquest of Corsica, see pp. 183–208. Also see, Rene Boudard "La Nation Corse et sa lutte pour la liberte entre 1744 et 1789," *Information Historique*, 41 (March 1979): 81–85, and Francis Beretti, *"Pasquali Paoli et l'image de la Corse au dix-huitieme siècle le témoinage des voyagers britanniques,"* Studies on Voltaire and the Eighteenth Century, no. 253 (Oxford: The Voltaire Foundation, 1988).

37. Charles-François Dumouriez, *Mémoires du General Dumouriez*, ed. Fs. Barriere, 2 vols. (Paris: Libraire de Firmin Didot Frères, 1848), 1:73. For the 1768 campaign, see pp. 59–77. For 1769, see pp. 78–92.

38. Hall, *France and the Corsican Question,* 200.

39. Baguenault de Purchesse, "La Conquète de la Corse et le Maréchal de Vaux," *Revue des questiones historiques* 28 (1880): 152–213. This article contains much of Vaux's correspondence and is the most-important published primary source for the 1769 campaign. For Vaux's background, see p. 5.

40. Ibid., 168.

41. Ibid., 179.

42. Boudard, *La Nation Corse,* 85.

43. Voltaire and Catherine the Great, *Voltaire and Catherine the Great: Selected Correspondence*, trans. and ed. A. Lentin (Cambridge: Oriental Research Partners, 1974), 69.

44. Pugachev's revolt is placed in perspective in Paul Avrich, *Russian Rebels, 1600–1800* (New York: Schocken Books, 1972). For Pugachev, see pp. 180–254.

45. In addition to Avrich, I have relied for my discussion of Pugachev on John T. Alexander, *Emperor of the Cossacks: Pugachev and the Frontier Jacquerie of 1773–1775* (Lawrence, Kans.: Coronado Press, 1973). I also wish to thank Brian Boeck for his advice.

46. Simon Schama, *Patriots and Liberators: Revolution in the Netherlands 1780–1813* (New York: Knopf, 1977), 100.

47. R. R. Palmer, *The Age of Democratic Revolution; a Political History of Europe and America* (Princeton: Princeton University Press, 1959–1964); Bernard Bailyn, *The Ideological Origins of the American Revolution* (Cambridge, Mass.: Belknap Press of Harvard University Press, 1992); J. C. D. Clark, *The Language of Liberty, 1660–1832: Political Discourse and Social Dynamics in the Anglo-American World* (Cambridge; New York: Cambridge University Press, 1994).

48. Charles Royster, *A Revolutionary People at War: The Continental Army and the American Character, 1775–1783* (Chapel Hill: University of North Carolina Press, 1979), 373–78.

49. Sylvia Frey, *The British Soldier in America: A Social History of Military Life in the Revolutionary Period* (Austin: University of Texas Press, 1981), 117.

50. Ira D. Gruber, "For King and Country: The Limits of Loyalty in the War for American Independence," in *Limits of Loyalty,* ed. Edgar Denton III (Waterloo, Ont.: Wilfred Laurier University Press, 1980); Stephen Conway, "British Officers and the American War for Independence," *William and Mary Quarterly,* 3d series, 41 (1984): 265–76.

51. Thomas Hughes, *A Journal by Thos: Hughes (1778–1789),* with an introduction by E. A. Benians (Cambridge: Cambridge University Press, 1947), 24.

52. *Letters from America 1776–1779, Being Letters of Brunswick, Hessian, and Waldeck Officers with the British Army during the American Revolution,* trans. Ray W. Pettengill (Port Washington, N.Y.: Kennicat Press, 1964), 181.

53. Ibid., 132.

54. Hugh Earl Percy, *Letters of Hugh Earl Percy from Boston and New York, 1774–1776,* ed. Charles Knowles Bolton (Boston: C. E. Godspeed, 1902), 37, 44.

55. W. Glanville Evelyn, *Memoirs and Letters of Captain W. Glanville Evelyn* (Oxford, 1879; reprint, New York: Arno Press, 1971), 51 (page citation is to the reprint edition).

56. Great Britain, Historical Manuscripts Commission, *Report on the Manuscripts of the Late Reginald Rawdon-Hastings,* 4 vols. (London, 1934), 3:185.

57. Frederick Mackenzie, *Diary of Frederick Mackenzie Giving a Daily Narrative of His Military Service as an Officer of the Regiment of Royal Welch Fusiliers During the Years 1705–1781 in Massachusetts, Rhode Island and New York,* 2 vols. (Cambridge: Harvard University Press, 1930), I:39.

58. Ibid., 1:111.

59. Ibid., 1:289–99.

60. Ibid., 2:395–98.

61. Stephen Conway, "To Subdue America: British Army Officers and the Conduct of the Revolutionary War," *William and Mary Quarterly,* 3d series, 43 (July 1986): 405-6. I have used the material discussed above in my article "War and Cul-

ture, a Case Study: The Enlightenment and the Conduct of the British Army in America, 1755–1781," *War and Society* 8 (May 1990): 1–28.

62. I have based this section on my article "Paoli to Stony Point: Military Ethics and Weaponry during the American Revolution," *Journal of Military History* 58 (January 1994): 7–27.

63. *The Revolution Remembered: Eyewitness Accounts of the War for Independence,* ed. John C. Dann (Chicago: University of Chicago Press, 1980), 149–50.

64. "The Actions at Brandywine and Paoli, Described by a British Officer," *Pennsylvania Magazine of History and Biography* 29 (1905): 368.

65. Thomas Robinson to his brother, 1 October 1778, Anthony Wayne Papers, 5, fol. 93, Historical Society of Pennsylvania. For British accounts of the Old Tappan action, see Sir Henry Clinton to Lord George Germain, [8] October 1778, Sir Henry Clinton Papers , 43:3, 4, William L. Clements Library, University of Michigan, Ann Arbor. For a detailed American description of British atrocities at Old Tappan, see James Thacher, *A Military Journal during the American Revolutionary War from 1775 to 1783....* (Boston, 1823), 179–81.

66. "An Officer Out of His Time: Correspondence of Major Patrick Ferguson, 1779–1780," ed. Hugh Rankin, in *Sources of American Independence: Selected Manuscripts from the Collection of the William L. Clements Library,* ed. Howard H. Peckham, 2 vols. (Chicago: University of Chicago Press, 1978), 2:313.

67. Mark Odintz, "The British Officer Corps, 1754–1783" (Ph.D diss., University of Michigan, 1988), 470.

68. Earl of Bute and Charles Stuart, *A Prime Minister and His Son from the Correspondence of the 3rd Earl of Bute and of Lt. General the Hon. Sir Charles Stuart, K. B.,* ed. Mrs. E. Stuart Worley (London: J. Murray, 1925), 137.

69. Ira O. Gruber, "On the Road to Poonamalle: An Irish Officer's View of the War for American Independence," *American Magazine and Historical Chronicle* 4 (spring–summer, 1988): 9. Officers expressing unqualified support for these actions included John André, the Chief Engineer John Montresor, and James Murray.

70. Banastre Tarleton, *A History of the Southern Campaigns of 1780 and 1781 in the Southern Provinces of North America* (London, 1787; reprint, New York: New York Times, 1968), 90 (page citation is to the reprint edition).

71. Franklin and Mary Wickwire, *Cornwallis: The American Adventure* (Boston: Houghton Mifflin, 1970), 172. For Clinton's distaste for terrorist methods, see William B. Willcox, *Portrait of a General* (New York: Knopf, 1964), 195, n. 1.

72. Lawrence Robert Campbell to Sir Henry Clinton, 24 July 1779, Clinton Papers, 63:32.

73. Wayne Papers, 7, fol. 82.

74. Ibid., 10, fol. 83.

75. Henry P. Johnston, *The Storming of Stony Point on the Hudson, Midnight, 15 July 1779* (New York: James T. White, 1900), 135.

76. Ibid., 131. Also published in *Collections for the Year 1877, Official Letters of Major General James Pattison* (New York: New York Historical Society, 1876), 96.

77. Gilbert Bodinier, *Les officers de l'Armée Royale combattants de la guerre d'Indépendence des Etats-Unis de Yorktown à l'an II* (Chateau de Vincennes: Service Historique de l'Armée de Terre, 1983), 193–200.

78. Johann Ewald, *Diary of the American War, A Hessian Journal,* trans. and ed. Joseph P. Tustin (New Haven: Yale University Press, 1979), 342.

79. Don Higginbotham, *The War of Independence: Military Attitudes, Policies, and Practice, 1763–1789* (New York: Macmillan, 1971), 414.

80. *Letters from America,* 113.

81. Ewald, *Diary,* 341.

CHAPTER 6

The Conflict of Cultures

In 1700 the Ottoman Empire remained one of Europe's great powers. As is true of modern Turkey, it appeared to be *in* Europe, but not *of* it. Thus, as we have seen, eighteenth-century discussions of the balance of power differed as to whether the empire belonged to the system. Culturally, the Ottoman Empire appeared distinct from European civilization. The majority of its subjects were Muslims, and memories of the Crusades remained fresh. Only in 1683 had a "sacred league" of European powers combined to block the last great eruption of Ottoman power deep into Europe. The failed Ottoman siege of Vienna and the subsequent collapse of the Ottoman army followed the high-water mark of Ottoman expansion. The Peace of Karlowitz of 1699 was the first of a series of agreements between the empire and alliances of Christian powers. These agreements represented a shift from the offensive to the defensive on the part of the Ottomans and the beginning of their withdrawal from Europe. Important territories were ceded to the Habsburgs, to Venice, to Poland, and to Russia. In 1700, however, it was not apparent that the Ottoman Empire was permanently in retreat, and European powers could still at least discuss the idea of a crusade against the Turkish menace. From a historical perspective, the eighteenth century reveals a decline in Ottoman military power vis-à-vis Austria and, more significantly, Russia. However, this decline was far from clear in the first half of the century, and the Ottomans retained the capacity to inflict sharp defeats upon Christian adversaries.

Following his defeat at Poltava in 1709, Charles XII of Sweden and his ally the Cossack leader Ivan Mazepa sought safety in Ottoman territory. Their arrival touched off a struggle within the Ottoman court among factions that resisted involvement in the great European wars of the day and those that sought to exploit apparent opportunities to recover lost lands. Among the latter there was debate over which front to reopen. Charles, with French assistance, lobbied for war with Russia. Citing the continued residence of Charles XII, Peter the Great settled this debate for them by moving against the principality of Moldavia, from whence he intended to advance through Bulgaria to Constantinople. However, he found that the Christian peasants of Moldavia showed little interest in being saved or in parting with their scanty food. Raids by Cossacks and Tatars made a shambles of the czar's logistics, forcing him to retreat. As he attempted to re-cross the Pruth River, he found his army completely surrounded by the Turks, who seized the high ground and commanded his camp with their artillery. Peter escaped total disaster only by signing a humiliating peace by which the Russians conceded all conquered territories to the Ottomans. In 1711 it was not evident that the Ottoman Empire was on the defensive.[1]

Jeremy Black observes that during the period 1711–1715 the Ottomans enjoyed more military success than any other European power. They drove the Venetians from the weakly defended Morea in 1715. In 1716 they resumed war against the Habsburgs in Hungary but were defeated by the great Austrian commander Prince Eugène of Savoy, Marlborough's companion in arms. He destroyed one Ottoman army at Peterwardein in 1716 and another at Belgrade in 1717. That city, along with significant Balkan gains, passed into Austrian hands through the Treaty of Passarowitz of 1718.[2] Although the Ottoman Empire became mired in a lengthy struggle with Persia, it was at peace with European powers in the period 1718–1735. It was the beginning of the tulip period, a time of extraordinary luxury and artistic flowering in Constantinople. The empire became more receptive to Western influences and Western visitors. Travelers were not confronted by an empire in crisis.

Among the vanguard of those visitors was Lady Mary Wortley Montagu, who accompanied her husband on his assuming the post of British ambassador at Constantinople and recorded her impressions in a series of letters that became famous when published in 1763. Her party traveled via Vienna through lands ravaged by the wars of preceding decades. Passing the field of Zenta, scene of Prince Eugène's victory of 1697, she found that "the marks of that Glorious bloody day are yet recent, the field being strew'd with Skulls and Carcases of unbury'd Men, Horses and Camels. I could not look without horror on such numbers of mangled humane bodys, and reflect on the Injustice of War, that makes murther not only necessary but meritorious. Nothing seems to me a plainer proofe of the irrationality of Mankind (whatever fine claims we pretend to Reason) than the rage with which they contest for a small spot of Ground, when such vast parts of fruitfull earth lye quite uninhabited. 'Tis true, Custom has now made it unavoidable, but can there be a greater demonstration of the want of reason than a Custom being firmly establish'd so plainly contrary to the Interest of Man in General? I am a good deal inclin'd to believe Mr. Hobbs that the State of Nature is a State of War, but thence I conclude Humane Nature not rational, if the word reasonable means common sense."[3]

Lady Mary's party had an Austrian escort until it approached Belgrade, still in Ottoman hands. It was then that she sensed she had crossed an exotic frontier, as Janissaries replaced the Austrian guards. On their way to Adrianople, they passed through a countryside stripped bare by the demands of war. She was struck by the poverty of the peasants and by the ruthless manner in which the Janissaries requisitioned supplies. Their conduct confirmed western notions of the harshness of Asiatic despotism. However, once past this military zone she encountered a worldly and sophisticated urban culture that confounded Western stereotypes. She found the Turks to be truthful and kind to their servants. After observing the lavishness that came to be associated with the tulip period, she concluded: "these people are not so unpolish'd as we represent them. Tis true their Magnificence is of a different taste from ours, and perhaps of a better. I am almost of the opinion they have a right notion of Life; while they consume it in Music, Gardens, Wine, and delicate eating, while we are tormenting our brains with some Scheme of Politics or studying some Science to which we can never attain, or if we do, cannot perswade people to set that value upon it we do ourselves."[4] She was charmed by the dress of Turkish women and concluded that their veils gave them greater freedom to pursue love affairs than was afforded women in the West. Perhaps more amazing was the naturalness of these women, who socialized while entirely naked in the elegant baths of the Ottoman cities. She could not help but find such life seductive.

But not all life was idle luxury. She found that smallpox had been virtually eradicated and arranged to have her son inoculated. As a result, she was to become known as one of the great advocates for inoculation in the West. She had numerous discussions with scholars about poetry and religion. Muslim scholars appeared to her as the mirror image of Britain's own enlightened clergy. On the one hand, they satisfied the people's needs for religious zeal by providing various sects. The scholars themselves shared a form of deism and moderation that would have appealed to divines such as Samuel Clarke or William Whiston. Lady Mary had penetrated a secret that explained much of the success of the Ottoman Empire as an institution: the tolerance and live-and-let-live attitude that preserved the fragile unity of peoples who spanned the continents of Europe, Asia, and Africa. Lady Mary's perspective was that of the early Enlightenment, and she found much in Turkish life that struck a resonant chord. Although Ottoman culture may not have been enlightened in the European sense, it was far from the enemy of civilization portrayed by intellectuals such as the Scottish historian William Robertson, who wrote that "the despotic system of Turkish government, founded on such illiberal fanaticism" had extinguished science in Egypt, Assyria, and Greece, "its three favorite mansions in ancient times."[5] Many Western intellectuals were unable to overcome stereotypes rooted in the crusades. We have seen the example of Voltaire, whose prescription for Turks was to kill them.

Lady Mary had the good fortune to pass through the harsh barrier imposed by war and see an aspect of Turkish life that few Westerners understood. For most, the face of the Turks was the face of war. In the seventeenth century the Ottoman military machine had achieved levels of efficiency that only Louis XIV had the capacity to rival. The empire's bureaucracy so managed its resources that it could pay and supply a large standing army that included the Janissaries, infantry with special skills in siege warfare, and the Sipahi regular cavalry. They were supplemented by a kind of feudal cavalry, the Timariots, and Tatar auxiliaries.[6] Raimundo Montecuccoli (1609-1680) was the most distinguished Habsburg commander in Austrian wars against the Ottomans during this period. His military writings, highly regarded by eighteenth-century military intellectuals, provided a good portrait of the Ottoman Empire's military sophistication. The Turks had many advantages over Habsburg armies, which were small ad hoc affairs before the expansion of the eighteenth century. Montecuccoli emphasized the sultan's ability to maintain a large, well-disciplined standing force. Superior numbers were the Ottomans' greatest military asset. The Sultan's great treasury meant that the troops were paid punctually and were always well supplied, conditions often lacking in Christian armies. In the end, Montecuccoli believed that everything depended on money: "If one were to inquire what was necessary in war, the answer would be three things: money, money, money."[7] At the heart of Ottoman power was the ability of its bureaucracy to efficiently transform money into well-disciplined, well-supplied soldiers. In contrast to Christian forces, the Turks also possessed a unified command and the ability to take decisive action. Montecuccoli observed that their wars were great and brief. The Turks always sought battle in order to achieve their objectives quickly and, he concluded, their opponents should adopt Fabian tactics to oppose them. Did they have any weaknesses? He criticized their exercise of arms and lack of instruction in firing by ranks, a technique he insisted on for his own troops, and he believed that they lacked modern fortification. In fact, as Rhoads Murphy points out, the Ottomans did commit great resources to fortification, but the vast extent of their frontiers strained even their means. Nevertheless, it is clear that Montecuccoli believed that the Christian powers dealt with the Ottomans from a position of weakness. It would require a "military revolution" or a "bureaucratic revolution" to achieve equality with what Murphy terms the European "super power."

The wars between the Ottomans and their Christian neighbors had characteristics different from the campaigns of western Europe. Light cavalry played a greater role in operations on the Asian steppe or on the Hungarian plain than in the West. A general marching into such a region confronted the prospect of starvation if he could not secure his communications with a strong cavalry force of his own. Logistics, never a strong point in the Russian and Habsburg armies, became a nightmare in the East, where armies marched long distances through lands with scant resources. Many more of their soldiers died from hunger and disease than from Turkish weapons. Linear tactics, the standard deployment in the West, were less effective on the treeless plains, where an army's flanks and rear were threatened by the enemy's light cavalry. Western generals needed new tactics to counter these conditions. Particularly successful was the Russian count Peter Rumyantsev, whose offensive campaign on the Pruth in 1770 featured infantry columns and squares, strengthened by mobile field artillery for attack and defense. While columns were a matter of academic discussion in the West, they were a reality in Eastern war.[8]

The Turkish way of war has been traditionally portrayed as cruel and inhumane, but there is no evidence that the Turks were harsher than their Western opponents. The Turks committed atrocities against Austrian opponents in the wars of the eighteenth century, particularly by decapitating prisoners, but the Austrians responded with equal brutality. Prince Eugène destroyed all of the Turkish villages he captured in Bosnia and sold the women and children into slavery.[9] John L. H. Keep finds that the Russo-Turkish wars of the period were fought with a savagery seldom achieved in the West. Russian soldiers fought to avenge the "Tatar yoke" and to punish Muslim infidels. It was rumored that the Turks took no prisoners (a charge commonly aimed at peoples of non-Western cultures), and Turkish prisoners were harshly treated.[10] The extensive use of irregular troops in the East probably made war less chivalric. Western writers usually believed that it was dishonorable, even murder, to aim at enemy officers or sentries. The Eastern school seems to have taught different values. Montecuccoli advised that fire should be aimed particularly at the officers.[11] When the Austrians introduced irregulars into Western campaigns during the War of the Austrian Succession, they brought with them a different military culture.

During the second half of the eighteenth century, the military balance shifted against the Ottoman Empire. The chief beneficiary of this new state of affairs was Russia. Although Austria had grown in military sophistication during the period, the Habsburgs were too distracted by central European concerns to mount a formidable challenge to the Ottomans. However, during the period 1768–1774, despite the distraction of the Pugachev revolt, the empire of Catherine the Great overcame the logistical and tactical obstacles and achieved a stunning victory over the

Turks. Not only did the Russians sweep away Turkish armies and fortresses, the Russian fleet entered the Mediterranean and destroyed the Turkish navy at Chesme in 1770. By the treaty of Kutchuk-Kainardi (1774), Russia reaped huge strategic gains: territory on the coast of the Black Sea, along with navigation rights. The sultan agreed to pay a large war indemnity and to allow Catherine to build and protect an Orthodox church in Constantinople, a thin edge for Russia's subsequent claims to intervene on the behalf of all of the Turks' Orthodox subjects. Perhaps most significant was the recognition of Crimean independence, a step toward Russian dominance. Loss of the Crimea deprived the sultan of the source of his most-reliable troops as the traditional forces of the empire failed to keep pace with the military reforms embraced by its Christian opponents.

The Turkish defeat in the war of 1768–1774 is attributable to a variety of reasons. Black points out that the grand vizier, Mehmed Emin Pasha, lacked military experience, had no effective plan, and was unable to provide adequate supplies or pay for the army.[12] The failure in leadership would be sufficient explanation in itself, but, at least from the midcentury, the Ottoman military machine was in decline relative to that of other European powers. Westerners, such as William Robertson, thought of the government as representative of an Asiatic despotism that reduced all subjects equally to a kind of slavery. No doubt such a system limited initiative, but Robertson concluded that the sultan's power was limited by the army and by religion.[13] These were the very institutions that resisted attempts to introduce military reforms. Originally, the Janissaries were a slave army recruited in conquered territory and transformed into an elite professional force. In the eighteenth century the Ottoman Empire ceased to be an expanding power, and the nature of the Janissary corps changed accordingly. They evolved into craft and merchant guilds in Constantinople and gave more time to business and politics than to military training. Large numbers of men claimed Janissary pay status, but only a small percentage of these claimants were military effectives. In retrospect, the 1768–1774 war marked the beginning of a transition period for the Turkish forces. The Janissaries declined in significance, and the Sipahi and feudal Timariot-style soldiers all but disappeared. The empire came to rely on locally recruited peasant-soldiers formed in regiments that paralleled traditional forces. They became the basis for the reforms of Selim III (sultan 1789–1807), under whom the Turkish army began to be recruited on a Western model.[14]

Prior to this time, successive viziers had recognized the need to match European military developments but failed in efforts to reform the established forces. European officers were introduced in an effort to effect modernization. During the 1730s, Claude-Alexandre, comte de Bonneval (1675–1747), a veteran of the French and Austrian armies, went to Constantinople, converted to Islam, and entered the service of a vizier interested in military reform. Bonneval presented the sultan with a comprehensive plan to restructure the army along Western lines and to increase the efficiency and professionalism of the Janissaries. He was thwarted by conservative forces in the army and by the uncertain nature of his political support; reform-minded viziers seldom lasted long. He succeeded in establishing a modern engineering school that provided the basis for a modern artillery service. Turkish military reform thus centered on the "scientific corps" outside the traditional system. Graduates of Bonneval's school, nevertheless, had to endure the jealousy of Janissaries, who had traditionally considered themselves the experts on siege warfare.[15] Another important European adviser was Baron Francois de Tott (1730–1793), a Hungarian who had risen in the French artillery service. De Tott was sent to Constantinople to learn Turkish and acted as an agent of the French embassy. He became a military adviser to the sultan during the 1768–1774 war and instituted important technical reforms, including the establishment of a rapid-fire artillery corps. The experience of these Western officers indicates that the Ottoman Empire did import Western technology but that the government could not carry out far-reaching reforms of the military system. Ottoman power also declined as the sultans lost power to provincial notables during the century in contrast to the centralizing trends in other European states. Contributions to the sultan's great treasury declined as a consequence. Inevitably, there were negative consequences for Ottoman military power.

Culturally the Ottoman Empire did not resemble a backward state during the eighteenth century. Its inhabitants lived in a more sophisticated and moderate society than did the majority of Catherine the Great's Russian subjects. Russia offers the comparative example of a state on the margin of Europe undergoing westernization. Russia's rulers understood that a reform of society was necessary if their state was to survive and flourish. The Ottoman elites felt no such compulsion. Both regimes sought Western technical assistance for their military forces. Peter the Great established the School of Mathematics and Navigation in 1701, two Moscow artillery schools (1701 and 1712), and two engineering academies (Moscow, 1712–1724, and St. Petersburg, 1719). The government continued to sponsor establishments of this type throughout the period. The empress Anna sponsored the establishment of the Noble Cadet Corps in 1732 (renamed the Noble Land Cadet Corps in 1742) in order to prepare officers for service in the field army. The Corps provided young nobles with a liberal education suitable as a background for many occupations. Many graduates entered the civil service. Even if all had joined the army, they would have provided only a fraction of the officers required. Russian military education did not provide a technical advantage over the Ottomans who founded schools under the direction of Western experts. More fundamental to Russian success was the development of an entirely new army of long-service regulars trained in Western methods. Thus the Russians achieved the program that Bonneval had vainly advocated in Constantinople. The single-minded pursuit of power by Russia's rulers and the ability of such commanders as Rumyantsev and Alexander Suvorov to adapt Western tactics to Eastern conditions contributed to Russia's military superiority over the Turks in the second half of the century.[16]

INDIA

William Robertson's simplistic view of the Turks stands in contrast to the greater sophistication and sympathy he displayed in his discussion of other non-Western peoples. Robertson, the moderator of the Church of Scotland, was one of the eighteenth century's great historians and one of the most distinguished figures of the Scottish Enlightenment. He wrote a history of Scotland that was free of the partisan and religious bias that had marred previous accounts and established himself as one the first global historians through his *History of the Reign of the Emperor Charles V* and *History of America.* With the exception of Edward Gibbon, no eighteenth-century scholar cast so wide a net, and none surpassed him in his dedicated research and spirit of philosophic detachment. He was convinced that European military resistance had saved civilization from the Turks, but he was less sanguine about the positive effects of European contact with other parts of the globe. He deplored European assertions of cultural superiority over non-Western peoples as founded on a narrow prejudice that served to justify crimes such as African slavery and what is now considered genocide in America.

Robertson was particularly shocked that such prejudices extended to India, a region that he believed possessed a civilization far advanced beyond that of Africa and America. This culture had been only recently revealed to Europeans as they learned to read Sanskrit and gain access to Brahmin texts. Yet "the colour of the inhabitants, their effeminate appearance, their unwarlike spirit, the wild extravagance of their religious tenets and ceremonies and many other circumstances, confirmed in Europeans such an opinion of their own pre-eminence, that they have always viewed and treated them as an inferior race of men."[17] Robertson argued that ancient Indian civilization compared favorably in its achievements with those of the Mediterranean world. Nor had Indian culture been stifled by Turkish-style despotism. He appealed to Europeans to consider "the Hindoos of the present times as a knowing and ingenious race of men…descended from ancestors who had attained to a very high degree of improvement, many ages before the least step towards civilization had been taken in any part of Europe."[18]

Robertson was aware that his appreciation of Indian culture was shared by only a few scholars, some of whom were servants of the British East

India Company, the chief agent of European intervention in Indian affairs. His enlightened remarks came at a time of increased European military activity on the subcontinent. During the Seven Years' War and the American War of Independence, Britain and France clashed for supremacy in the region. Few European troops were involved, but both powers recruited Indian mercenaries, the famous Sepoys, whom they trained in European tactics. The struggle between Britain and France was a near thing, particularly during the War of American Independence. British naval power was the deciding factor in this conflict. However, as Britain emerged victorious over France, the East India Company came into conflict with indigenous military powers that represented a challenge of a very different nature. Europeans who fought against native armies found nothing effeminate or unwarlike in their opponents. These native powers sought European military advisers in order to make their armies competitive with those of the British East India Company. In turn, British commanders adapted to local methods. The result was both a conflict and an exchange between military cultures.

There was nothing inevitable about the British domination of India. Although European trading posts were long established on the subcontinent, they had not been intended as platforms for territorial expansion. The decline of the Mogul Empire and the conflict between native successor states opened a potential vacuum that might be exploited by the European powers. Due to these conditions, the global wars of the eighteenth century affected India in ways avoided by China or Japan. Otherwise, the small numbers of European troops, thousands of miles removed from their homelands, could have made but slight impression. The introduction of European weapons and methods was significant in determining British success in India, but it must be considered a secondary factor. Western methods were not the only new influences on Indian warfare. A recent study demonstrates that Afghan military innovation, featuring mounted musketeers and light camel-mounted artillery, also revolutionized traditional military practice.[19] The Afghans successfully adapted firearms technologies to the desert conditions prevailing in much of the Middle East, and their style of mobile warfare provided a model for armies in the area. This approach stood in contrast to Western infantry and artillery armies depending on slow bullock transport. The latter were well adapted to tropical conditions in much of India but floundered when matched against cavalry armies in arid environments. Topography played at least an equal role with technology in determining the course of military innovation.

However, Anglo-French warfare was the catalyst for European military expansion in India. The disputes between native rulers in the Carnatic region of southeastern India in the 1740s inspired a struggle between France and Britain for influence. Britain prevailed because of superior resources, but the margin of superiority was slight. Robert Clive defeated the French-backed nawab of the Carnatic and captured his capital with a force of only 500 men. French attempts to regain control of the area during the Seven Years' War were decisively defeated by 1760.[20] Bengal was the scene of some of the most-memorable events in Britain's wars in India during the period. In 1756 the nawab Sirā j-ud-Dawlah captured the East India Company's Fort William and confined his prisoners to the "black hole of Calcutta." This event acquired notoriety on the scale of the Bataan Death March and gave Indian warfare a reputation for exceptional brutality. Clive entered the list of imperial heroes by avenging this act. With 890 Europeans and 2,100 Sepoys, supported by British warships, he recaptured Fort William. He then marched on the nawab's capital and defeated a far-larger army at the celebrated battle of Plassey. The nawab's army showed little initiative—perhaps because his best troops were deployed elsewhere against the Afghans—and Clive prevailed by well-directed artillery and infantry fire that prepared the way for his capture of the enemy camp. As in Europe, artillery began to assert itself as a decisive weapon on the battlefield. Infantry battles in India appear to refute the claims that eighteenth-century firearms and linear tactics were ineffective.

The Europeans' superiority in firepower was partially the result of the Indian tradition of large cavalry armies. Anglo-Indian conflicts were thus asymmetrical, with both sides required to adapt to the tactics of the other. The East India Company's reliance on infantry and artillery worked well in areas near coastal forts that assured naval support and supply by sea. The marshy conditions of Bengal favored infantry over cavalry. However, as the Company's forces launched campaigns into the desert lands of the interior, native commanders could employ their superior light cavalry to play havoc with logistics and to cut off and destroy detachments.[21] Indian rulers were impressed with Western technology and tactics and sought expert assistance, usually that of French officers, to meet the challenge posed by the East India Company's forces. One of the Company's most formidable opponents was the kingdom of Mysore, which fought four major wars with the British between 1767 and 1799. Mysore was led by able and aggressive rulers: Hyder Ali, who came to power in 1761, and subsequently by his son Tipu Sultan. Hyder's army remained a cavalry-dominated force in the Mogul tradition, but he hired French and other European officers to assist in his artillery and technical services. Europeans thus played an important, yet marginal, role. Hyder did not attempt to create an infantry army along European lines. His army of some 50,000 included only about 1,000 Europeans during the First Anglo-Mysore War. Constant warfare may have prevented Hyder from seeking a more-significant change in his forces. Even absolute rulers find it difficult to effect rapid radical change in military organization without social change.

However, the rulers of Mysore had 30 years to perfect their military institutions. Tipu was able to create an efficient system, with most commands filled by salaried officers and an infantry of long-service volunteers trained and equipped in the European manner. Europeans assisted in this training but did not hold commands in the field. Both Hyder and Tipu relied on cavalry action to achieve success. Their campaigns featured mobility and surprise. Hyder forced the surrender of Madras in 1769 and, during the Second Anglo-Mysore War, cut off and destroyed a British force of 3,720 men. Small European armies relying on linear fire tactics were not guaranteed victory against native opponents. Both Hyder and Tipu effectively used their light cavalry to play havoc with British supplies. In 1791, Tipu allowed General Charles Cornwallis to advance to his capital at Seringapatam, but lack of supplies forced a British retreat. In 1792, Cornwallis recruited 12,000 Maratha light cavalry to protect his communications and supply lines. Only then did his superior artillery compel Tipu to sign the Treaty of Seringapatam, which deprived him of half of his kingdom and three-quarters of his population. European methods were decisive, but only when adapted to local conditions.

In the 1780s the leader of the Maratha Confederacy in northern India, Mahadji Sindhia, was sufficiently impressed by the power of the East India Company's infantry to develop a Sepoy army of his own. He hired a Savoyard officer, Benoit de Boigne, who formed a 2,000-man force with artillery that was instrumental in Mahadji Sindhia's becoming the chief warlord in northern India. This initial force was expanded into a formidable army in the 1790s, but the British were able to undermine it by bribing its European officers to desert. British success in India rested on the size of their armies, their weapons, training and discipline, the superiority of their artillery, their knowledge of local conditions and their ability to adapt to them, and astute political intrigue and bribery. Indian rulers strove to adapt essentially feudal regimes to meet the challenge, but they lacked the time to overcome the inertia present in all societies, not just those considered feudal or traditional.[22] One scholar suggests that the European attitude toward war, rather than technical innovation, was a deciding factor in British military success against the native princes. Indian warfare was often decided by intrigue and sedition that led to a peaceful resolution of conflict. The British, while proving adept at intrigue, sought decisive military victories. Thus the Western way of war prevailed on the subcontinent, although its reach was limited by the mountains and deserts of Afghanistan.[23]

Britain's victories over native princes had political ramifications at home. In the last decades of the century, India occupied a greater share of parliamentary attention than at any time before or since. There was recognition that India was an important asset, even if had yet to become a crucial prop of British world power. However, the British presence was in the form of a private trading company that in the course of the conflicts of the time began to exercise the powers of government. The East India Company monopoly was a vestige of a time when the state could not ensure the safety of long-distance commercial enterprises. The chartered monopoly company was the device by which seventeenth-century states pursued imperial or colonial enterprises without having to make a substantial investment. States at this time had achieved a remarkable level of privatization in their overseas expansion. Now, however, the East India Company's success raised questions about these arrangements. Britain had not prevailed over France in India by private means alone, for British naval power had been critical to the decision of that struggle. The period of warfare of the second half of the century ensured that India could not be simply regarded as the concern of a private company. Many of the debates in the House of Commons concerned constitutional arrangements. These were not merely matters of academic theory, since political patronage was at stake. The Company was subjected to the scrutiny of select committees in 1772 and in 1782, each of which was followed by an attack on an important individual, first Robert Clive and then Warren Hastings, the man who had met the challenges presented by the American War of Independence. Hastings's impeachment trial was a long and exhausting affair, but, as in the case of Clive, it was concluded that his services outweighed any faults. These investigations led to important parliamentary legislation that tightened parliamentary control over the Company and set in motion a reform of the civil service.[24]

The impeachment and trial of Warren Hastings, 1786–1795, is memorable because of the role of Edmund Burke, who served as Hastings's most-aggressive prosecutor. Burke believed that Britain's role in India raised serious moral questions. He was a critic of those "nabobs" who extracted wealth from India while in the Company's service and returned home to a life of luxury and political influence. The focus of his attack was on the misgovernment of the people of India. Like Robertson, Burke believed that India was an ancient and sophisticated civilization. The recent wars, however, had thrown India into turmoil and had exposed the inhabitants to chaos and to harsh and arbitrary rule. The chief culprit in this sad state of affairs was the East India Company, more interested in acquiring wealth than in securing the welfare of the people. Burke argued that the Company sought political power from motives of avarice. Native princes such as the nawab of the Carnatic ran up debts to the Company, which in turn used the nawab's authority to extort money. These devious maneuvers, he insisted, were at the root of the wars in which the Company engaged. Burke derided Hastings's defense, in which he pled the need for expediency in times of danger and within the context, that is, the existing practice in India. Such practice, Burke concluded, conformed neither to the laws of India or England.[25]

Burke admitted that he had no hope in securing Hastings's conviction. He was condemned at the time for his lengthy and exhausting pursuit of a man who many believed had rendered Britain distinguished service. Burke's knowledge of India paled beside that of Hastings, who was an accomplished Orientalist as well as a dynamic political and military leader. Although the Company's directors in London opposed aggressive military action in India as inconsistent with commercial profit, Hastings, the man on the spot, concluded that only a vigorous forward policy could secure the revenues essential for military security.[26] The prosecution ignored the complexity and difficulties confronting a governor who could communicate with England only with difficulty and who was plagued by factions within his own council. East India Company politics lay behind the prosecution, as Burke relied on Hastings's bitter enemy Philip Francis for the details of the case. Burke's prosecution was therefore compromised by its partisan zealotry. However, it is perhaps best to view Hastings as a symbol of what Burke believed to be the failure of Britain's imperial mission. Hastings himself had condemned the corrupt nature of the East India Company's practices in India, calling it "a system charged with expensive establishments, and precluded by the multitude of dependents and the curse of patronage, from reformation; a government debilitated by the various habits of inveterate licentiousness" and referring to India as "a country oppressed by private rapacity, and deprived of its vital resources by the enormous qualities of current specie annually exported in the remittance of private fortunes."[27] Hastings had attempted reform, but wartime and partisan opposition prevented him from achieving much. Ironically, both Burke and Hastings looked forward to the nineteenth-century administration of India, which took more seriously its responsibility for the welfare of the inhabitants. The Hastings trial reminds us, however, that greed and force were the essential characteristics of Britain's role in India during the eighteenth century.

NORTH AMERICA

What did enlightened European opinion make of the native people of North America? Again, William Robertson, author of *The History of North America*, provides us with an excellent guide. Robertson developed his picture of Native Americans through a careful study of travelers' accounts, such as that of Louis-Antoine de Bougainville, a famous Pacific explorer who had written an important journal of his experience as an aid to General Montcalm in Canada during the Seven Years' War.[28] He submitted these reports to a discriminating analysis, dismissing early Spanish accounts of Native American life as the product of illiterate adventurers whose views were distorted by prejudice. Roberston drew upon what we would call branches of social science for insights into native society. He was inclined to follow the French naturalist Georges-Louis Buffon's view that animal life was less active and vigorous in America than in Europe. Thus the Native Americans seemed to be a different breed of men, "more remarkable for agility than strength. They resembled the beasts of prey, rather than animals formed for labour."[29] They were feebly made and treated their women coldly. Robertson noted that there was more than one explanation for the differences observed between the people of Europe and America. Some believed that the Native Americans had emerged later than had Europeans and thus had yet to evolve to a higher order. Others argued that the climate of America was enervating and that men there remained animals of an inferior order. Robertson was aware of Rousseau's idealization of the noble savage, but he pointed out that others regarded the most perfect state of man as that which was most civilized. Robertson's conclusion was appropriate for one of the founders of the modern study of history: It was all very well for philosophers such as Rousseau to create systems, but he would stick to the facts!

Nevertheless, Robertson's outlook was distinctly Lockean. The nature of men was determined by the conditions of society, and he saw little difference between a tribe of savages on the Danube and one on the Mississippi. With the exception of Mexico and Peru, the peoples of America were savages, he believed. They consisted of small tribes of hunters who required a large area in which to exist. These circumstances led to a high state of independence and equality. The most-important factor in their political institutions was the lack of private property, for without property there could be no defined subordination, no law, and, except for external relations and war, no government. Robertson shared the general belief that Native American wars were motivated by the spirit of revenge and thus especially ferocious. "When polished nations have obtained the glory of victory, or have acquired an addition of territory, they may terminate a war with honour. But savages are not satisfied until they extirpate the community which is the object of their hatred. They fight, not to conquer, but to destroy.... The desire of vengeance is the first, and almost the only principle, which a savage instills in the minds of his children."[30]

Robertson could have drawn on many eighteenth-century soldiers, such as Bougainville, for a view that Native Americans were cruel, undisciplined, inconstant, and unreliable in war. This was a simplistic view. Bougainville, who believed that all of these things were true, never took the time to try to understand Native American culture on its own terms. However, Robertson also provided a much more sophisticated discussion of Native American military practice than one would expect to find in a work drafted in an eighteenth-century Scottish study. Indeed, some findings were fully consistent with those of modern ethnohistorians. For example, Robertson understood that Native Americans distinguished between private wars conducted by individuals or chiefs with small parties and national war. In the latter, he wrote, when "undertaken by public authority, the deliberations are formal and slow. The elders assemble, they deliver opinions in solemn speeches, they weigh with maturity the nature of the enterprise, and balance its beneficial or disadvantageous consequences with no considerable portion of political discernment or sagacity. Their priests and soothsayers are consulted, and sometimes they ask advice even of their women."[31] He was also aware that there were tribes that sought to replace their population, which had been reduced by war, by adopting prisoners. He thus understood the principle of "mourning war" as conducted by the Iroquois and correctly observed that this was not a universal practice. While Robertson's generalizations on Native American warfare will appear superficial to a modern expert, many of his details seem strikingly current.[32]

Robertson had to reconcile his description of the wise deliberations that preceded national war among the Native Americans with his simplistic revenge-motivation thesis. He could not believe that true political institutions could exist without private property. Thus, he wrote, "It is the genius of savages to act from the impulse of present passion." The lengthy deliberations of tribal councils therefore were less the result of wisdom than "the coldness and phlegm of their temper."[33] In the end, Robertson was unable to allow his data to carry him beyond entrenched eighteenth-century stereotypes.

His description of Native American tactics reveals a similar gap. He accurately observed that the Indians moved in a loose and unencumbered manner. "Even in their hottest and most active wars, they proceed wholly by stratagem and ambuscade.... War and hunting are their only occupations, and they conduct both with the same spirit and the same arts."[34] He understood that the Indians refused to risk unnecessary casualties and did not believe that flight was dishonorable. Death in battle was considered a misfortune, one that might subject a warrior's memory to the charge of rashness. Robertson provided a good discussion of the Indian practice of scalping for trophies, of the torture or adoption of prisoners, and of cannibalism. He may have been near the mark in saying that cannibalism may have been motivated by revenge (the reasons for cannibalism among Native Americans continue to be not fully understood) and that women and children were spared. However, he criticized Native American warriors for their lack of discipline and staying power that resulted from the absence of a system of subordination: "Destitute of that foresight which discerns and provides for remote events, strangers to the union and mutual confidence no less requisite in carrying such plans to execution, savage nations may astonish a disciplined enemy by their valour, but seldom prove formidable to him by their conduct; and whenever the contest is of long continuance must yield to superior art."[35] Experienced American frontier fighters knew better: "I have often heard the British officers call the Indians undisciplined savages," wrote one, "which is a capital mistake—as they have all the essentials of discipline.... Could it be supposed that undisciplined troops could defeat Generals Braddock, Grant, etc.?"[36] Robertson did not understand the nature of Indian military discipline, but neither did many European soldiers who opposed them.

Vattel believed that the laws of war did not apply to savage peoples, thus justifying what we may today perceive as atrocities committed by Europeans against native peoples. However, despite categorizing the latter as savages, Robertson was concerned about the moral dimension of European settlement, or what has come to be called "the European invasion of America." He deplored the Spanish conduct in Mexico, stained by the avarice of Hernán Cortés and his followers, writing. "Under the sanction of those ill-founded maxims they violated every right that should be held sacred between hostile nations."[37] However, Robertson was not simply restating "the Black legend." He believed that the Spanish monarchy was solicitous for the welfare of the inhabitants but that its policies were neutralized by the greed of the conquistadors. As far as North America was concerned, he condemned the colonists who adopted the Spanish conduct as their model. During Virginia's Powhatan War, he commented, disregarding the "principles of faith, honour, and humanity, which regulates hostility among civilized nations and set bounds to its rage, the English deemed everything allowable that tended to accomplish their design. They hunted the Indians like the wild beasts, rather than enemies."[38] The two peoples seemed to have reversed their cultural values. Robertson was equally harsh in his judgment of English atrocities during the 1637 Pequot War in New England. Here they sought to exterminate an independent people gallantly attempting to preserve their land and freedom.

As in India, European–Native American warfare was complicated in the eighteenth century by the great conflicts between European states and their colonists for the control of the continent. Native Americans participated in these wars as allies. European generals, such as the unfortunate James Braddock, found that expeditions to the frontier came to grief if they did not have the support of experienced Native American frontier warriors. European professionals adapted to this environment with difficulty. Bougainville, who served as an aid to the marquis de Montcalm during the Seven Years' War, often expressed his concern over this dilemma. He arrived in Canada in 1756 as an inexperienced but opinionated young officer who quickly adopted the views of his mentor Montcalm, who was involved in a dispute with the governor, the marquis de Vaudreuil. The latter was an advocate of vigorous frontier raiding by Canadian militia and Native American allies as a means of inciting panic in the British colonies and casting them on the defensive. Montcalm espoused a more conventional strategy of attacking British frontier forts and, when forced on the defensive by superior forces, of buying time through the defense of fortified positions. This dispute set off a conflict among the French over the nature of "true war." Bougainville robustly defended the "professional" corner. He argued that "they never made war in Canada before 1755. They had never gone into camp. To leave Montreal with a party, to go through the woods, to take a few scalps, to return at full speed once the blow was struck, that is what they called war, a campaign, success, victory. Now," he continued, "war is established here on the European basis. Projects for the campaigns, for armies, for artillery, for sieges, for battles.... What a revolution!" This was a business for professionals rather than amateurs. Unfortunately, "townsmen, bankers, merchants, officers, bishops, parish priests, Jesuits, all plan this [war], speak of it, discuss it, pronounce on it. Everyone is a Turenne or a Folard."[39]

When Montcalm advanced against the frontier forts of Oswego on Lake Ontario and William Henry on Lake George, he led a mixed force of professionals (regulars recently dispatched from France and marines permanently stationed in the colony) and irregulars (Canadian militia with considerable experience in frontier warfare, and Native Americans). The Native Americans consisted of Christian mission Indians and Native allies from the Great Lakes region, the latter of whom participated in hopes of acquiring plunder and prisoners. The Native Americans were led by the celebrated La Corne St. Luc, who had terrorized the British frontier in the previous war and who would later command General John Burgoyne's native allies during the American War of Independence. Bougainville was deeply disturbed by his association with the Indians. He admitted that they possessed indispensable skills, but he considered them an undisciplined and parasitical mob, rather than soldiers. He witnessed chilling scenes of cannibalism that led him to conclude, "What a scourge! Humanity shudders at being obliged to make use of such monsters. But without them the match would be too much against us."[40] He was not alone in his belief that Native Americans were useless in pitched battles and were prone to desert after the first engagement. The siege of Fort William Henry in August 1757 revealed the strain between allies of two cultures. Montcalm's native allies were useful in attacking the communications of enemy forts, but they were unsuited for siege work and consistently refused to participate in assaults on fortified positions, on the grounds that they produced excessive casualties. The French general also employed them as a psychological weapon by threatening the defenders with Native American terror if they did not capitulate. The surrender of Fort William Henry was rendered notorious by Montcalm's inability to enforce the terms of the capitulation when the Indians plundered, captured, or killed British prisoners.

This incident remains an issue of historical controversy. The historian Francis Jennings blames Montcalm who, he believes, cynically knew that the Native Americans would violate the capitulation. Ian Steele argues that the Native Americans regarded the capitulation negotiated between European commanders as a violation of the Franco–Native American alliance, depriving them of their rightful booty and captives. The idea of a capitulation was foreign to the Native American warriors. When the French confiscated their prisoners, many concluded that their partici-pation in the war was at an end. Francis Parkman blamed La Corne St. Luc, who one witness reported as standing by while the Native Americans plundered wounded men. Some French officers blamed the British, who had retained their arms, for not standing up to the Native Americans, but the British appear to have been too disorganized and demoralized to pro-tect themselves.[41]

   Montcalm seems to have been genuinely embarrassed by this episode and did his best to reclaim the prisoners seized by the Native Americans. Bougainville, who was not present at the "massacre," called the violation of the capitulation a national disgrace.[42] Lord Loudon, the British com-mander in chief, denounced the French conduct as barbarous and protested to Vaudreuil that a general who could not control his troops was in no position to negotiate a capitulation: "Whatever Troops you bring into the Field are to me French, therefore if any Part of them break through the Rules of War, it will immediately lay me under the disagreeable necessity to Treat the whole of your People in the same manner."[43] Regular officers found it difficult to impose their rules of war on the frontier, particularly when they dealt with a people whose definition of war and whose military culture was radically different. La Corne St. Luc had so adapted himself to the Native American way of war that he probably considered their conduct at Fort William Henry to have been normal. Experienced frontier officers such as Sir William Johnson and James Bradstreet understood that their Native American allies followed their own rules and interests. At the sur-renders of the French fort Frontenac (August 1758) and Fort Niagara (July 1759), the British commanders recognized that the Native Americans would plunder the forts without regard for the terms of the capitulation. They gave them free rein and concentrated on protecting the prisoners. This seems to have satisfied the Native Americans and drew praise from French officers.[44] On the other hand, British regular officers could be as obtuse as their French counterparts. Sir Jeffrey Amherst, who orchestrated Britain's North American triumph in the Seven Years' War, never under-stood or appreciated his Native American allies. His journal is peppered with complaints about their conduct. At the surrender of Fort Levis in 1760, he ordered his grenadiers to bar the Native Americans from entering the fort. Within days, large numbers of Native Americans appropriated the army's precious whaleboats and abandoned the campaign.[45] They com-plained that Amherst had not allowed them "to prosecute the Warr [sic] agreeable to their own Custom and seem'd not to want their services."[46]

Amherst's disregard for Native American interests cost him more dearly in the years following the Peace of Paris of February 1763. The French cession of their Canadian empire shocked the native inhabitants, who did not consider that France had the right to give away their land. The continuation of the British garrison at Fort Pitt demonstrated that the British would not honor promises to withdraw from the Ohio country at the end of the war. Failing to take the Native Americans seriously, Amherst pursued the worst combination of policies. He asserted Britain's rights by establishing a network of weakly garrisoned posts across the Great Lakes region. At the same time he cut back on the presents that represented the symbolic bonds of alliance thus undermining the influence of native leaders who wished for a peaceful accommodation with the British. Amherst neglected diplomacy at a time when he lacked the means to force the natives to accept British authority. This policy was exacerbated by the obvious contempt that Amherst and fellow officers displayed toward the Native Americans. Experts such as the Indian superintendent Sir William Johnson warned of the perils of Amherst's approach, but the latter remained adamant until the outbreak of the uprising known as Pontiac's Rebellion, in which British forces were fought to a standstill during 1763–1765.[47]

The foregoing demonstrates that Native Americans had different ideas of war and peace than did Europeans of the Age of Enlightenment. Native Americans do not appear to have drawn a fine distinction between hunting animals and killing human beings, although both actions were governed by a regime of ritual. Nor do Native Americans appear to have drawn a distinction between killing one's enemy within or without the context of war. Native American social and religious customs and the nature of Indian warfare determined the moral conduct of their warriors. These warriors resembled the modern commando or guerilla fighter. This is a form of warfare that even today cannot be easily waged according to the principles of international conventions and military codes. Fighters not in uniform or not under formal state authority may be denied prisoner-of-war status and may themselves find it unsafe to take prisoners while operating behind enemy lines. As we have seen, during the eighteenth century, European irregulars might be denied the protection of the laws of war. This was even more the case with people of an alien or "savage" culture. This created an unusual paradox. European readers of numerous captivity narratives chilled at the reports of rough treatment and brutal torture inflicted by Native American communities. Yet, as Francis Jennings has asked provocatively, what happened to Native Americans captured by Europeans? There seem to have been very few, and those taken in the seventeenth century at least were frequently enslaved. Furthermore many European prisoners adopted by Native families chose to remain among them. Even returning prisoners remarked on the remarkable internal peace of Native communities, where theft or the corporal punishment of children was unknown. The contrast between such harmony and the hard face of Indian warfare adds to the paradox. Most Europeans, however, failed to penetrate beyond that hard face.

The record of European–Native American warfare demonstrates that military success owed much to cross-cultural exchange. Native Americans acquired significant numbers of firearms by 1675 and were keen to adopt the latest technological advances: flintlocks in place of matchlocks, light-weight fusils, and rifled barrels. They were often in advance of European opponents in this regard, and they displayed a skill in marksmanship superior to European soldiers, who were trained to deliver rapid volleys of unaimed fire. Native American military leaders would probably have been puzzled by those European military pundits who advocated the restoration of the pike as the primary infantry weapon. As James Smith, quoted above (see note 36), observed, Native American warriors were disciplined, but their discipline was based on lifelong training and their leaders chosen on grounds of demonstrated merit. Operations in loose order in the woods required self-discipline and individual initiative, the very qualities that late-eighteenth-century European military reformers advocated for their own light troops. Forest operations forced European commanders to adapt to Native American methods. The most adaptable were the most successful, but the experience of Robert Rogers, who commanded Rangers under General Amherst, demonstrated the limits of adaptability by regulars. Rogers was never as successful as the legend that he, and later Kenneth Roberts, sought to create. However, his mixed force of colonists and Stockbridge Indians had the capacity to strike deep within enemy territory, including the village sanctuary of the St. Francis Indians. Rogers's men adopted Native commando techniques, but regular officers were critical of their lack of subordination and discipline in camp. Although they were under the Articles of War, Rogers's authority was personal. Colonel Thomas Gage sought an alternative by dressing regulars in brown uniforms and training them in loose order, but without substantial results. His regiment, the 80th foot, were not woodsmen and could not replace the Rangers. Gage's experiment was ephemeral, and the regiment was disbanded in 1764. Brigadier General John Forbes, who led the successful British advance on Fort Duquesne in 1758, thought of his wild Highland troops as the Indians' cousins and hoped that they would be the Indians' equals in the forest. This interesting anthropological observation proved unfounded, however, for Forbes's successor, the able Swiss professional Henry Bouquet, complained that the Highlanders lost their way as soon as they set foot off a path.[48]

American nationalist writers have often disparaged the ability of European regular officers to adapt to frontier conditions, but by the Seven

Years' War they had gained considerable experience in irregular warfare. The War of the Austrian Succession and the Jacobite Rebellion of 1745 offered many lessons and provoked an outpouring of treatises on *petite guerre* beginning in the 1750s, including those of Turpin de Crissé (1754), Hector de Grandmaison (1756), and Capitaine de Jeney (1759). This background has led some historians to conclude that the line between European and American warfare was less distinct after 1750 than before and that officers were better prepared to adapt to American conditions than has often been maintained.[49] There is considerable truth in this view. Many commanders demonstrated greater skill in maneuvering in the forest than did the unfortunate Edward Braddock, whose army was shot to pieces by the French and Native Americans in 1755, in which battle the latter employed their classic tactics of an enveloping horseshoe and moving, aimed fire. At Bushy Run in 1763, Henry Bouquet proved that regulars could withstand a similar attack. However, one must be cautious in drawing a connection between North American warfare and the development of European military thought. Treatises on *petite guerre* were written in response to European rather than American developments and thus emphasized different things. For example, Bouquet was familiar with Turpin de Crissé's *Essai sur l'art de la guerre*, one of the most influential of such treatises. This experienced hussar officer provided practical advice for setting and avoiding ambushes in the woods, but from the point of view of a cavalryman, a branch almost useless and therefore nonexistent on the American frontier. Thus Crissé advised that troops attacking from ambush should fall upon the enemy with swords and bayonets rather than open fire. Such an attack would achieve greater surprise than a musket volley and avoid alerting other enemy troops. Crissé's book reflects the skepticism of many eighteenth-century soldiers about the benefits of firepower. He believed that light troops should consist of infantry and cavalry. In this mix, cold steel was the offensive weapon, the musket a defensive one in the hands of infantry, whose role was to protect and support the cavalry.[50] For the most part, European interest in light forces developed independently of American conditions. British light infantry in this period were "flank companies" of regular regiments, consisting of men chosen for difficult and dangerous operations but who received no special training as Rangers. They were an evolutionary step in the development of true light infantry at the end of the century.[51]

The writings of Robert Rogers provided a better guide for forest warfare than those of his European contemporaries. Rogers's biographer credits him with having successfully compressed the shapeless mass of backwoods fighting experiences into a simple exposition of small-unit tactics soundly based on timeless principles: mobility, security and surprise."[52] However, he acknowledges that even Rogers failed to provide an understanding of how to survive the most-dangerous enemy in the forest: nature itself. Hunger and exposure were greater threats to survival than man-made weapons. Rogers's men endured expeditions in midwinter conditions: snow, ice, freezing rain, and subzero temperatures, and often without fires. Rogers learned his survival skills from the Native Americans but did not discuss them in his writings. In addition, there were details of frontier war that regulars did not know: "How did the rangers hide their own tracks or follow an enemy's trail? What were the signals in the woods? How were boats hidden? How were trees and bushes used for concealment? The rules have a deceiving simplicity; they actually could only be applied by expert woodsmen."[53]

The most-successful frontier commanders were those who emulated their Native American opponents' skills and tactics. This could result in other unusual forms of cross-cultural exchange. In 1779 during the American War of Independence, George Rogers Clark won fame by his 250-mile march from Kaskaskia to Vincennes in present-day Indiana. There he laid siege to and captured the British lieutenant governor Henry Hamilton, whom he held responsible for all of the atrocities committed by Native American raiders on the frontier. Clark treated Hamilton, whom he referred to as "the Hair Buyer," as a war criminal and shipped him in irons for trial in Virginia. Clark's case against Hamilton appears weak from a historical perspective and is further compromised by his own behavior. He and his men adopted Native American dress and styles of warfare. British officers were shocked when Clark personally tomahawked a Native American prisoner in full view of the besieged Fort Vincennes. Hamilton recalled that when he met Clark to discuss surrender terms, "He had just come from his Indian triumph all bloody and sweating…and, while he washed his hands and face still reeking from the human sacrifice in which he had acted as chief priest, he told me with great exultation how he had been employed."[54] On the frontiers the moral lines between cultures sometimes became indistinct.

AFRICA

The three areas discussed above experienced large-scale European military intervention during the eighteenth century. There was much less European military activity in Africa. During our period only Portugal possessed an established colony of significance. Contact between the great European powers and Africa was, for the most part, restricted to the western portion of the continent. Commerce and the slave trade, rather than territorial ambition, inspired European involvement in Africa. European traders and slave forts existed at the sufferance of African states, which possessed considerable military power of their own. The military powers of West Africa possessed armies well adapted to their environments, including cavalry on the savannah, infantry in the forest regions, and marines in coastal and river areas. These soldiers continued to use traditional weapons such as poisoned arrows and javelins but had also integrated firearms into their forces. Artillery and fortifications were employed by African states and thus testify to considerable technical knowledge. European technical experts occasionally served in African forces, but it does not appear that African rulers believed that westernization was the key to military progress.

The bulk of African firearms were imported, thus leading to the conclusion that there was a connection between the firearms trade and that in slaves. Did the demand for firearms encourage African rulers to attack their neighbors in order to capture slaves that might be used to pay for those weapons? This cycle was condemned as particularly odious by the antislavery movement of the time. On the other hand, the slave trade has also been considered as a fallout of wars undertaken by African states for political reasons. European commerce could be disrupted by these wars, and merchants found themselves lamenting their loss of trade. On the Gold Coast, Europeans preferred to exchange their commercial wares for gold. Political upheavals on the Gold Coast redirected African payments in the form of slaves. John Thornton has concluded that African leaders may very well have been motivated to exchange enemy captives for European technology, but they also may have been motivated by the desire to reduce the size of a hostile population.[55]

The overwhelming majority of slaves were victims of African warfare whatever the motivation. European slave traders were on the periphery of these conflicts. The enslavement of prisoners stood in sharp contrast to European treatment of prisoners and is but one way in which African attitudes toward war differed from those of Europe. The use of poisoned weapons was another. The slave trade represents the adoption of a morality that differed sharply from that evolving in Europe in the eighteenth century, at least as far as military ethics were concerned. Enlightenment writers universally condemned slavery, although their uncertainty as to whether Africans shared a common ancestry with Europeans provided ammunition for defenders of slavery, who contended that Africans were not true human beings.[56] The antislavery movement, however, was centered in the Evangelical movement rather than the intellectual circles of the Enlightenment. The slave trade predated the period covered in this book and met its first severe critics in the eighteenth century. European forces were deployed to protect interests in the slave trade and the tropical commerce that depended on its existence. Eighteenth-century cultural leaders were unhappy about the resulting inhumanity and called attention to the departure from moral norms. However, the slave trade underscores the extent to which naked self-interest prevailed on the policies of European governments. Slavery represents the dark side of European culture but also represents a graphic picture of cultural exchange.

THE VOYAGE OF THE *CENTURION*

On June 15, 1744, the 60-gun warship *Centurion,* commanded by George Anson, cast anchor at Spithead, England, after a circumnavigation of the globe lasting three years and nine months. The *Centurion* was the only vessel of a squadron of six warships and two supply vessels to complete the voyage. Only 145 of the *Centurion*'s crew were original members of the squadron, the remainder consisting of a multiethnic lot recruited along the way. A total of 1,300 crewmen were dead—four through combat, the others as a result of disease and accidents. In spite of this grim toll, the *Centurion*'s return was an occasion for national celebration, for she bore a treasure of £400,000 in silver coin and plate seized from Spain's fabled Manila galleon on its return voyage from Acapulco. It was an exploit worthy of Sir Francis Drake, and it fired the British imagination after a series of disappointments in the war against Spain. Spain's global empire had proven itself remarkably resistant to British naval assault. A massive amphibious expedition launched under Admiral Edward Vernon had failed to take Cartagena, and attempts on Panama and Guantánamo Bay had also come to grief.[57] In February 1744, Admiral Thomas Mathews had failed to destroy the Franco-Spanish fleet in the Mediterranean in an action that left Mathews squabbling with his principal subordinate over the blame. Mathews may have been saddled with an unimaginative set of fighting instructions, but his court-martial concluded that he did not fight hard enough.[58] Now Anson emerged from these wrecked hopes with reassurance that the great days of British sea power were not past. Indeed, in the person of this extraordinary commander, the great days were yet to come.

For Anson, the voyage of the *Centurion* brought wealth, fame, and rapid professional advancement. In 1746–1747 he assumed command of the Western Squadron, a fleet stationed almost permanently at sea in western approaches to the English Channel. This fleet and its detachments ensured that enemy vessels would be intercepted on their way to and from continental ports, and thus it became the linchpin of British naval strategy. Other commanders had recognized the benefits of such a deployment, but Anson possessed the leadership qualities and administrative skills to realize its potential.[59] By 1751 he was first lord of the Admiralty, a post that, with the exception of one year, he occupied throughout the Seven Years' War and one in which he became the architect of British naval victory. Anson is known principally by his deeds. Unlike Frederick the Great and Maurice de Saxe, he was notoriously averse to writing. Thus he is not included in *The Makers of Modern Strategy*,[60] a work that does not consider naval thought until it arrives at Alfred Thayer Mahan. This is unfortunate, for Anson possessed a clear and broad strategic vision. In contrast with Frederick the Great, whose sphere was confined to central Europe, Anson's mind embraced the globe.

The voyage of the *Centurion* played a significant role in the shaping of this vision. Despite the parallels with the celebrated Drake, Anson was a serious naval professional rather than a buccaneer. He viewed the voyage as a first step in the projection of British power into the Pacific and sought to profit from its lessons. Although he was no writer himself, he oversaw the publication of a detailed account published in 1748 as *The Voyage Round the World*.[61] Glyndwr Williams, editor of the 1974 edition of *The Voyage*, recognizes Richard Walter, chaplain of the *Centurion,* and Benjamin Robins as the actual authors, but it is clear that the work advanced a project near to Anson's heart: the promotion of British expeditions to the Pacific. It is fair to say that *The Voyage* provides an accurate representation of Anson's ideas. It gives an account of a heroic exploit while providing detailed descriptions of the lands and peoples encountered and vital navigational data. Anson foresaw the need for accurate charts, sailing instructions, and bases such as the Falkland Islands to secure Britain's long-term presence in Pacific waters. The Anson expedition was thus more than a naval raid; it served as a forerunner of the voyages of Cook, Bougainville, and other Pacific explorers of the late eighteenth century. It provided a window into a world unfamiliar to European readers and offered a concrete alternative to the fanciful notions of intellectuals such as Voltaire, who created a Chinese world of virtue that stood in sharp contrast to European vice. Anson's perspective on China, which he twice visited to secure repairs and stores, was narrow, but at least it was based on contact with real people. *The Voyage* thus made a significant contribution to the Enlightenment's consideration of Chinese culture.[62]

Anson's expedition reveals much about the nature of British naval reach in the mid-eighteenth century. It was based on an ambitious plan: to sail around Cape Horn and to attack and capture major Spanish cities in Chile, Peru, Panama, and Mexico. Land forces were to be embarked for this purpose, along with arms and presents that might be used to raise the native population against their masters. Having cut this swathe along the Pacific coast of Latin America, Anson was to capture the Manila galleons that carried Asian luxury goods to Acapulco in return for silver. In the end he was to rendezvous with another squadron sailing east from the Cape of Good Hope in order to capture Manila. Spain's Pacific empire was to be swept away.

Had this plan been executed promptly and with the intended force, that goal might have been achieved. But the new war imposed too many demands on limited resources. The second squadron was soon cancelled, and Anson's departure was long delayed. It was difficult to find sufficient men to carry out all of the government's plans; Anson's land force was recruited from the invalids of Chelsea Hospital (none of whom survived the hardship of the voyage) and newly recruited marines without experience with either ships or firearms. The delay in fitting out allowed the Spanish government to learn of the mission and to organize a squadron that narrowly missed an opportunity to intercept the British force. Most critically, Anson's delayed departure in mid-September 1740 resulted in his arrival at Cape Horn at the worst season of the year, when the vessels could make no way against the prevailing westerly winds and savage seas. Cape Horn at this time of year meant ceaseless agony for men in sailing vessels. Storm damage and mountainous seas were a continuous threat to the safety of the best-designed, maintained, and manned ships. Men were in constant peril from iced decks and spars, hurricane force winds, and vast waves that broke over their ships. Not until April did Anson gain the Pacific. One ship had foundered and two had turned back. More seriously, scurvy had broken out in the fleet. It was a disease the causes of which were not well understood and against which seamen were helpless. Hundreds of crewmen perished, and others were too weak to work vessels in conditions that demanded maximum effort from all hands. Although Anson had escaped his Spanish pursuers, his expedition had nearly foundered upon the most powerful defenses of Spain's American empire: nature and disease.[63]

The *Centurion* became separated from its consorts during the struggle to gain the Pacific. Anson had arranged a rendezvous at one of three uninhabited islands of the Juan Fernández group, which he knew to have been used by earlier buccaneers as a haven for repair and a source of fresh food, water, and firewood. Finding this island was no easy matter. There were no accurate charts or sailing instructions, and the inability of navigators to determine longitude compelled Anson to sail along the given latitude to find the island. This took him so far to the east that he encountered the coast of Chile before he discovered his error. All of May was consumed in this quest, with the men continuing to die from scurvy. Not until June 9 did they sight the island, and they were fortunate to find a secure anchorage. Men continued to die as they were transferred to hospital tents erected onshore, but the survivors were soon restored by fresh food. Another ship, the *Gloucester,* was even less fortunate. It arrived off the island having lost two-thirds of its crew. Unfavorable winds kept this square-rigged ship at bay, and the *Centurion*'s crew watched with dismay as the *Gloucester* hovered off the coast for weeks. Anson dispatched boats with fresh water and provisions, but, even with extra hands from the *Centurion* and with the officers sharing the work, the *Gloucester* lacked sufficient crew. By the time it dropped anchor off the island, it was a virtual death ship.

These circumstances are a reminder that long-distance navigation had not far advanced in the 250 years preceding the mid-eighteenth century. It remained a perilous business to set forth on a voyage almost certainly threatened by disease, the dangers of wind and weather, and navigational uncertainty. Theoretically, a sailing ship could remain at sea for as long as its stores held out, but wooden vessels were under constant threats from the elements and required careening to clean bottoms and repair leaks. The voyage of the *Centurion* brought home these technical limitations to its commander. The Royal Navy's success in meeting the challenges of scurvy and longitude, along with progress in the accuracy of charts and the securing of adequate bases, were the greatest military technical triumphs of the late eighteenth century.[64]

In retrospect, Anson seems to have worked miracles in bringing his expedition this far. He now possessed but three warships: *Centurion*, *Gloucester*, and the small *Tryal* sloop, and his land force of Chelsea invalids had been among the first to die. The lost ship, the *Wager*, had carried the arms and supplies required for land operations, and Anson found himself reduced to operations that resembled those of the buccaneers. He bitterly lamented lost opportunity. *The Voyage* makes it clear that Anson regarded Chile as poorly defended and ripe for revolution by its Creole and Indian inhabitants. Had the squadron arrived in its full strength, Anson was certain that Spanish rule would have collapsed.[65] Still Anson persevered to do what damage he could to Spanish interests. He took a number of Spanish ships (which were essentially valueless as prize money since they had to be burned) and with a landing party of only 58 men attacked and burned the Peruvian town of Paita, where he sacked the treasury. But big projects continued to elude him. He hoped to make contact with Vernon's men at Panama, being without news of that expedition's failure, and he cruised unsuccessfully, hoping to intercept the Manila galleon off Acapulco. Frustrated by the defeat of his plans and in need of a friendly port, he at length departed the Mexican coast and sailed west, for China.

In China, he said, "we expected to meet with many *English* ships, and numbers of our countrymen; and hoped to enjoy the advantages of an amicable well frequented port, inhabited by a polished people, and abounding with the conveniences and indulgencies of a civilized life; blessings, which now for near twenty months had never been once in our power."[66] After a scurvy-racked voyage of six months (rather than the anticipated two), the *Centurion*, by then the only survivor of the squadron, did reach Macao, where Anson found ships of the East India Company and, after many travails, supplies and repair facilities. However, the Chinese did not live up to Anson's expectations as a polished people. After sighting the Chinese mainland, Anson vainly sought to secure a Chinese pilot for the *Centurion* from one of the many fishing vessels in the vicinity. Not only were the fishermen uncommunicative, they showed no interest in the *Centurion*. At the very least, Anson thought, they might have demonstrated a mariner's curiosity in such an unfamiliar ship. The account of this encounter set the tone for Anson's impression of the Chinese: "which insensibility, especially in maritime persons, about a matter in their own profession, is scarcely to be credited, did not the general behaviour of the *Chinese*, in other instances, furnish with continual proofs of a similar turn of mind: It may be perhaps doubted, whether this cast of temper be the effect of nature or education; but, in either case, it is an uncontestable symptom of a mean and contemptible disposition, and is alone a sufficient confutation of the extravagant panegyrics, which many hypothetical writers have bestowed on the ingenuity and capacity of this Nation."[67] So much for Voltaire's China of the imagination!

Anson's subsequent dealings with the Chinese confirmed this impression. He found himself in an unusual situation. As commander of a 60-gun ship of war, he thought that he might defy the whole force of China, but he depended on the cooperation of Chinese authorities to secure vital repairs if he was to take the sea again. He could look to the representatives of the East India Company at Canton for assistance, but they in turn were fearful of incidents that might disrupt their trading relationships. The Chinese were unaccustomed to dealing with any but merchant ships, and it seems they were uncertain what to make of Anson. They expected him to pay the port duties required of merchant vessels, a demand rejected by Anson as the commander of a royal ship of war and representative of his king. Their only experiences with armed ships had been with pirates. Was Anson a merchantman or a pirate? His subsequent capture of the Manila galleon may have pointed to the latter. Anson was confident that the *Centurion*, objectively the most formidable fighting machine in Asian waters, commanded respect and fear. It appears that the Chinese were not as impressed as he assumed they would be. Nevertheless, as a result of difficult negotiations across this cultural divide, he was able to careen his ship and repair a dangerous leak. Other repairs were made and supplies secured, allowing the *Centurion* to depart for the Philippines to intercept the Spanish galleon on its return from Acapulco.

On this occasion fortune at last smiled on the *Centurion* for, after cruising for a month off Cape Espíritu Santo, she encountered the galleon *Nostra Signora de Cabadonga*. The galleon was a large ship with a more numerous crew than that of the *Centurion*. She was armed with 36 guns and numerous small arms sufficient to fend off piratical attacks but was no match for a specialized warship and a highly trained and motivated crew. The contest once joined was unequal with the galleon, striking its flag after 67 of her crew had been killed and 84 wounded. The *Centurion* had suffered 19 casualties. As a battle it was a minor affair, but the account provided in *The Voyage* illustrates certain themes explored in this work. First, there was Anson's professionalism and his commitment to training his men. Although he lacked sufficient men to man all his guns, he devised a plan by which two men only were attached to each gun for loading. Fuller crews moved from gun to gun to ensure that the *Centurion* would maintain a continuous fire throughout the action. This plan was perfected through intense training as the *Centurion* cruised in quest of its quarry. Anson also recognized the importance of small-arms fire. He indicated in *The Voyage* that the need for proficiency with small arms "seems so plain and natural a conclusion, that a person unacquainted with these affairs would suppose the first care of a Commander to be the training his people to the use of their arms." He continues:

But human affairs are not always conducted by the plain dictates of common sense. There are many other principles which influence our transactions: And there is one in particular, which though of a very erroneous complexion, is scarcely ever excluded from our most serious deliberations; I mean custom, or the practice of those who have preceded us. This is usually a power too mighty for reason to grapple with; and is the most terrible to those who oppose it, as it has much of superstition in its nature, and pursues all those who question its authority with unrelenting vehemence. However, in these later ages of the world, some lucky encroachments have been made on its prerogative; and it may be reasonably hoped, that the Gentlemen of the Navy, whose particular profession hath of late been considerably improved by a number of new inventions, will of all others be the readiest to give up those practices, which have nothing to plead but prescription, and will not suppose that every branch of their business hath already received all the perfection of which it is capable. Indeed, it must be owned, that if a dexterity in the use of small arms, for instance, hath been sometimes less attended to on board our ships of war, than might have been wished for, it hath been rather owing to unskillful methods of teaching it, than to negligence: For the common sailors, how strongly soever attached to their own prejudices, are very quick sighted in finding out the defects of others, and have ever shewn a great contempt for the formalities practiced in the training of land troops to the use of their arms; but when those who have undertaken to instruct the seamen with inculcating only what was useful, and that in the simplest manner, they have constantly found their people sufficiently docile, and the success hath even exceeded their expectation. Thus on board Mr. *Anson's* ship, where they were only taught the shortest method of loading with cartridges, and were constantly trained to fire at a mark, which was usually hung at the yard-arm, and where some little reward was given to the most expert, the whole crew, by this management, were rendered extremely skilful, quick in loading, all of them good marksmen, and some of them most extraordinary ones; so that I doubt not but, in the use of small arms, they were more than a match for double their number, who had not been habituated to the same exercise.[68] (The murderous fire of the *Centurion's* top men inflicted many of the Spanish casualties during the attack on the galleon.)

This enlightened pragmatism stands out in bold relief against the background of eighteenth-century theoretical military speculation. Strict disci-

plinarian that he was, Anson understood that success came from capital-
izing on the abilities and limitations of his men. It would be no exaggera-
tion, therefore, to view *The Voyage* as one of the great works of the Military
Enlightenment. The enlightened nature of this work is also evident in
Anson's concern that his actions be considered humane. He stressed that
Spanish prisoners taken on the coast of Latin America had been well
treated. The *Nostra Signora de Cabadonga*'s crew presented a more difficult
problem since they outnumbered their captors. Thus Anson found it necessary to lock them below in stifling heat and unsanitary conditions. Their
lot was made worse because of water shortages. With the crew limited to
a pint and a half per day, the Spaniards had to make do with a pint. Anson
admitted that when the prisoners were discharged at Canton after a
month at sea "they were reduced to mere skeletons; and their air and
looks corresponded much more to the conceptions formed of ghosts and
specters, than to the figure and appearance of real men."[69] Nevertheless,
with the exception of three men wounded in the battle, all of the prisoners
survived and gained their freedom when Anson reappeared at Canton.
According to Anson, the Chinese officials asked the Spaniards how they
came to be overcome by inferior numbers and why, since Britain and
Spain were at war, the British had not killed their captives. The Spaniards
replied that they could not resist a specialized ship of war and that it was
not the custom in Europe to kill those who surrendered. Anson believed
that this point made a powerful impression on the Chinese and led them
to conclude that he was not a pirate.

Nevertheless, Anson found himself locked once again in difficult negotiations over port duties, supplies, and repairs. He could not return to
England without Chinese cooperation, which seemed to him sufficient
incentive if they wanted to be rid of him. Yet he found it almost impossible to have what he considered straightforward dealings with Chinese
officials, a problem that he concluded was rooted in the Chinese character.
In his concluding remarks on the Chinese, Anson rejected the notion that
they were exemplars of a superior sense of humanity and morality:

Indeed, the only pretension of the *Chinese* to a more refined morality than their
neighbours is founded, not on their integrity or beneficence, but solely on the
affected evenness of their demeanor, and their constant attention to suppress all
symptoms of passion and violence. But it must be considered, that hypocrisy and
fraud are often not less mischievous to the general interests of mankind, than
impetuosity and vehemence of temper: Since these, though usually liable to the
imputation of imprudence, do not exclude sincerity, benevolence, resolution, nor
many other laudable qualities. And perhaps, if this matter was examined to the
bottom, it would appear, that the calm and patient manner of the *Chinese*, on which
they so much value themselves, and which distinguishes the Nation from all others, is in reality the source of the most exceptionable part of their character; for it
has been often observed by those who have attended to the nature of mankind,

that it is difficult to curb the more robust and violent passions, without augmenting, at the same time, the force of the selfish ones: So that the timidity, dissimulation, and dishonesty of the *Chinese*, may, in some sort, be owing to the composure, and external decency, so universally prevailing in that Empire.[70]

Anson's greatest contempt was reserved for the inability of the Chinese government to protect its people. When a fire broke out in the merchant quarter of Canton, he was astonished that Chinese authorities stood by and did nothing. Only the energetic intervention of Anson's seamen saved the day. Indeed, Chinese merchants asked that he post sentries to protect their property. Even more striking was the government's military weakness: "Since that form of Government, which does not in the first place provide for the security of the public against the enterprizes of foreign powers, is certainly a most defective institution: And yet this populous, this rich and extensive country, so pompously celebrated for its refined wisdom and policy, was conquered about an age since by a handful of *Tartars*; and even now, by the cowardice of the inhabitants, and the want of proper military regulations, it continues exposed not only to the attempts of any potent state, but to the ravages of every petty invader."[71]

In December, as it departed on its voyage for England, the *Centurion* passed the forts guarding Canton. The fortifications were crowded with soldiers armed with pikes and matchlock muskets. Numerous banners of many colors were displayed, and a giant soldier clad in armor and brandishing a battle-ax stalked the ramparts. Observers on the *Centurion* concluded that the giant's armor was fashioned not from steel but from a kind of glittering paper.

Thus ended the West's most significant military contact with China during the period covered in this book. Anson departed for home a rich man. He carried with him Spanish charts that would prove of value when Britain captured Manila in 1762 to complete its astonishing sweep of global prizes during the Seven Years' War. Most significant for the long term, he carried with him an attitude toward China. He had not fought the Chinese, but he was convinced of their military weakness and pusillanimity. This view, disseminated through Europe with the publication of *The Voyage*, led to a sharp readjustment of attitudes toward China. Montesquieu for one cited Anson as an authority when he concluded that China's government possessed principles of neither honor nor virtue.[72] The country was weak, corrupt, and ripe for the taking. Anson's was the first British man-of-war to visit China. The trip had been an arduous one, but the *Centurion* would not be the last British warship to make the journey.

During the eighteenth century, European observers of non-Western cultures often saw either hard or soft faces, depending on their particular perspective. Soldiers almost invariably saw the hard face of war and did not penetrate much beyond that. Europeans adopted into Native American communities found a "soft" culture that inspired admiration. It was this face of the Native Americans that Enlightenment writers idealized. Lady Mary Wortley Montagu encountered and admired the soft culture of the Ottoman Empire. She interpreted it through the perspective of the early Enlightenment, which allowed her to seek universal values. Anson also encountered the soft culture of China, but his mind was that of the Military Enlightenment. China's softness inspired only contempt. This should serve as a reminder of the many facets of that culture we call the Enlightenment.

NOTES

1. Stanford Shaw, *History of the Ottoman Empire and Modern Turkey,* vol. 1, *Empire of the Gazis: The Rise and Decline of the Ottoman Empire, 1280–1808* (Cambridge: Cambridge UniversityPress, 1976), 299–331.

2. Jeremy Black, *War and the World: Military Power and the Fate of Continents 1450–2000* (New Haven: Yale University Press, 1998), 102–3.

3. Mary Wortley Montagu, *The Complete Letters of Lady Mary Wortley Montagu,* 3 vols. (Oxford: Clarendon Press, 1965), 1:305.

4. Ibid., 414–15.

5. William Robertson, *An Historical Disquisition Concerning the Knowledge which the Ancients had of India....,* in *The Works of William Robertson,* 12 vols. (Edinburgh: Peter Hill, 1818), 12:192–93.

6. For Ottoman military power at its height, see Rhoads Murphy, *Ottoman Warfare 1500–1700* (New Brunswick: Rutgers; London: UCL Press, 1999).

7. Raimundo Montecuccoli, *Mémoires de Montecuccoli Généralissme de troupes de l'empereur* (Paris, 1751), 67. For his discussion of Ottoman warfare, see pp. 225–32, 257–343.

8. Black, *War and the World,* 108.

9. Peter H. Wilson, *German Armies: War and German Politics, 1648–1806* (London: UCL Press, 1998), 84–85.

10. John L. H. Keep, *Soldiers of the Tsar: Army and Society in Russia 1462–1874* (Oxford: Clarendon Press, 1988), 217.

11. Montecuccoli, *Mémoires,* 200.

12. Black, *War and the World,* 108.

13. William Robertson, *The History of the Reign of the Emperor Charles V with a View of the Progress of Society in Europe from the Subversion of the Roman Empire to the Beginning of the Sixteenth Century,* in *Works,* 4:224–28.

14. See Virginia H. Afsan, "Whatever Happened to the Janissaries? Mobilization for the 1768–1774 Russo-Ottoman War," *War in History,* 5, no. 1 (1998): 23–36.

15. Shaw, *History of the Ottoman Empire,* 240–42.

16. For Russia's military development, see Christopher Duffy, *Russia's Military Way to the West: Origins and Nature of Russian Military Power 1700–1800* (London: Routledge & Kegan Paul, 1981).

17. Robertson, *Historical Disquisition,* 288.

18. Ibid.

19. Jos Gommans, "Indian Warfare and Afghan Innovation during the Eighteenth Century," *Studies in History*, 11, no. 2, n. s. (New Delhi and London: Sage Publications, 1985), 261–80.

20. Black, *War and the World*, 111. For details of the British military triumph to 1789, see pp. 111–14.

21. See G. J. Bryant, "The Cavalry Problem in the Early British-Indian Army, 1750–1785," *War in History* 2, no. 1 (1995): 1–21.

22. For this section I have relied on Pradeep Barua, "Military Developments in India, 1750–1850," *Journal of Military History* 58 (October 1994): 599–616. See also, Bruce Lenman, "The Transition to European Military Ascendancy in India, 1600–1800," in *Tools of War: Instruments, Ideas, and Institutions of Warfare, 1445–1871*, ed. John Lynn (Urbana: University of Illinois Press, 1990), 100–130.

23. Gommans, "Indian Warfare." 279–80.

24. *The Cambridge History of India*, 6 vols. (Cambridge: Cambridge University Press, 1929), 5:181.

25. Burke's views on the East India Company and the condition of India at this time are best stated in a series of speeches, notably "Speech on Mr. Fox's East India Bill, December 1, 1783," in *The Writings and Speeches of Edmund Burke*, 12 vols. (Boston, 1901), 2:438 ff.; "Speech on the Nabob of Arcot's Debts, February 28, 1785," Ibid., 3:15 ff.; and "Speech in Opening the Impeachment [of Warren Hastings]," Ibid., 9:332 ff.

26. This issue is well developed in G. J. Bryant, "The Military Imperative in Early British Expansion in India, 1750–1785," *Indo-British Review* 21 (1996): 18–35. For Hastings, see pp. 28–32.

27. *Cambridge History of India*, 5:198. For the rivalry of Hastings and Francis, see Sophia Weitzman, *Warren Hastings and Philip Francis* (Manchester: Manchester University Press, 1929).

28. See Louis-Antoine de Bougainville, *Adventure in the Wilderness: The American Journals of Louis-Antoine de Bougainville, 1756–1760*, trans. and ed. E. P. Hamilton (Norman: University of Oklahoma Press, 1964).

29. Robertson, *The History of North America*, in *Works*, 9:61.

30. Ibid., 9:147.

31. Ibid., 9:150.

32. This is my view in comparing his account with my own chapter "The Indian Way of War," in Armstrong Starkey, *European and Native American Warfare, 1675–1815* (London: UCL Press; Norman: University of Oklahoma Press, 1998). For modern discussions of "private and national war" and of "mourning war," see L. V. Eid, "National war among Indians of northeastern North America," *Canadian Review of American Studies* 16 (summer 1985): 125–54, and Daniel Richter, "War and Culture: The Iroquois Experience," *William and Mary Quarterly*, 3d series, 40 (1983): 528–59.

33. Robertson, *History of North America*, in *Works*, 10:222.

34. Ibid., 9:151.

35. Ibid., 9:172.

36. James Smith, *Scoouwa: James Smith's Captivity Narrative* (Columbus: Ohio Historical Society, 1978), 161.

37. Robertson, *History of North America*, in *Works*, 10:88–89.

38. Ibid., 11:209.

39. Bougainville, *Adventure in the Wilderness*, 251–53.

40. Ibid., 191.

41. Francis Jennings, *Empire of Fortune: Crowns, Colonies, and Tribes in the Seven Years' War* (New York: Norton, 1988), 318; Ian Steele, *Betrayals: Fort William Henry and the "Massacre"* (New York and Oxford: Oxford University Press, 1990), 184–85; Francis Parkman, *Montcalm and Wolfe in North America*, 2 vols. (New York: Atheneum, 1983), 2:1492; F. Pouchot, *Memoir upon the Late War in North America between the French and English, 1755–1760*, ed. and trans. F. B. Hough, 2 vols. (Roxbury, Mass.: 1866), 1:91, 204.

42. Bougainville, *Adventure in the Wilderness*, 172.

43. Lord Loudon to the Marquis de Vaudreuil, 8 November 1757, Loudon Papers, LO 4788, Huntington Library, San Marino, Calif. This was wartime rhetoric. A British professional officer who wrote a history of the war exonerated Montcalm. See Thomas Mante, *The History of the Late War in North America and the Islands of the West Indies* (London, 1772; reprint, New York: Research Reprints, 1970), 91 (page citation is to the reprint edition).

44. James Bradstreet, *An Impartial Account of Lieut. Col. Bradstreet's Expedition to Fort Frontenac* (Toronto: Toronto and Mann Ltd., 1940), 21–22; Bougainville, *Adventure in the Wilderness*, 276; Pouchot, *Memoir*, 1:264.

45. Jeffrey Amherst, *The Journal of Jeffrey Amherst, Recording the Military Career of General Amherst in America from 1758 to 1763*, ed. J. Clarence Webster (Toronto: Riverson Press; Chicago: University of Chicago Press, 1931), 133.

46. "George Croghan's Journal, 1759–1763," *Pennsylvania Magazine of History and Biography* 81 (January 1947): 409–10.

47. For a discussion of Pontiac's Rebellion, see Ian Steele, *Warpaths: Invasions of North America* (New York: Oxford University Press, 1994), chap. 12.

48. John Forbes, *Writings of General John Forbes Pertaining to His Service in North America*, ed. A. P. James (Menosha, Wisc.: Collegiate Press, 1938), 117, 191, 198; Henry Bouquet to General Amherst, 26 July 1763, and Henry Bouquet to Lieut. Colonel Robertson, 26 July 1763, in D. Brymmer, "Before and after the Battle of Edge Hill [Bushy Run]," *Report on the Canadian Archives* (1889), n. D (Ottawa, 1890), 61–62.

49. Peter Russell, "Redcoats in the Wilderness: British Officers and Irregular Warfare in Europe, 1740 to 1760," *William and Mary Quarterly*, 3d series, 35 (October 1978): 629–52. According to Peter Paret, the earliest of these treatises appeared in 1752; he has identified 50 such works in the period 1752–1800. See his "Colonial Experience and European Military Reform at the End of the Eighteenth Century," *Bulletin of the Institute of Historical Research*, 37 (1964): 57.

50. See Lancelot, Comte Turpin de Crissé, *Essai sur l'art de la guerre*, 2 vols. (Paris, 1754).

51. See David Gates, *The British Light Infantry Arm* (London: B. T. Batsford, 1987). The limited success of British regulars in adapting to frontier war is discussed by Matthew C. Ward, "The British Method of Warring Is Not Practiced Here: The Failure of British Military Policy in the Ohio Valley, 1755–1757," *War in History* 4 (July 1997): 247–63, and by Steve Brumwell, " 'A Service Truly Critical': The British Army and Warfare with the North American Indians, 1755–1764," *War in History* 5 (April 1998): 146–75.

52. J. R. Cuneo, *Robert Rogers of the Rangers* (New York: Oxford University Press, 1959), 59. For Rogers's directions for forest warfare see his "Methods used in disciplining the Rangers … with their manner and practices in scouting and fighting in the woods," 25 October 1757, Loudon Papers, LO 4701, and "Instructions for New Rangers, 1757," in *Journals of Major Robert Rogers* (Readex Microprint, 1966), 56–70.

53. Cuneo, *Rogers*, 59–60.

54. *The Spirit of 'Seventy-Six': The Story of the American Revolution as Told by Participants*, ed. H. S. Commager and R. B. Morris, 2 vols. (Indianapolis: Bobbs-Merrill, 1958), 2:1050. For a defense of Hamilton, see J. D. Barnhart, *Henry Hamilton and George Rogers Clark in the American Revolution with the Unpublished Journal of Lieut. Gov. Henry Hamilton* (Crawfordsville, Ind.: R. E. Banta, 1951). For Clark, see J. Bakeless, *Background to Glory: The Life of George Rogers Clark* (Lincoln: University of Nebraska Press, 1957; reprint, 1992). In the 1992 edition, J. P. Ronda provides an introduction that places the book within the context of recent scholarship.

55. I have relied on John Thornton's *Warfare in Atlantic Africa, 1500–1800* (London: UCL Press, 1999), which casts light on a relatively unknown topic. For eighteenth-century British attitudes toward Africa, race, and slavery, see Philip Curtin, *The Image of Africa: British Ideas and Action, 1780–1850* (Madison: University of Wisconsin Press, 1964), especially pp. 3–119.

56. The issue of slavery is peripheral to the subject of this book. Enlightenment writers deplored slavery, and their views are best captured in Denis Diderot and Jean Le Rond d'Alembert, *L' Encyclopédie, ou Dictionnaire raisonné des sciences, des arts et des métiers*, 28 vols. (1751–72; facsimile of the first edition, Stuttgart-Bad Cannstatt: Frommann, 1969), 5:941–43. However, they also noted that African rulers themselves were responsible for the sale of their inhabitants to European slavers. See *Encyclopédie*, 15:13. British abolitionists were inspired by religion. A good sense of the debate over slavery may be gained from Granville Sharp, *Tracts on Slavery and Liberty* (Westport: Negro Universities Press, 1969). Mungo Park, an astute traveler of the 1790s, commented on the indigenous nature of African slavery and concluded that abolition of the European slave trade would not produce the beneficial effects anticipated by the abolitionists. See *Life and Travels of Mungo Park with a Full Narrative and Subsequent Adventure in Central Africa* (Edinburgh: Chambers, 1841), 252–53.

57. Vernon's expedition against Cartagena that included American troops will not be considered here. It is covered by H. W. Richmond, *The Navy in the War of 1739–48*, 3 vols. (Cambridge: Cambridge University Press, 1920), 1:101–37. Richmond blamed the government for the debacle, but see the reappraisal of Richard Harding in *Amphibious Warfare in the Eighteenth Century: The British Expedition to the West Indies 1740–1742* (The Royal Historical Society: Boydell Press, 1991). Harding focuses most of the blame on Vernon.

58. Richmond, *Navy in the War of 1739–48*, 2:54–55.

59. For Anson's role in the creation of the Western Squadron, see Richmond, *Navy in the War of 1739–48*, 1:xix; Ruddock Mackay, *Admiral Hawke* (Oxford: Clarendon Press, 1965), 53; Richard Harding, *Seapower and Naval Warfare, 1650–1830* (London: UCL Press, 1999), 199–200.

60. *The Makers of Modern Strategy from Machiavelli to the Nuclear Age*, ed. Peter Paret (Princeton: Princeton University Press, 1986).

61. All references to this work are from Richard Walter and Benjamin Robins, *The voyage Round the World in the Years MDCCXL, I, II, III, IV by George Anson,* ed. Glyndwr Williams (London: Oxford University Press, 1974).

62. For Anson's contribution to the European image of China, see Jonathan Spence, *The Great Chan's Continent: China in Western Minds* (New York: W.W. Norton, 1998), 51–56. I wish to thank my colleague Cristina Zaccarini for directing me to this book.

63. The limitations imposed on British naval operations by nature and disease are discussed in Duncan Crewe, *Yellow Jack and the Worm: British Naval Administration in the West Indies* (Liverpool: Liverpool University Press, 1993).

64. For advances in the mastery of longitude and the prevention of scurvy, see N. A. M. Rodger, *The Wooden World: An Anatomy of the Georgian Navy* (Annapolis: Naval Institute Press, 1986), 51–53, 100–3. Eighteenth-century diets made scurvy a problem on land as well as at sea. Fleets near their bases may have been less afflicted by scurvy than were many landsmen, for they received frequent supplies of fresh food. As Anson's voyage makes clear, however, scurvy was the scourge of long-distance voyages.

65. Walter and Robins, *A Voyage,* 255–59.

66. Ibid., 254.

67. Ibid., 313.

68. Ibid., 335–56.

69. Ibid., 343.

70. Ibid., 368–69.

71. Ibid., 369.

72. Spence, *Great Chan's Continent,* 92. For Voltaire, see pp. 95–98. Voltaire believed that Anson's contact with China was superficial because it was restricted to contact on the frontier.

CHAPTER 7

Conclusions

A discussion of the eighteenth-century "culture of force" involves ideas, values, and human interaction. In warfare, values are tested under the most-extreme circumstances, and generalizations about eighteenth-century culture are incomplete unless we consider this harsh proving ground. Perhaps it is best to say that those things we truly believe are those for which we are prepared to die. Our conduct under stress, fear, and danger reveals our values stripped cleanly of hypocrisy. It is my hope that the preceding chapters have revealed the complex dimensions of eighteenth-century culture. No single strand of ideas provided a unity within the culture of force. Today, scholars perceive the Enlightenment as more complex and perhaps less progressive than previously thought. The Military Enlightenment was but one facet of a broader cultural phenomenon. So we must recognize that this Military Enlightenment, often studied as the foundation of modern strategic thought, possessed many strands that produced creative tensions. Thus, writers of the Military Enlightenment sought classical models for modern warfare, as well as the scientific principles that might guide its conduct. The best writers were as interested in the psychological dimension of war as they were in tactical deployments and marching tables. Some embraced the technological innovations of the "military revolution." Others sought victory by rekindling the warrior spirit in the human heart. Today, when one reads of the skepticism expressed by some veteran soldiers about a so-called revolution in military affairs—which seems to be about an increased reliance on high technology in warfare—the tension within the eighteenth-century Military Enlightenment does not appear so arcane.

What was the influence of the Military Enlightenment? Eighteenth-century states sought to base the professionalization of their officer corps on this philosophy. They founded schools to transmit military knowledge, and enlightened commanders such as Frederick the Great encouraged their officers to read authorities such as Folard. Clearly, this had an effect: Maurice de Saxe was a household name among eighteenth-century officers, even if not so well known today. Nevertheless, no state was capable of educating all of its officers, and many remained unenlightened. The officer corps remained aristocratic in style if not in actual makeup. The great expansion of eighteenth-century armies meant that men of nonaristocratric background were assimilated into a culture that was only partially shaped by the Military Enlightenment. The continuing practice of the duel as a confirmation of officer status was denounced by some military writers and affirmed by others. It was an integral part of a code of honor that was rooted in the traditions of chivalry but was regarded by writers such as Vattel as a guarantee of good officer conduct. The duel was clearly at odds with the humane trends of what we consider Enlightenment thought, but ironically it may have gained in significance in the eighteenth century as officers of nonaristocratic background found it necessary to defend their status within the corps. A young officer most frequently depended on his mentors within the regiment for his values and his military education. There was a great variety in the lessons that might be offered. The complexity of the culture of honor mirrors that of eighteenth-century culture at large.

Great battlefield commanders such as Saxe were emblematic of the Military Enlightenment. Saxe was one of a rare breed of intellectuals who were also men of action. At Fontenoy he gave his ideas concrete form. Of course, he could not reorganize his army into legions, because he had to work with the material at hand. Fontenoy was a hallmark of Saxe's genius—a battle won in spite of inferior officers and troops. Saxe was not one of Tolstoy's generals, who exercised no control and whose orders only confirmed events. Fontenoy demonstrates that a great commander does count in battle. Nevertheless, it was a close fight, and the courage and discipline of the Anglo-Hanoverians almost prevailed. Fontenoy also demonstrated that success in battle was not just about the great captains, and thus it continued to be a battle that was intensely studied throughout the period. Many writers saw it as a struggle between technology (in the form of cannon) and the human spirit. Thus it was a focal point for many debates in the Military Enlightenment. The events of Fontenoy have little application for modern warfare, but the underlying issues perhaps justify its study even today.

We have also seen that the eighteenth-century military experience was much more complex than the rococo battle portraits of the age might suggest. Military service was widespread, and war placed a heavy burden on the civilian population. Although Enlightenment writers envisioned replacing mercenaries with citizen-soldiers, such soldiers were actually in their midst in various forms. Unfortunately, Highlanders and Cossacks did not serve an Enlightenment agenda. The people in arms often rose in opposition to centralizing states that seemed to serve the cause of enlightenment. Many eighteenth-century Scots, as do some modern historians, regarded the Hanoverian regime as brutal, corrupt, and authoritarian. However, the Highlanders received little support for their uprisings from enlightenment circles. After all, the Hanoverian monarchs could be seen as guarantors of parliamentary government, rule of law, Protestantism (tempered by toleration), and a sound financial system. The Highlanders' fight for their own version of freedom was dismissed as a threat to civilization. The Pugachev rebellion against Catherine the Great's "enlightened" regime provoked only hysterics. Thus there was much ambiguity toward the idea of the people in arms. They represented a threat to the social fabric that frightened even Rousseau. Many British officers believed that the American Revolution represented just such a threat in its attack on law and its reliance on mob rule. But American leaders were able to explain their actions in terms that enlightened intellectuals could understand. Thus the Americans became citizen-soldiers, a category denied many of those in the eighteenth century who took up arms against the power of the state. American officers adopted the code of honor as their own and adapted it to a republican ideology. Outside the boundaries of this study is the question of the effect of French revolutionary ideas on the officer culture. It is a question that deserves further investigation.

Eighteenth-century Europe did not exist in isolation. European contact with the non-Western world had existed long before 1492, and the great Spanish and Portuguese empires had come into being long before the Enlightenment period. Those empires had come about through conquest and adaptation, and they had expanded European knowledge of other cultures. During the sixteenth and seventeenth centuries, other European states began to rival the Iberian powers' imperial greatness. The Spanish Empire proved remarkably resilient in fending off invaders throughout the eighteenth century. For the most part, the other European powers made imperial headway in areas outside those under Spanish control. There they encountered determined resistance from warlike peoples, and their victories were far from inevitable. Success came through adaptation of European techniques to local conditions. This meant adaptation to local cultures as well. One is struck by how little Europeans knew about the rest of the world in the eighteenth century, despite centuries of exploration. Spain kept much important knowledge as state secrets, and some areas, such as sub-Saharan Africa, were impenetrable to most European travelers. William Robertson's knowledge and appreciation of other cultures was impressive, but it also reveals the limits of European understanding.

Soldiers and sailors had little to guide them when they encountered non-Western peoples, and they had to make up their own minds about them. In many cases, the military provided the most-detailed—if distorted—sources of knowledge of non-Western cultures. Military contact was also one of the most-important engines of cultural exchange.

What factors produced the eighteenth-century culture of force? The foregoing chapters suggest that the military environment was shaped by material and intellectual influences that laid the foundation for modern perceptions of war and peace. The most-important factor was the increased power of the state, which to a great degree succeeded in gaining a monopoly over the exercise of military force. This development was recognized in international law and was the linchpin of international order. Abbé Saint-Pierre based his plan for perpetual peace on a collective security agreement between European states. Others believed that peace, or at least security, rested on equilibrium in the European state system. Even a critic of the political order such as Rousseau seems to have despaired of any fundamental change on the grounds that it might prove too dangerous. Enlightenment writers were ambivalent about the state system. They understood that the polite diplomacy of the age masked the avarice and lust for power of contemporary rulers. Enlightenment luminaries, such as Voltaire, who hobnobbed with the "great," frequently suffered for their association. Voltaire, however, believed that the enlightened culture had humanized the conduct of war. One can only conclude that this is very difficult to demonstrate. Regular armed forces, increased respect for military law and discipline, and a new sense of professionalism on the part of officers played a more important role in improving conditions. However, the new age of "humanity in war" existed within narrow parameters. The century experienced many outbursts of popular conflict in which the rules of interstate warfare did not apply.

The power of the state was not a force for peace. Monarchs such as Louis XIV brought about internal peace at the expense of liberty. Even if they had but modest success in creating new wealth, bureaucratic establishments had great extractive power that allowed them to find the men and money to wage war on an unprecedented scale. The wars of religion in preceding centuries had produced much misery. Relatively speaking, eighteenth-century soldiers were better behaved than the poorly paid mercenaries of the Thirty Years' War. Nevertheless, eighteenth-century governments wielded much more destructive forces than did their seventeenth-century predecessors—and employed them on a global scale. The eighteenth century saw accounts settled between the weak and the strong. Small German states that looked to the empire for protection were on their way to extinction before the arrival of Napoleon. The fate of Poland and of Corsica exposed the true nature of enlightened monarchy.

We have seen how science, technology, and rational thought were har-nessed in the service of force. The Military Enlightenment, the foundation of modern military thought, sought to apply these developments to achieve victory in war. The eighteenth century debate over the "military revolution" illustrates this fact. However, it also reveals the tensions in the military culture. Was technology more important than moral factors? Could the stasis produced by linear fire tactics be overcome by more-imaginative offensive techniques, such as the column? How were officers to motivate soldiers? By severe discipline and intensive training, on the Prussian model, or by encouraging self-sufficiency and dedication on the part of the individual soldier? How should soldiers be recruited? Should they simply be servants of the king or citizens of the nation? Thus the military-revolution debate found its way into the broader political dis-course of the time. Military and nonmilitary intellectuals had pondered these questions for three generations before the year 1789 created a new environment for the application of their ideas. The debate over the nature of honor also seems to have been at least partially resolved by 1789. Writ-ers who defined honor as self-sacrifice and virtue contributed to the new republican spirit.

Many eighteenth-century technical developments contributed to the success of French revolutionary and Napoleonic armies: the column as an offensive infantry formation, permanent divisional and corps organiza-tion, artillery reform, and specialized light troops. The *levée en masse* had been introduced by Paoli in Corsica, and the concept of the citizen-soldier had been widely discussed. The spirit of Folard, Saxe, and Guibert ener-gized French military development after 1789. Much has been made of the increased size of armies in the post-1789 period. However, the reader should remember that the management of campaigns on a Napoleonic scale was a task dependent on the experience gained in the preceding cen-tury, which saw unprecedented continental and global conflict. Staff offi-cers and logistical departments do not appear overnight. The French Revolution produced new talent and sources of energy, but it may be said that the new commanders had a playbook ready to hand. Continuity is much more evident in naval matters; the line between Anson and his later contemporaries Jervis and Nelson is perfectly clear. When war broke out with France, the Western Squadron was ready for deployment. Behind this lay a century of professional naval development: the creation of a bureaucracy and an industry to support the fleet, tactical experience, and strategic thought. These continuities existed in the French army as well.

Chapter 5 raises the question of an eighteenth-century crisis. Big con-cepts such as these tend to evaporate before discriminating analysis. Yet, two themes ran through the popular rebellions of the eighteenth century: (1) resentment of the burden that war imposed on the human and material

resources of eighteenth-century society and (2) opposition to centralization of state power by minorities and those who lived on the borders of
eighteenth-century empires. Although it possessed an almost-unique ideology, the American Revolution does conform to these themes. Ironically,
the border peoples of the American colonies were as likely to resist the
centralizing authority of the new American government as they were to
resist control from London. Thus the rebellions did not share a common
ideology, and established governments usually retained support from
their core populations. Although they advocated reform, few eighteenth-
century intellectuals favored the overthrow of the established order. After
all, that order was perceived as the defender of enlightened civilization in
such places as Scotland and Russia. The French Revolution was the
extraordinary event of the century. The financial burden imposed by more
than a century of war, fiscal mismanagement, and military ineptitude
undermined the legitimacy of the regime and cost it the support of its core
population. For good or bad, the hopes and fears of eighteenth-century
intellectuals were about to be realized. The ideal of the people in arms,
combining patriotic zeal and technical proficiency, had been anticipated
by writers for 50 years. It was thus a child of the eighteenth century, born
to shake the continent and then the world.

Index

About the Author

ARMSTRONG STARKEY is Professor of History and former Dean and Provost at Adelphi University. His special research interest is the relationship between ideas, values, and war in the 18th century. He lives in Huntington, New York.